The Economics of Military Spending

AF835191

The Economics of Military Spending offers a comprehensive analysis of the effect of military expenditures on the economy. It is the first book to provide both a theoretical and an empirical investigation of how military spending affects the profit rate, a key indicator of the health of a capitalist economy.

The book presents a general discussion on the economic models of the nexus of military spending and economic growth, as well as military Keynesianism and the military-industrial complex. Including an account of the Marxist crisis theories, it focuses on military spending as a counteracting factor to the tendency of rate of profit to fall. Using a range of econometric methods and adopting a Marxist perspective, this book provides comprehensive evidence on the effects of military spending on the rate of profit for more than thirty countries. The findings of the book shed light on the complex linkages between military spending and the profit rate by considering the role of countries in the arms trade.

Offering a Marxist perspective and an emphasis on quantitative analysis, *The Economics of Military Spending* will be of great interest to students and scholars of defence and peace economics, as well as Marxist economics.

Adem Yavuz Elveren is Associate Professor at Fitchburg State University, U.S.A. His research focuses on gender and social security and the effect of military spending on the economy.

Routledge Frontiers of Political Economy

251 Commodity
The Global Commodity System in the 21st Century
Photis Lysandrou

252 Uncertainty and Economics
A Paradigmatic Perspective
Christian Müller-Kademann

253 Discourse Analysis and Austerity
Critical Studies from Economics and Linguistics
Edited by Kate Power, Tanweer Ali and Eva Lebdušková

254 A Macroeconomic Analysis of Profit
Andrea Carrera

255 The Dark Places of Business Enterprise
Reinstating Social Costs in Institutional Economics
Pietro Frigato and Francisco J. Santos Arteaga

256 Economic Woman
Gendering Economic Inequality in the Age of Capital
Frances Raday

257 The Economics of Military Spending
A Marxist Perspective
Adem Yavuz Elveren

258 Political Pluralism, Disagreement and Justice
The Case for Polycentric Democracy
Julian F. Müller

For more information about this series, please visit: www.routledge.com/books/series/SE0345

The Economics of Military Spending

A Marxist Perspective

Adem Yavuz Elveren

Routledge
Taylor & Francis Group
LONDON AND NEW YORK

First published 2019
by Routledge
2 Park Square, Milton Park, Abingdon, Oxon OX14 4RN

and by Routledge
605 Third Avenue, New York, NY 10017

First issued in paperback 2020

Routledge is an imprint of the Taylor & Francis Group, an informa business

British Library Cataloguing-in-Publication Data
A catalogue record for this book is available from the British Library

Library of Congress Cataloging-in-Publication Data
Names: Elveren, Adem Y. (Adem Yavuz), author.
Title: The economics of military spending : a Marxist perspective / Adem Yavuz Elveren.
Description: Abingdon, Oxon ; New York, NY : Routledge, 2019. | Series: Routledge Frontiers of Political Economy | Includes bibliographical references and index.
Identifiers: LCCN 2019003325 (print) | LCCN 2019006562 (ebook) | ISBN 9780429430947 (Ebook) | ISBN 9781138365063 (hbk) | ISBN 9780429430947 (ebk)
Subjects: LCSH: War—Economic aspects. | National security—Economic aspects. | Marxian economics.
Classification: LCC HC79.D4 (ebook) | LCC HC79.D4 .E48 2019 (print) | DDC 330—dc23
LC record available at https://lccn.loc.gov/2019003325

ISBN 13: 978-0-367-72888-5 (pbk)
ISBN 13: 978-1-138-36506-3 (hbk)

Typeset in Bembo
by Apex CoVantage, LLC

To my eldest brother, Mehmet Ali

Contents

Figures

Tables

Foreword

Interest in particular economic topics and approaches ebbs and flows under the influence of economic conditions. What were once topics of great research interest get neglected only to be rediscovered when the conjuncture changes. In this book, Adem Yavuz Elveren examines the interaction of military expenditure and the rate of profit and their contribution to capitalist crises. It not only redirects attention to an increasingly relevant older literature but also makes an original theoretical and empirical contribution to the analysis.

In recent years, in many countries there has been a tendency for inequality to increase, for the share of wages in total income to fall, and for median incomes to stagnate. This pattern has increased interest in the determinants of the rate of profit, which for long had been relatively neglected. In fact, the centrepiece of most growth theories, the Cobb-Douglas production function, assumes that the shares of profits and wages are constant. Slowing growth has also revived interest in theories of secular stagnation. Alvin Hansen (1939) writing a decade after the Wall Street Crash and subsequent crisis now sounds very topical with his warnings of the danger of secular stagnation driven by declining incentive to invest. However, he did not anticipate the offsetting effects of the subsequent war and the baby boom. After the most recent financial crisis, Summers (2015) echoed Hansen in warning of the dangers of secular stagnation. He noted the long-term decline in real interest rates since the 1980s and raised the concern that the equilibrium real rate may now have become negative and that a zero nominal rate would then become a chronic and systemic inhibitor of economic activity holding economies back below their potential. Unusually, these low real interest rates have coincided with high real rates of profit.

In a similar manner, the end of the Cold War and the falling shares of military expenditure in GDP in many countries meant that the role of military expenditures had also been neglected. Recent geo-strategic developments around Russia, China, and in the Middle East have signalled that the world remains a dangerous place and have revived interest in military topics. Adem Yavuz Elveren's book is at the intersection of defence economics and Marxist economics. This was once a crowded intersection with many asking how military expenditures, capitalist accumulation, and the rate of profit interacted. It is worth considering the longer-run pattern of fluctuating interest. Although

Marx had not given military spending a central role in the theory of capitalist accumulation, subsequent Marxists did. Early contributions reflecting the central role of militarism in the early 20th century included Rosa Luxemburg in *The Accumulation of Capital* published in 1913 and Lenin in *Imperialism, the Highest Stage of Capitalism* published in 1917. The interwar depression seemed to confirm a crisis in capitalism, even to orthodox thinkers like Alvin Hansen.

At the end of World War II, many on both the left and right predicted that the capitalist world would sink back into depression. The fact that it did not posed a problem for the left, many of whose theories had centred on the inability of capitalism to generate adequate demand. These theories argued that the drive for profit was contradictory; by depressing wages it also depressed the demand that would enable capitalists to realise those profits. To many it appeared that military expenditure provided an alternative source of demand. This appeared superficially plausible both because of the large share of output taken by military expenditure – around 9 percent in the mid-1960s – and because the U.S. had achieved full employment during the Korean and Vietnam Wars. This led to a theory of military Keynesianism, the idea that U.S. governments regulated the economy by varying the level of military spending; an interpretation reinforced by the Reagan military build-up of the early 1980s. The argument against military Keynesianism was that the variations in military expenditure were better explained by strategic than economic factors, and the economic effects were often inconsistent with the theory.

The importance of analysing military spending was also reinforced by the power of what, in his 1961 farewell address before ceasing to serve as U.S. president, General Eisenhower had labelled "the military-industrial complex". Adem Yavuz Elveren has a nice 1969 quote from John Kenneth Galbraith about how anyone who spoke to the problem of military power took the thoughtful precaution of first quoting President Eisenhower, to avoid being labelled as a communist sympathiser.

The turbulent 1970s were generally seen as a time of low and falling profitability. But from the mid-1980s in the U.S., and later in many other capitalist countries, one saw less turbulence as the Great Moderation got underway. One also saw a tendency for inequality and the share of profits to increase. With the end of the Cold War, military spending in many countries declined substantially, freeing resources for other uses. In the U.S. it fell from 6.3 percent of GDP in 1986 to 2.9 percent in 2000, allowing President Clinton to balance the budget. The share of military spending in GDP began rising again after 9/11, though not to Cold War heights. During the Great Moderation there was little interest in theories of crises, though their prevalence was ably documented in Reinhart and Rogoff (2009). Similarly, the low shares of military expenditure meant that there was little interest in theories of military expenditure. This has now changed.

The current conjuncture makes this book a timely one. It reviews the theories of the effect of military expenditure on growth, Military Keynesianism, crisis, and the effect of military expenditure on profitability. It examines the institutional structure that mediates this relationship, in particular the military-industrial complex. Adem Yavuz Elveren asks how strongly military expenditure can function as a surplus-absorbing entity and whether it can counteract any tendency of the rate of profit to fall. The book combines theoretical analysis with detailed econometric investigations for 30 countries over 60 years. Compared with the discussion in the 60s and 70s, there is more data and more powerful econometric techniques, both for large N panel studies and for specific case studies on individual countries. The book contains a careful discussion of the difficult issues involved in choosing a measure of the rate of profit, which has been a matter of controversy in both the orthodox and Marxist literatures. As one would expect, the effects of military expenditure on profits are mixed: responses are contingent on the historically specific structural context. In particular, the estimated effects appear to differ between arms importers and arms exporters, for whom military industries have a different significance. The effects also differ over different periods.

Adem Yavuz Elveren has produced a very careful analysis of an interesting topic, the role of military expenditure in growth, emphasising the special role of the rate of profit. It deserves a wide readership.

Ron Smith
Birkbeck, University of London
January 2019

References

Hansen, A. (1939). Economic progress and declining population growth. *American Economic Review*, 29(1), pp. 1–15.

Reinhart, C. M. and Rogoff, K. S. (2009). *This time is different: Eight centuries of financial folly*. Princeton: Princeton University Press.

Summers, L. H. (2015). Have we entered an age of secular stagnation? IMF fourteenth annual research conference in honor of Stanley Fischer, Washington, DC. *IMF Economic Review*, Palgrave Macmillan, International Monetary Fund, 63(1), May, pp. 277–280.

Acknowledgements

Several people contributed to this book. Among them, I owe a special thank you to Ron Smith, who not only kindly wrote the foreword but also provided invaluable feedback on each chapter. I truly appreciate the help of Al Campbell, a great mentor, whose dedication to his profession has always been inspiring to me. Becoming friends with Ali Cevat Taşıran has been invaluable, as I am indebted for his constant support. I would also like to thank Deepankar Basu, Eric Budd, Ceyhun Elgin, Duncan Foley, James K. Galbraith, Gülay Günlük-Şenesen, Sara Hsu, Gökçer Özgür, Ünal Töngür, Ramaa Vasudevan, and Matías Vernengo for their helpful comments. I am grateful to Andy Humphries of Routledge for his encouragement and kindness. Finally, another special thank you goes to my daughter, Asya, for picking the cover design.

Any remaining errors, of course, remain my own responsibility.

Abbreviations

AMECO	Annual macroeconomic database of the European Commission's Directorate General for Economic and Financial Affairs
AR	Autoregression
ARDL	Autoregressive distributed lag model
CADF	Cross-section Augmented Dickey-Fuller
CCC	Civilian Conservation Corps
CIPS	Cross-sectionally augmented IPS test
DARPA	Defense Advanced Research Projects Agency
DFE	Dynamic Fixed Effect
EPWT	Extended Penn World Tables
GDP	Gross Domestic Product
GMM	Generalized method of moments
IPS	Im-Pesaran-Shin unit root test
LDCs	Least Developed Countries
LLC	Levin-Lin-Chu unit root test
MENA	Middle East and North Africa
MG	Mean Group
MIC	Military-industrial complex
MRT	Marginal rate of transformation
MSAR	Markov Switching Autoregression model
NASA	National Aeronautics and Space Administration
NATO	North Atlantic Treaty Organization
OECD	Organisation for Economic Co-operation and Development
OLS	Ordinary least squares
PAYG	Pay-as-you-go
PIM	Perpetual Inventory Method
PMG	Pooled Mean Group
PPF	Production possibility frontier
PPP	Purchasing power parity
PWT	Penn World Tables
R&D	Research and development

SIPRI	Stockholm International Peace Research Institute
USSR	Union of Soviet Socialist Republics
UTIP	University of Texas Inequality Project
VAR	Vector autoregression
WMEAT	U.S. World Military Expenditures and Arms Transfers

1 Introduction

What is the driving force of capitalism – consumption or profit? If it is consumption, then a shotgun or a rifle is just like any other private good, used for personal security or 'pleasure' (e.g. hunting), while a fighter jet or a nuclear missile is a 'public good', providing national security. If the driving force of capitalism is profit, then arms are again not so different from other private goods, but perhaps with one crucial advantage: they may be more functional than civilian goods in that they can reinforce political and economic hegemony and are either rapidly used or rendered obsolete, which guarantees endless demand, thereby helping to absorb surplus. This book adopts the latter approach, in which the driving force of capitalism is profit. The book stands at the junction of defence economics and Marxist economics, examining the effect of military expenditures (milex hereafter) on the rate of profit, an indicator of the health of capitalist economy.

Defence economics is a subfield of economics that studies the causes and consequences of conflicts and military production (e.g. milex).[1] The term militarism[2] is a wider concept, with social and political roots. In addition to high milex, the term refers to the dominance of military power and values over society and governance, including but not limited to the exaggeration of external and internal threats as a means of justifying a large military and/or high milex, the adoption of aggressive foreign policies and repressive internal security measures, and the extensive use of militarist symbols and procedures[3] (Smith, 2009, p. 28). Thus, there are several ways the military influences society, which requires environmental, philosophical, psychological, sociological, and feminist perspectives to fully understand the causes and consequences of the military. Taking an economic perspective, this book employs various quantitative methods to perform a modest task: to examine the effect of milex on economic performance from a Marxist perspective. Although there has been an ever-growing literature on the effect of milex on economic growth, there have been very few studies examining the role of milex on profitability. Therefore, this book aims to fill this gap by providing comprehensive evidence on the mechanisms by which milex affects the rate of profit, thereby aiming to contribute to 'quantitative Marxism'.

A brief history of military expenditure

Global milex in 2017 was $1.74 trillion, or about $229 per person per year. As Smith (2009) noted in reference to earlier data, this is a tragic figure when one considers that there are several hundred million people living on less than a dollar a day. In fact, the 10 countries with the highest milex accounted for 73 percent of the total (SIPRI, 2018): the U.S., China, Saudi Arabia, Russia, the U.K., India, France, Japan, Germany, and South Korea. Table 1.1 presents some valuable figures for the top 20 spending countries in 2015, based on the U.S. World Military Expenditures and Arms Transfers (WMEAT).

Table 1.1 shows some important indicators of milex. High milex per capita is notable in the cases of Saudi Arabia, the U.S., Israel, and Australia. Milex per capita shows the cost of milex per person. The ratio of milex to the armed forces may be considered a rough measure of the capital intensity of the military (Smith, 2009, p. 93). The ratio of armed forces to the population shows the proportion of people who serve in the military. It is important to observe the indicators of milex and the military burden (e.g. the share of milex in GDP) together. For instance, although China is the second largest spender, the ratio of milex to GDP is just 1.9 per cent, below several countries with high ratios, such as Saudi Arabia, Israel, Russia, Pakistan, the U.S., South Korea, India, and the U.K.

Table 1.1 Military spending in 2015

	Milex (2015 $ bn)	*Milex per capita (2015 $)*	*Armed Forces (AF) (thousands)*	*Milex/ AF (millions)*	*Milex/ GDP (%)*	*AF/ Pop. (%)*
U.S.	641	1,997	1,310	489	3.6	0.41
China	215	156	1,920	112	1.9	0.14
Saudi Arabia	85	3,040	260	325	13.1	0.94
Russia	67	470	900	74	5.0	0.63
U.K.	60	928	160	372	2.1	0.25
India	48	39	1,410	34	2.3	0.11
France	44	653	210	207	1.8	0.31
Japan	41	322	240	170	0.9	0.19
Germany	40	492	180	221	1.2	0.22
South Korea	36	719	660	55	2.6	1.3
Australia	26	1,132	60	430	1.9	0.25
Brazil	25	123	350	71	1.4	0.17
Italy	20	317	180	109	1.1	0.29
Canada	19	533	75	249	1.2	0.21
Israel	17	2,099	180	94	5.6	2.2
Turkey	12	151	400	30	1.7	0.5
Pakistan	10	49	750	13	3.6	0.38
Mexico	8	63	270	29	0.7	0.22
Indonesia	8	30	400	19	0.9	0.15
Egypt	5	59	440	12	1.6	0.48

Source: 2015: WMEAT

Figure 1.1 shows regional share of milex in total world milex. Whereas the share of the Americas, the highest-spending region, has declined slightly (considering its enormous size), there have been remarkable increases in Asia and Oceania, the Middle East, and Africa, corresponding with a substantial decline in Europe. The share of the Americas declined from 45.5 percent to 42.3 percent from 1988 to 2014. The increase for the same period in Africa was nearly 1.5 times, from 1.1 percent to 2.5 percent. Similarly, the increase in the Middle East was more than two times, from 5.3 percent to 11.2 percent, and in Asia it was about three times, from 9.3 percent to 24.9 percent. These increases corresponded with a significant decline in Europe, from 38.9 percent to 19.1 percent.

Figure 1.2 shows the share of milex for major countries during the Cold War era. There are two notable patterns. First, while there has been an overall decline in the military burden in the last decade, Russia has sustained its high spending ratio. Second, except for the U.S. and Russia, there has been a steady decline in the military burden in other major countries. Although the end of the superpower conflict led to an initial decline in milex, conflicts in the post–Cold War era became intra rather than interstate (D'Agostino et al., 2016).

Table 1.1 shows that U.S. milex in 2015 was $641 billion, which is nearly three times that of the second highest spender, China, and larger than the next nine biggest military spenders combined.[4] Figure 1.3 shows the U.S.'s military burden for 1949–2017.

Figure 1.3 shows that milex in the U.S. rose to as high as 13 percent in 1953 due to the Korean War, followed by a steady decline until the Vietnam War. After that, milex declined to 4.8 percent in 1979. This downward trend

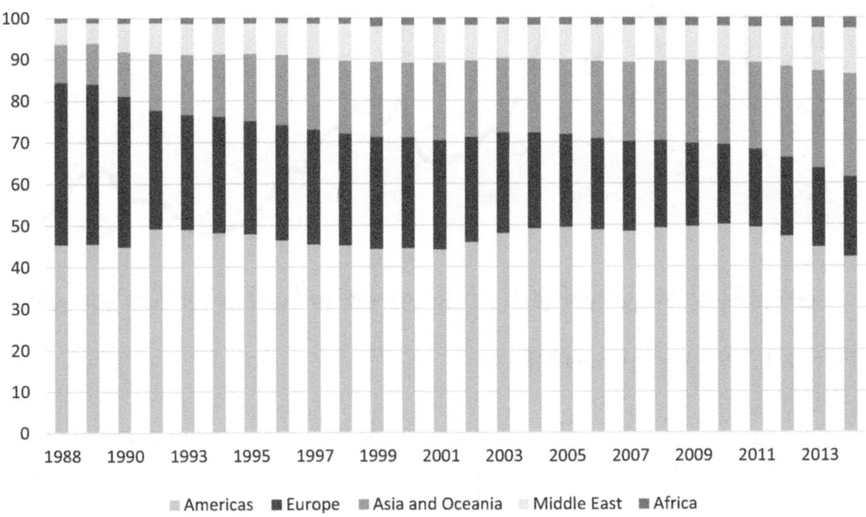

Figure 1.1 Regional share of milex

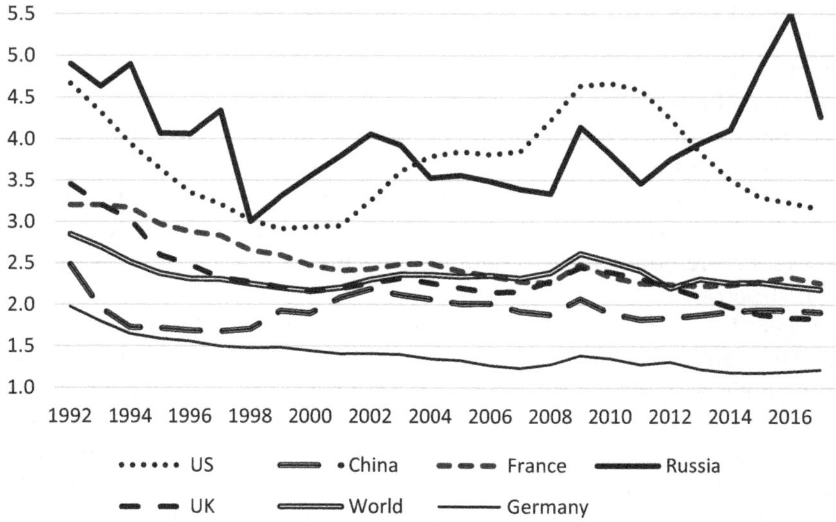

Figure 1.2 Milex share in GDP – selected countries (%)

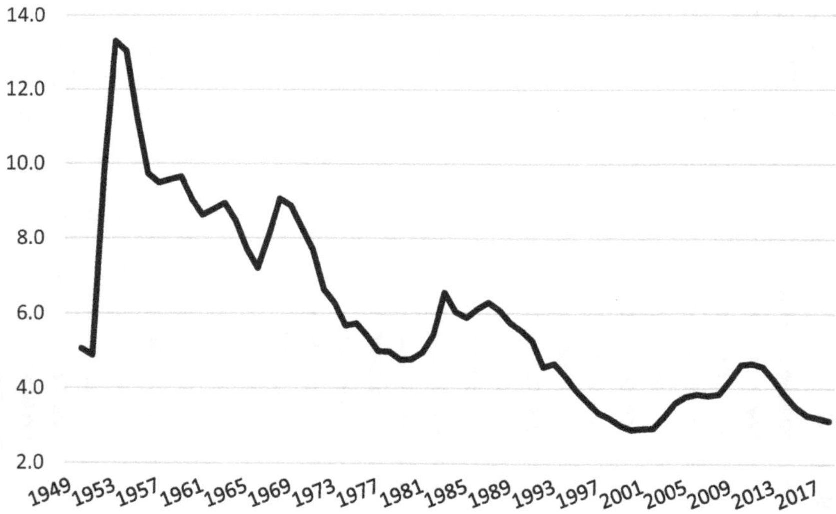

Figure 1.3 U.S. milex share in GDP (%)

was broken due to the Soviet invasion of Afghanistan in 1980 and the election of President Reagan, which pushed milex to the peak of 6.3 percent in 1986. The end of the Cold War led to a steady and significant decline in milex as a share of GDP, dropping to 2.9 percent in 1999–2000. This was followed by a steady increase throughout the 2000s, triggered by the September 11 attacks and the subsequent global war on terrorism. Currently, milex has again decreased since the 2010s, falling to 3.1 percent in 2017. Figure 1.4 shows this general pattern in terms of average spending over decades along with the other main variables in the study: profit rate, unemployment, and economic growth.

Profit rates both in the U.S. and other major economies rose in the post–WW II era up until the mid-1960s. This rise was followed by a fall until 1982 when profit rates recovered again during the neo-liberal period. After a short fall from 1997 to 2001, profit rates once again rose in the credit boom up to 2005–6. In the 1970s, there was a substantial transfer of profit from the non-financial to the financial sector in the U.S., which continued at an increasing rate under the full neo-liberal paradigm (Bakir and Campbell, 2013).

A sizeable literature has examined the effect of milex on economic growth and unemployment in the U.S. and other major countries. While there is an evident positive effect of milex on unemployment (Tang et al., 2009), the effect on economic growth is inconclusive. One part of the literature finds a negative effect, suggesting that milex impedes economic growth because it crowds out productive spending, such as public and private investments and education. Another part of literature argues for a positive effect. According to this view, milex leads to fiscal expansion and higher aggregate demand, thereby increasing employment and output if there is spare capacity, while technology-intensive military production may have a spill-over effect on the civilian sector. Overall, the literature provides inconclusive evidence due to various factors, such as degree of utilisation, how milex is financed, and externalities from milex (Dunne et al., 2005, pp. 450–451).

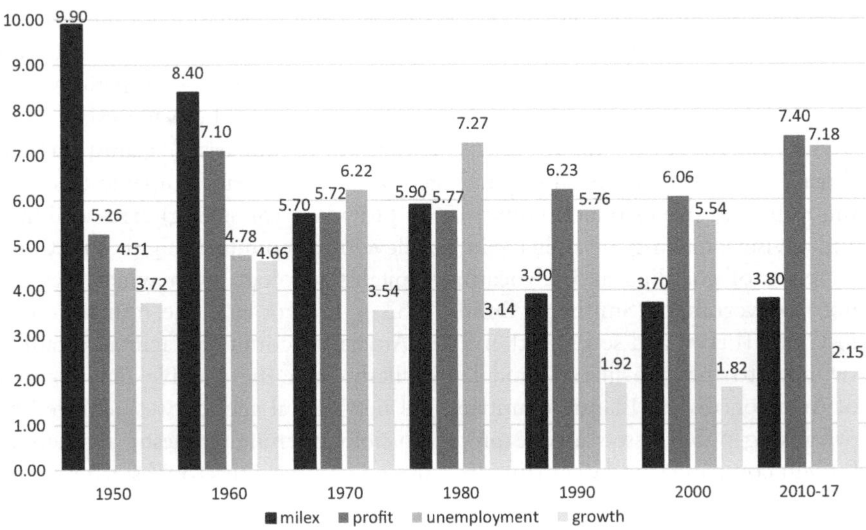

Figure 1.4 U.S. milex share in GDP (decadal averages)

Strategic and economic motives for military expenditure

There are three main economic views regarding conflict (Smith, 2009). First, according to the materialist view, wars between countries as well as civil wars in poor countries result from the battle for natural resources like oil, water, or diamonds. Second, the liberal[5] view suggests that free trade and economic integration lead countries to reduce their milex, which in turn promotes peace and prosperity as they avoid conflict spirals and devote more resources to social spending. Wars, on the other hand, cause large budget deficits because of increasing milex and declining tax revenues due to disruptions in trade. The origin of the liberal approach goes back to Immanuel Kant's view that citizens governed by effective, democratically representative regimes that promote individual freedoms and rights become less willing to sacrifice themselves in military conflicts. Democracies are also less likely to go to war with each other: the so-called *democratic peace* or *peace dividend*.[6] Third, the mercantilist-Leninist view, on the other hand, can be best summarised by the famous aphorism of Carl von Clausewitz, the 19th-century Prussian general and military theorist, that "war is the continuation of politics by other means". According to the orthodox Marxist view, however, war is the product of the capitalist system, a product to *protect* itself because the system must expand its markets. As Luxemburg noted, the direct coercive power provided by the military and the ideological influence of militarism were key mechanisms of primitive accumulation in the history of capitalism (Rowthorn, 1980). War creates additional demand, helps to eradicate stock surpluses, and counteracts the tendency of profit rates to fall.

There are several strategic and economic motives for milex (Smith and Smith, 1983), with three aspects of the strategic requirement for milex in capitalist systems. First, capitalist states must protect the international capitalist system from external threats, such as communism or radical Islamic terrorism. Second, military power is used to sustain the hegemony of core nations over peripheral capitalist countries and to regulate the rivalry between core countries. Third, states use military power (and promote militarism) against internal threats to protect the social order. Core countries also build organic ties with the militaries of peripheral countries by providing (or selling) arms, training, and advisers, making the military in less-developed countries highly functional in terms of guarding and advocating capitalist ideology, even when they are not in government (Smith and Smith, 1983, p. 43). For example, military coups in Chile, Turkey, and several other Latin American countries facilitated radical switches to the neo-liberal model.[7] Similarly, after the forcible liberalisation of Arab socialist or Islamic countries, the neo-liberal agenda was achieved by privatising public assets as cheaply as possible, opening domestic markets to foreign companies, and exporting low-priced commodities to Western markets (Galbraith, 2004, p. 299).

External or internal threats are considered major determinants of milex. In this sense, during the Cold War, the key determinant of the milex in both the

U.S. and U.S.S.R. was the arms race. In an arms race, both countries spend more but neither can increase their security.[8] Arms races also occurred between India and Pakistan, Greece and Turkey, North Korea and South Korea, and China and Taiwan. However, even in the absence of external and internal threats, countries may prefer to have high milex for status reasons because a powerful state is commonly associated with having a strong military. In this sense, the military-industrial complex (MIC) theory offers an institutional perspective to understand milex and conflict. The MIC, a concept popularised by U.S. President Eisenhower, refers to a coalition of vested interests across the bureaucracy, the armed forces, and large arms producer firms. (See Chapter 3 for a detailed discussion.) This symbiotic coalition, which has an autonomous structure within the state, promotes and lobbies for high milex in the name of 'national security' by using actual or perceived internal or external threats. In fact, even within the military there is rivalry between the army, navy, and air force for more power and resources, pushing their own agenda regarding new weapons in the case of the U.S. (Smith, 2009, p. 27). At the global level, NATO, a part of the MIC, also favours higher milex.

Economic effect of military expenditure

To analyse the effect of milex on the economy, neoclassical economists use the tools of production possibility frontier (PPF), opportunity cost, and cost-benefit analysis. Basically, the state, a rational actor, tries to maximise the national interest by measuring the marginal benefits and marginal costs of milex.[9] The state considers that there is trade-off between different expenditures in the budget, with the benefits of milex generally considered as increased security. The opportunity cost of milex is what could be gained if that money was spent on social security, such as health and education, or used to reduce taxation to allow higher private consumption. Therefore, there is a clear trade-off between civil spending and milex if national defence[10] (i.e. milex) is treated as a pure public good in a rational-choice setting. The neoclassical approach's well-known pros and cons are highly pronounced in this context. The approach is very appealing to researchers as it allows consistent formal theoretical models to be developed to inform empirical work (Dunne, 2000). However, this supply-side analysis tends to be ahistorical and ignores the internal role of the military and military interests (i.e. the military-industrial complex, MIC). In other words, the neoclassical approach assumes that there is a national consensus over the 'utility function'. Moreover, this approach is also unrealistic in terms of measuring marginal security benefits and the costs of decisions made by these 'rational actors' (Dunne, 2000). Elements within the MIC who benefit from higher milex have an interest in exaggerating military threats. In contrast, the general public tends to be either unaware of such threats or unwilling to engage in making such strategic estimates (Smith, 2009, p. 88).

There are two main views regarding the economic effects of milex: while one group argues that increasing milex raises aggregate demand and boosts economic growth, the other emphasises its long-term negative effects on economic growth through crowding out civilian resources. Keynesian and some Marxist arguments overlap in terms of the role of milex in the economy. Marxists emphasise that the capitalist mode of production is prone to economic crises because the growth of production inherently runs ahead of aggregate demand since the former depends on suppression of wages, which is the source of the latter. In other words, there is a chronic lack of aggregate demand, preventing capitalists from realising surplus as profit. Competition within the capitalist system forces firms to reduce their cost of production by increasing the degree of mechanisation in production, leading to enhanced productivity of labour. However, replacement of labour by machines leads to a rise in the organic composition of capital and, absent a rise in surplus value, this can lead to a decline in the rate of profit.

Against this background, Baran and Sweezy (1966) suggested an underconsumptionist theory of milex: through milex, capitalists can obtain higher profit rates and lower levels of competition, reducing the economic surplus of the economy. From this perspective, milex, including military aid to allies, is an important component of the monopolistic post-war capitalist system by increasing aggregate demand and absorbing surplus. Milex, contrary to other forms of state spending, is useful in that it absorbs the surplus without harming the interests of any powerful faction of the ruling class and without raising wages or capital.

This view is parallel to Keynes's main argument that there is a need for an active government to maintain aggregate demand. Thus, the argument is that high milex in the U.S. (and U.K.) provides the extra demand the system requires, thereby preventing slumps and generating sustained economic growth. This argument is commonly called *military Keynesianism*. The underconsumptionist view in Marxist thought (Baran and Sweezy, 1966; Kidron, 1970; Mandel, 1968) and military Keynesianism in general became popular to understand the role of milex in the capitalist system. However, this view has been criticised from a Marxist perspective by the seminal work of Smith (1977). He showed that milex actually reduces economic growth by crowding out investment that could have increased productivity otherwise, thereby challenging the underconsumptionist view. He concluded that it is more plausible to explain high milex in the 1960s in terms of its strategic role in maintaining capitalism than its economic role. Although the military did not have a substantial influence to repress and control domestic labour in the U.S. (Baran and Sweezy, 1966, p. 179), it was obviously significant in the case of most developing countries. Milex also has an impact on the economy through its international role in terms of expanding the capitalist system into non-capitalist systems and conflict between capitalist powers.

Marxist scholars have also dealt with the direct economic channel through which milex operates, while emphasising different aspects of this channel. For instance, while Engels noted the cost of arms production, Luxemburg and

Baran and Sweezy stressed the role of milex in offsetting a lack of aggregate demand. Similarly, Kidron argued that milex counteracts the permanent threat of overproduction by focusing on the effect of milex on the organic composition of capital through cheapening constant capital and the spin-off effect.[11] Thus, the Marxist literature suggests various linkages between milex and economic growth and profit rates while empirical studies remain inconclusive.

Above discussion therefore involves some major questions: how does milex affects economic growth? What are the pros and cons of economic models on the nexus of milex and economic growth? What is the role of milex in capitalism according to Marxist thought? More specifically, how does milex affect the rate of profit, a key indicator of health of capitalist economy? Does the effect change with respect to the development level of economies or to their role in the arms trade? For example, is it more likely for arms-exporting countries to enjoy the positive effect of arms production as arms exports contribute to the balance of payments and create jobs? This book aims to answer these questions.

Following this introduction, Chapter 2, *Economic Models of the Military Expenditure-Growth Nexus*, presents a general review of econometric models on the nexus of milex and economic growth. Chapter 3, *Military Keynesianism and the military-industrial complex*, through the works of John Kenneth Galbraith, offers a novel way to examine the origin and development of the MIC. Chapter 4, *Marxist Crisis Theories*, briefly summarises Marxist crisis theories that explain the long-term economic crisis caused by the internal contradictions of capitalism, leading to the potential for underconsumption or overproduction and the tendency for the profit rate to fall. Chapter 5, *The Effect of Military Expenditure on Profitability in Marxist Theories*, provides a brief discussion on the essential role of milex in capitalism to reveal direct linkages between milex and the profit rate. Chapter 6, *An Econometric Analysis of the Nexus of Military Expenditure and the Profit Rate*, provides comprehensive evidence on the effect of milex on profit rates, covering 31 major countries for 1950–2014. Chapter 7, *Analysis of the Nexus of Military Expenditure and Profit: Country Cases* provides further evidence based on time-series analysis for the same set of countries with alternative profit rates. Finally, the *Conclusion* summarises the main arguments and findings of the book.

Notes

1 Throughout the book, I use defence economics, defence and peace economics, and military economics interchangeably, as well as defence spending and military spending. While the literature includes both *defence* and *defense*, I prefer to use *defence*.

2 The term also refers to military dictatorship or government by martial law.

3 Among many others, the U.S.A. in general, and particularly with Trump's administration, Russia with 'the new tsar' Putin, and Erdoğan's Turkey, with its Neo-Ottomanism (i.e. imperial nostalgia) can be considered examples of contemporary militarist states.

4 The U.S. hosts 38 of the largest 100 arms firms, followed by 27 in Europe (the majority in the U.K. and France), 10 in Russia, and 7 in South Korea (SIPRI, 2018).

5 Here and throughout the book (unless otherwise indicated), *liberal* is used in the classical sense of those who believe in free markets and free trade. In the U.S., however, the term refers to the Left, associated with social liberalism.

6 The sizeable literature on the negative relationship between democracy level and milex shows that democratic or liberal regimes spend less on the military than autocratic regimes (Töngür et al., 2015). Covering 37 countries over 1988–2003, Töngür and Elveren (2015) found a significant negative relationship between social democratic welfare regimes and milex. They also found that social democratic political regimes have significantly lower milex, whereas communist nations, nations experiencing civil war, and conservative democracies tend to spend more on the military. Covering 130 countries for 1963–2000, Töngür et al., 2015 confirmed the negative relationship between democracy level and milex, finding that social democratic political regimes tend to spend less on the military. They also showed that higher income inequality is associated with higher milex.

7 For example, Chile's full privatisation of social security (replacing the "pay as you go" system, PAYG, with a private system) in 1981 under the Pinochet dictatorship is one of the most radical transformations in the history of privatisation of social security. It is also perhaps the most hypocritical case because all Chile's armed forces, including the military and police, continued to enjoy their old PAYG pensions. Moreover, Chile was praised by international organisations led by the World Bank as a "miracle" from the very early day of the system, and aggressively promoted as a role model for other developing countries – until they revised their view in the early 2000s (Holzmann, 2002; Elveren, 2008). Likewise, the 1980 military coup was the breakpoint in the formation of contemporary Turkey. It facilitated the establishment of the neo-liberal paradigm by repressing the voice of civil society and shutting down the largest labour union, promoting Islamic values against a rising left-wing stance. After three years of harsh repression, the military regime allowed a civilian successor to follow the same neo-liberal model. This transformation paved the way for Erdoğan's current Islamic regime.

8 Arms races increase costs for rival nations, not just in terms of total sales (i.e. total cost), but also in terms of advanced technology (i.e. unit cost) because it occurs not just in terms of volume of weapons but in terms of their technology. The historically rising unit cost is a distinctive characteristic of the arms industry (Hartley, 2017, p. 44).

9 Arms markets have a different structure than other markets, allowing arms firms to enjoy high profits. By the nature of the industry, there are few large corporations in the market, which form duopolies or oligopolies (e.g. Boeing, Lockheed Martin, and Northrop Grumman in the U.S. combat aircraft market) or monopolies (e.g. nuclear-powered submarine suppliers in France and the U.K.) (Hartley, 2017, p. 42). Therefore, being isolated from competition, these companies enjoy more than the general rate of profit. Arms firms do not compete over prices but rather on the technological level of their product. They are R&D intensive firms whose R&D efforts are funded by governments. Private firms are not willing to undertake major arms projects because these are high-technology projects that involve large costs, and the government is the only buyer. However, such a 'great' interdependence between the State and private arms firms is not the only model in the arms market since major arms firms can also be either fully or partly state owned, as for example in France, Italy, Spain, and India (Hartley, 2017, p. 42).

10 A good (e.g. defence or peace) is called a public good if one person's consumption does not affect other people's consumption (non-rivalry) and, once it is provided, if no individual can exclude others from its consumption (non-excludability). Smith (2009) contends that national defence cannot be considered a public good. In the case of deterrence, defence is a public good because milex prevents an attack by enemies, thereby protecting everyone without any exclusion. However, protection from attack does not meet these two qualifications of a public good. "The Spitfires that were defending airfields during the Battle of Britain were not defending London, so there was rivalry in

consumption" while "the benefits of the defence budget may be private benefits that accrue to those that determine it" (Smith, 2009, p. 37).

11 Arms industries may benefit the economy through the spin-off effect as high technology produced in the military sector spills over into the civilian sector. However, some argue that while military technology led civilian technology until the 1980s, civilian technology had overtaken military technology in many areas by the 1990s, particularly in electronics (e.g. IT and mobile phones). That is, these scholars argued that there is no spin-off effect from the military to the civilian sectors; on the contrary, technology transfer is from the civilian to the military sector (Dunne and Sköns, 2011).

References

Bakir, E. and Campbell, A. (2013). The financial rate of profit: What is it, and how has it behaved in the United States? *Review of Radical Political Economics*, 45(3), pp. 295–304.

Baran, P. A. and Sweezy, P. M. (1966). *Monopoly capital: An essay on the American economic and social order*. New York and London: Monthly Review Press.

D'Agostino, G., Dunne, P. and Pieroni, L. (2016). *Military spending and contemporary capitalism*. Available at: www.cpes.org.uk/dev/wp-content/uploads/2016/06/Agostino_Dunne_Pieroni_Milex_and_Contemporary_Capitalism.pdf

Dunne, P. (2000). *The economic effects of military expenditure in developing countries*. London: Economics Group Middlesex University Business School.

Dunne, P. and Sköns, E. (2011). *The changing military industrial complex*. Available at: http://ideas.repec.org/p/uwe/wpaper/1104.html

Dunne, P., Smith, R. P. and Willenbockel, D. (2005). Models of military expenditure and growth: A critical review. *Defence and Peace Economics*, 16(6), pp. 449–461.

Elveren, A. Y. (2008). Social security reform in Turkey: A critical perspective. *Review of Radical Political Economics*, 40(2), pp. 212–232.

Galbraith, J. K. (2004). The worldly philosophers and the war economy. *Social Research*, 71(2), pp. 293–304.

Hartley, K. (2017). *The economics of arms*. Croydon: Agenda Publishing.

Holzmann, R. (2002). The world bank approach to pension reform. *International Social Security Review*, 53(1), pp. 1–34.

Kidron, M. (1970). *Western capitalism since the war revised edition*. Harmondsworth: Pelican Books.

Mandel, E. (1968). *Marxist economic theory*. 2nd ed. London: Merlin.

Rowthorn, R. (1980). *Capitalism conflict & inflation essays in political economy*. London: Lawrence and Wishart.

Sandler, T. and Hartley, K. (1995). *The economics of defense*. Cambridge: Cambridge University Press.

SIPRI (Stockholm International Peace Research Institute). (2018). Available at: www.sipri.org/

Smith, D. and Smith, R. (1983). *The economics of militarism*. London: Pluto Press.

Smith, R. (1977). Military expenditure and capitalism. *Cambridge Journal of Economics*, 1(1), pp. 61–76.

Smith, R. (2009). *Military economics the interaction of power and money*. New York: Palgrave Macmillan.

Tang, J. H., Lai, C. C. and Lin, E. S. (2009). Military expenditure and unemployment rates: Granger causality tests using global panel data. *Defence and Peace Economics*, 20(4), pp. 253–267.

Töngür, Ü. and Elveren, A.Y. (2015). Military expenditures, income inequality, and welfare and political regimes: A dynamic panel data analysis. *Defence and Peace Economics*, 26(1), pp. 49–74.

Töngür, Ü., Hsu, S. and Elveren, A.Y. (2015). Military expenditures and political regimes: Evidence from global data, 1963–2000. *Economic Modelling*, 44, pp. 68–79.

WMEAT (World Military Expenditures and Arms Transfers). (2015). Available at: www.state.gov/t/avc/rls/rpt/wmeat/

2 Economic models of the military expenditure-growth nexus

Introduction

This chapter briefly presents major economic models to explain the effect of milex on economic growth. Assessing the importance of milex to the economy is the core task of defence economics. A key empirical question that has been addressed is whether milex has a positive impact on economic growth mainly by boosting aggregate demand or a negative impact mainly by crowding out public and private investments. Milex influences economic growth in several ways. In the short run, the main effect is substitution between milex and other government expenditure. In the long run, milex influences economic growth through different channels due to its effect on labour, capital, technology and debt, and through external relations, socio-political effects and conflicts (D'Aogstino et al., 2018).

The literature on the nexus of milex and economic growth is led by the seminal work of Emile Benoit (1973). Since Benoit's study, different growth models have been used to explain this nexus based on different growth theories, most of which do not assign an explicit role for milex. Numerous studies have also investigated this relationship by utilising causality tests. The following section summarises these models and the extensive literature, which yields conflicting results on the effects of milex on economic growth.

Economic models

Using time-series, cross-section, or panel studies, researchers have adopted different econometric models, such as the Feder-Ram model (Feder, 1983; Biswas and Ram, 1986), the Deger-type model (Deger and Smith, 1983; Deger, 1986), the endogenous growth model (Barro, 1990); the augmented Solow growth model (Mankiw et al., 1992); and the new macroeconomic model (Romer, 2000; Taylor, 2000).

The Feder-Ram model

Feder (1983, 1986) introduced a model to analyse the effects of imports and exports on economic growth in developing countries. Ram (1986) and Biswas and Ram (1986) developed this model to examine the effect of the military sector on economic growth. The model incorporates milex as an explanatory variable in a single-equation growth regression analysis (Dunne et al., 2005).

Below is a two-sector version of this model, including the civilian sector (*C*) and military sector (*M*), basically taken from Dunne et al. (2005):

$$M = M(L_m, K_m), C = C(L_c, K_c, M) = M^{\theta}c(L_c, K_c) \tag{1}$$

Where *L* and *K* refer to homogenous labour and capital, and military production has external effects on civilian production.

The factor endowment constraints are given by

$$L = \sum_{i \in s} L_{i,} K = \sum_{i \in s} K_{i,} S = \{m, c\} \tag{2}$$

And domestic income, Y, is

$$Y = C + M \tag{3}$$

Where *C* and *M* are in monetary output values.

In the equivalent form, equation (3) can be written in terms of the monetary values of marginal products of labour and capital:

$$Y = P_c Cr(L_c, K_{c,} M) + P_m Mr(L_m, K_m) \tag{3'}$$

Where P_c and P_m refer to the money prices of the real output quantities *Cr* and *Mr* and where the marginal products of labour (M_L, C_L) and capital (M_K, C_K) change by a constant uniform proportion. Therefore,

$$\frac{P_m Mr_L}{P_c Cr_L} = \frac{P_m Mr_K}{P_c Cr_K} = 1 + \mu \tag{4}$$

Equation (4) shows that the marginal factor productivities of capital and labour depend on the prices used in outputs across sectors.

The derivation of equation (3) proportionally with equations (1) and (2) yields the growth equation:

$$\dot{Y} = \frac{C_L L}{Y}\dot{L} + C_K \frac{1}{Y} + (\frac{\mu}{1+\mu} + C_M)\frac{M}{Y}\dot{M} \tag{5}$$

Where dot denotes the rate of growth of the variable and I = d*K* is net investment. Equation (5) can be restated by using the elasticity of civilian output with respect to military output, *θ*, in equation (1) in the following form:

$$\dot{Y} = \frac{C_L L}{Y}\dot{L} + C_K \frac{1}{Y} + (\frac{\mu}{1+\mu} - \theta)\frac{M}{Y}\dot{M} + \theta\dot{M} \tag{5'}$$

The variations of this equation have been used is many cross-country, time-series and pooled cross-sectional studies. However, Dunne et al. (2005) showed that the model has important problems in terms of interpreting the results and its econometric techniques. There are some flaws with the interpretation of the marginal factor productivity differential between sectors, μ, in empirical studies. It is commonly considered that a non-zero μ shows the existence of efficiency or productivity differentials between the civilian and military sectors. According to this interpretation, if the implicit price ratio ($P = P_m/P_c$) is less than the marginal rate of transformation (MRT) between *Cr* and *Mr*, (P < MRT) – which measures the amount of *bread* that must be given up in order to produce more *guns* – then negative μ suggests that GDP would increase if resources were moved from military to civilian production, or vice versa if P>MRT and μ>0. However, Dunne et al. (2005) note that the increase in GDP is not a result of shifting resources from an inefficient sector to the efficient one. Rather, GDP increases because, at the initial production level, "the value of a unit of *Cr* in terms of *Mr* goods (1/P) used in the calculation of *Y* is higher than the social cost of producing another unit of *Cr* in terms of *Mr* (1/MRT)". In fact, the model is "by construction, incapable of accounting for intra-sectoral organizational inefficiencies" (p. 455).

The authors also note several important problems in the estimation of the following equation (5") derived from equation (5).

$$\dot{Y} = \beta_1 \dot{L} + \beta_2 \frac{M}{Y} + \beta_3 \frac{M}{Y} \dot{M} + \beta_4 \dot{M} \ \varepsilon \qquad (5'')$$

First, while capital enters as a share of investment in this estimation, labour enters as the growth rate, creating asymmetry. Second, the model neither justifies nor clarifies the error term. Third, the growth rate of milex on the right-hand side leads to a simultaneity problem: if the share of milex is constant, then the change in output growth will determine the growth of milex. Fourth, the final two terms generate a multicollinearity problem (p. 456). The Feder-Ram model has lost popularity, particularly following Dunne et al.'s (2005) critique (Smith, forthcoming).

Deger-Smith model

A demand-side model was proposed by Smith (1980). Based on the Keynesian view, total output is represented as the summation of aggregate consumption (*C*), investment (*I*), milex (*M*), and the balance of trade (i.e. exports minus imports, *B*).

$$Y = Q - W = C + I + M + B \qquad (6)$$

Where *W* is the gap between actual output, *Y*, and potential output, Q. Resetting the equation for *I* by dividing with Q yields

$$i = 1 - w - c - m - b \qquad (7)$$

Smith then defines $c = \alpha_0 - \alpha_1 u - \alpha_2 g$ (8)

Where *u* and *g* denote the unemployment rate and the growth rate of actual output, respectively. Smith assumes that "the balance between domestic demand and potential supply is directly related to the unemployment rate", so that

$$\beta u = w + b \tag{9}$$

Thus, substituting (8) and (9) in equation (7), coupled with several other transformations, he derives the following estimatable equation:

$$i = (1 - \alpha_0) - (\beta - \alpha_1)u + \alpha_2 g - m \tag{10}$$

Equation (10) shows the negative relationship between milex and investment. That is, it allows us to empirically test the crowding-out effect of milex. The basic flaw of this demand-side approach is that it is likely to be associated with the negative effect of milex, just like the supply-side Feder-Ram model, which tends to yield positive results by its construction (Sandler and Hartley, 1995, p. 211).

This problem is addressed by the model suggested by Deger and Smith (1983) and Deger (1986), which considers both the supply and demand effects of milex in a simultaneous equations model, allowing both direct and indirect effects of milex on the civilian sector. A general form of the four-equation model can be presented as follows:

$$g_{it} = a_0 + a_1 s_{it} + a_2 m_{it} + a_3 B_{it} + \sum_j \alpha_j^g x_{j,it}^g + u_{it}^g \tag{11}$$

$$s_{it} = b_0 + b_1 m_{it} + b_2 g_{it} + b_3 B_{it} + \sum_k \alpha_k^s x_{k,it}^s + u_{it}^s \tag{12}$$

$$B_{it} = c_0 + c_1 m_{it} + c_2 g_{it} + \sum_l \alpha_l^B x_{l,it}^B + u_{it}^B \tag{13}$$

$$m_{it} = d_0 + \sum_n \alpha_n^m x_{n,it}^m + u_{it}^m \tag{14}$$

Where *g* is the growth rate of income per capita, *s* is the saving ratio, *m* is milex, *B* is the balance of trade, *x* denotes all predetermined variables in each equation, and *u* is the error term (Deger and Sen, 1995; Alptekin and Levine, 2012).

Augmented Solow-Swann growth model

One way to analyse the effect of milex on economic growth is to use the Cobb-Douglas production function and add milex in its logarithmic form. However, this approach is criticised as milex is added without any theoretical or empirical justification.

An alternative approach is a model based on the augmented Solow-Swan growth model, introduced by Mankiw et al. (1992) and used by Knight et al. (1996). The model below is taken from Dunne et al. (2005) and Töngür and Elveren (2017).

A human capital augmented Solow-Swan growth model with Harrod-neutral technical progress is presented as follows:

$$Y(t) = K(t)^{\alpha} H(t)^{\beta} \left[A(t)L(t)\right]^{1-\alpha-\beta} \tag{15}$$

Where Y is aggregate income, K is the capital stock, H denotes human capital stock, L is labour, A is the technology parameter, and AL refers to effective labour. α, β and $(1-\alpha-\beta)$ refer to the share of income of capital (i.e. capital-output elasticity), human capital and effective labour, respectively. Parameters α and β follow the following restrictions: $0<\alpha<1$, $0<\beta<1$, $\alpha+\beta<1$).

The technology parameter evolves according to

$$A(t) = A_0 e^{gt} m(t)^{\theta} \tag{16}$$

where g is the exogenous rate of technological progress, which allows a constant K/Y ratio over time, m is the share of milex in aggregate output, and θ is the elasticity of steady-state income with respect to the long-run military burden. Within this specification, Dunne et al. (2005) claim that a permanent change in milex does not affect long-run steady-state growth rate but it might have a permanent level effect on per capita income along the steady-state growth path to the new steady-state equilibrium.

Given the standard Solow model of an exogenous saving rate (s), a constant labour force growth rate (n), and a depreciation rate for both physical and human capital (d), the dynamics of physical capital per effective worker ($k_e = K/AL$) and human capital per effective worker ($h_e = H/AL$) can be derived from the model:

$$\begin{aligned} k_e(t) &= s_k y_e(t) - (n+g+d)k_e(t) \\ h_e(t) &= s_h y_e(t) - (n+g+d)h_e(t) \end{aligned} \tag{17}$$

where s_k and s_h denote the shares of physical capital and human capital investment in aggregate income and y_e refers to Y/AL. The steady-state levels of physical and human capital stock are:

$$\begin{aligned} k_e^* &= \left[\frac{s_h^{\beta} s_k^{1-\beta}}{n+g+d}\right]^{1/(1-\alpha-\beta)} \\ h_e^* &= \left[\frac{s_h^{1-\alpha} s_k^{\alpha}}{n+g+d}\right]^{1/(1-\alpha-\beta)} \end{aligned} \tag{18}$$

The transitory dynamics of income per effective worker in a neighbourhood of the steady state are approximated by

$$\frac{\partial \ln y_e}{\partial t} = (\alpha + \beta - 1)(n + g + d)\left[\ln y_e(t) - \ln y_e^{*}\right] \tag{19}$$

where y_e^{*} is the steady-state level of aggregate output. Then, the equation for observable per capita income ($y = Y/L$) in a suitable form for empirical analysis can be specified as follows:

$$\begin{aligned}\ln y(t) &= e^{z} \ln y(t-1) + \left(1 - e^{z}\right) \\ &\quad \times \left\{ \ln A_0 + \frac{\alpha}{1-\alpha-\beta} \ln s_k + \frac{\beta}{1-\alpha-\beta} \ln s_h \right. \\ &\qquad \left. - \frac{\alpha+\beta}{1-\alpha-\beta} \ln(n+g+d) \right\} \\ &\qquad + \theta \ln milex(t) - e^{z} \theta \ln milex(t-1) + \left(t - (t-1)e^{z}\right) g\end{aligned}$$

where $z = (\alpha + \beta - 1)\ (n + g + d)$ (20)

To investigate the impact of milex on growth in a panel data context, Dunne et al. (2005) proposed the following empirical form:

$$\ln y_{it} = \alpha_0 + \beta_0 \ln y_{it-1} + \sum_j \beta_j \ln x_{jit} + u_{it} \tag{21}$$

where the subscripts i and t denote countries and years, respectively, while x_j denotes standard explanatory variables in a Solow-type defence-growth model, which includes saving rate, growth rate of effective labour plus depreciation, human capital, and military burden.

There is a sizable literature examining the effects of milex on economic growth based on equations (20) and (21) and their extensions. According to this model, the share of milex to GDP influences the factor productivity of inputs through the effect on the efficiency coefficient of labour-augmenting technological progress (Dunne et al., 2005).

Endogenous growth model

Another major model analysing the effect of milex on economic growth is based on the endogenous growth model originally introduced by Barro (1990). The following outline was presented by Pieroni (2009). The model begins with the aggregate production represented as the Cobb-Douglas function:

$$y = A k^{1-\alpha-\beta} g_1^{\alpha} g_2^{\beta} \qquad 0 < \alpha,\ \beta < 1 \tag{22}$$

Where A is the exogenous rate of technology, k is private capital stock, g_1 is military government expenditure, and g_2 is non-military government expenditure.

The growth of private capital, $\dot{k}$, is

$$\dot{k} = (1-\tau)y - c \tag{23}$$

Where τ denotes the flat-rate income tax and c is private consumption. The agent chooses the amount of consumption (c) and capital (k) to maximise future utility functions, presented as:

$$U = \int u(c)e^{-\rho t}dt \tag{24}$$

Where ρ is the rate of time preference. Utility increases and the concave function of c is
$\partial(c) > 0$ and $\partial^2(c) < 0$, and is represented as

$$u(c) = \frac{c^{1-\sigma} - 1}{1-\sigma} \tag{25}$$

Where σ refers to the intertemporal elasticity of substitution of consumption. Since $\sigma > 0$, the marginal elasticity is $-\sigma$.

The government finances military and non-military expenditure by using a flat-rate income tax, τ. Therefore, the budget constraint is given as follows:

$$G = \tau y = g_1 + g_2 = \varnothing \tau y + (1-\varnothing)\tau y \tag{26}$$

Where $\varnothing$ and $(1 - \varnothing)$ are the proportions of military and non-military expenditure.

The steady-state growth rate of consumption, $\frac{\dot{c}}{c}$, can be found by substituting (25) in (24) and maximising the subject to (22), (23), and (26):

$$\frac{\dot{c}}{c} = \gamma = \left[(1-\alpha-\beta)(1-\tau)\varnothing^{\alpha}(1-\varnothing)^{\beta} A\left(\frac{G}{k}\right)^{(\alpha+\beta)} - \rho\right] \tag{27}$$

Solving for G/k, equation (27) can be rewritten in terms of the parameter $\varnothing$:

$$\frac{G}{k} = \left(\tau A\varnothing^{\alpha}(1-\varnothing)^{\beta}\right)^{1-\alpha-\beta} \tag{28}$$

Inserting (28) into (27) and differentiating with respect to $\varnothing$ yields the following result:

$$\frac{\partial\gamma}{\partial\varnothing} = \frac{1}{\theta}\left[\varphi\,\varnothing^{\frac{\alpha}{1-\alpha-\beta}}(1-\varnothing)^{\frac{\beta}{1-\alpha-\beta}}\left[\alpha\varnothing^{-1} - \beta(1-\varnothing)^{-1}\right]\right] \tag{29}$$

Where $\varphi = (1-\alpha-\beta)(1-\tau)A^{\frac{1}{1-\alpha-\beta}}(\tau)^{\frac{\alpha+\beta}{1-\alpha-\beta}}$

Finally, by differentiating (29) with respect to the share of milex and recalling that $0 < \varnothing < 1$, one obtains some restrictions on the expected sign of milex:

$$\left\{\frac{\alpha}{\varnothing} < \frac{\beta}{1-\varnothing} \qquad \frac{d\gamma}{d\varnothing} > 0\right\}$$
$$\left\{\frac{\alpha}{\varnothing} > \frac{\beta}{1-\varnothing} \qquad \frac{d\gamma}{d\varnothing} < 0\right\} \tag{30}$$

The implication of this is that the productivity parameters for milex's initial share of spending affect its influence on economic growth. More specifically, milex reduces growth if $\varnothing$ exceeds its optimal level. The model suggests that milex, because it is tax-funded state spending, can increase economic growth by improving social welfare. Consequently, milex has non-linear effects on economic growth due to the interaction between positive productivity and negative taxation (Pieroni, 2009).

New macroeconomic model

Atesoglu (2002) suggested an alternative approach to analyse the effect of milex on economic growth[1] by incorporating it into the new macroeconomic model introduced by Romer (2000) and Taylor (2000). This augmented Keynesian cross model is presented as

$$Y_t = C_t + I_t + X_t + M_t + G_t \tag{31}$$

Where Y_t is real aggregate output, C_t is real consumption, I_t is real investment, X_t is real net exports, G_t is real civilian government expenditure, and M_t is real milex. With a given real interest rate, R_t, based on the Keynesian cross model, they can be written as

$$C_t = a + b(Y_t - T_t) \tag{32}$$
$$T_t = c + dY_t \tag{33}$$
$$I_t = e - fR_t \tag{34}$$
$$X_t = g - hY_t - iR_t \tag{35}$$

Where, in addition to the defined variables above, T_t is real taxes and I_t is real investment. Solving equations (31) – (35) for Y_t and adding a stochastic error term yields i.

$$Y_t = \alpha_1 + \alpha_2 G_t + \alpha_3 M_t + \alpha_4 R_t + u_t \tag{36}$$

Where $\alpha_1 = \frac{(a - bc + e + g)}{(1 - b(1 - d + h))}$, $\alpha_2 = \alpha_3 = \frac{1}{(1 - b(1 - d + h))}$,

$\alpha_4 = \frac{-(f + i)}{(1 - b(1 - d + h))}$,

and α_2, $\alpha_3 > 0$ and $\alpha_4 < 0$

Causality approach

Many milex-growth studies have used causality tests. Granger causality tests can determine the direction of causation between variables (Granger, 1969). Whereas structural models pre-specify relationships between variables, Granger causality methods are free of such theoretical assumptions. In short, Granger causality tests investigate the presence of a relationship between the current value of X_t, its lagged values; and another variable, Y_t, in the following form:

$$X_{i,t} = \Sigma_{k=1}^{p} \alpha_i^k X_{i,t-k} + \Sigma_{k=1}^{p} \beta_i^k Y_{i,t-k} + u_{i,t} \quad (37a)$$

$$Y_{i,t} = \Sigma_{k=1}^{p} \gamma_i^k Y_{i,t-k} + \Sigma_{k=1}^{p} \delta_i^k X_{i,t-k} + v_{i,t} \quad (37b)$$

If the lagged values of *X* and *Y* are better predictors of X_t than just the lagged values of *X*, then *Y* Granger causes *X*, and vice versa. Therefore, (37a) and (37b) may yield no causality, unidirectional causality (either running from X to Y or from Y to X), or bidirectional causality.

If more than two variables are examined, then vector autoregression models (VAR) are used[2]. (See Chapter 7 for other time-series methods applied to the U.S. and other major countries.)

$$Y_t = a + \Pi_1 Y_{t-1} + \Pi_2 Y_{t-2} + \cdots + \Pi_1 Y_{t-p} + \varepsilon_t \cdots\cdots\cdots t = 1, \ldots T \quad (38)$$

Where $Y_t = (y_{1t}, y_{2t}, \ldots y_{nt})$ is the (nx1) vector of variables, Π_i is (nxn) coefficient matrices, and ε_t is a vector of errors with expected value zero and covariance matrix.

Brief literature survey

There are three groups in the literature on the milex-economic growth nexus. One part contends that milex impedes economic growth due to misallocation of resources. There is a trade-off between different types of expenditure, such that increasing milex, which is considered unproductive spending, may crowd out productive outlays, such as public and private investments and education. According to this strand, milex is detrimental to economic growth because it siphons off resources that otherwise would increase the economy's productive capacity. In addition, in the case of arms-importing countries, milex can distort the balance of payments, reducing potentially growth-promoting capital inflows (Sandler and Hartley, 1995, p. 202).

The second view argues for a positive effect as milex leads to fiscal expansion and higher aggregate demand, thereby increasing employment and output if there is spare capacity. Through R&D, milex may also have spill-over effect on the civilian sector. Finally, the third group argues for no causal relationship between milex and economic growth. There have been conflicting results on the effect of milex on economic growth because these positive and negative mechanisms are contingent on various factors, such as degree of utilisation, how milex is financed (i.e. cuts in other public expenditure, increased taxes, increased borrowing, or expansion in the money supply), externalities from military spending, and the effectiveness of milex in countering threats (Dunne et al., 2005, pp. 450–451). These factors tend to vary not just with respect to countries but also for the same country over time.

A sizeable and growing literature has investigated the relationship between milex and economic growth since the seminal work of Benoit (1973, 1978), which argued that milex enhances economic growth. Later studies using Keynesian, neoclassical, and structuralist models have provided conflicting results on the issue for different sets of countries (*inter alia* Dunne, 1996; Knight et al., 1996; Smith, 2000; Yakovlev, 2007; Hou and Chen, 2013; Dunne and Tian, 2015; Töngür and Elveren, 2017).

Early reviews of the extensive literature on the milex-economic growth nexus (Sandler and Hartley, 1995; Deger and Sen, 1995; Ram, 1995; Dunne, 1996; Smith, 2000) and recent ones (Dunne and Uye, 2010; Alptekin and Levin, 2012; Yesilyurt and Yesilyurt, 2014; Churchill and Yew, 2018) have yielded conflicting results due to several factors (Smith, forthcoming). First, model specification is the core of the analysis because it determines the functional form and how milex is measured (e.g. share in GDP, growth rate, level, or logarithm). It also determines which control variables are used, which significantly affects the outcome of the estimation. A second challenge is simultaneity because of the bidirectional relationship between output and milex, in that output affects demand for milex, and milex influences aggregate demand and supply (Smith, forthcoming). A third central issue is the choice of time-series, cross-section, or panel data because the results are highly sensitive to the time period covered (e.g. Cold War versus post–Cold War) and country selection (e.g. developed versus developing). Finally, it is crucial whether non-linearity has been taken into account because results may differ across countries with different income levels and across different income levels within the same country.

Dunne and Uye (2010) surveyed 102 studies to show that negative effects of milex were reported in 39 percent of cross-country and 35 percent of case studies. While 20 percent of these studies suggested positive effects, 40 percent had ambiguous results. In a follow-up study, Dunne and Tian (2013) examined 168 studies of an extended set of countries to show that almost 44 percent of cross-country studies and 31 percent of case studies reported that milex impairs economic growth, whereas 20 percent of cross-country studies and 25 percent of case studies reported negative effects. In addition, recent studies were more likely to find a negative impact. While 38 percent of Cold War cross-country studies found a negative effect, almost 53 percent of post–Cold War studies did. Similarly, for case studies, the percentage of studies reporting a positive effect also increased between the two eras, from 21.4 to 30 percent. Dunne and Tian also found that 63 percent of 72 case studies were based on only five countries: Greece, Turkey, India, Pakistan, and the United States. As they noted, the first four countries of this group with a beneficial economic effect of milex form two pairs in conflict (Dunne and Tian, 2013, p. 8).

Alptekin and Levine (2012) used a meta-analysis – a statistical method to systematically analyse the reported results of various empirical studies by taking into account the structural differences in findings of individual studies – to investigate the effect of milex on economic growth. They included 32 empirical studies with 169 estimates to apply bivariate and multivariate meta-regression analysis. Their findings suggest, first, that the combined effect of milex-growth studies is positive. Second, while their findings failed to confirm the negative impact of milex on economic growth in LDCs or generally, the positive effect is significantly common for developed countries. Third, there is a non-linear relationship between the variables in question. Fourth, the main methodological differences generating the varied results in the milex-growth nexus are the sample, time periods, and functional forms. Overall, the authors conclude, the findings confirm those of Ram (1995) and Dunne (1996). However, according to Dunne et al. (2005), while the relationship is mostly either insignificant or negative for developing countries, there is an even more pronounced negative relationship for developed countries. They also conclude that this negative effect occurs at the expense of investment rather than consumption.

Another meta-analysis (Churchill and Yew, 2018) covered 48 studies with 272 estimations to extended and mostly confirmed Alptekin and Levine (2012). The only exception was that Churchill and Yew found that there was no longer a positive relationship between milex and economic growth. Rather, their extended data set suggests a generally negative relationship. They suggest two possible factors for this. First, milex has increased consistently since 1998, except for a slight decline in 2011 during the significant recession. Second, they refer to Mauro (1998), who contends that corruption may have inflated the proportion of government military spending.

In a major study, Dunne and Tian (2015) took heterogeneities and non-linearity into account. They compiled a comprehensive data set for 106 countries for 1988–2010 to analyse the effect of milex on economic growth using the modelling framework suggested by Dunne et al. (2005). They found a significant short- and long-term negative impact of milex on economic growth. This negative effect remained after grouping countries as developed and developing, except for an insignificant long-run effect for developed countries. The short-run effect was negative and significant for low-, medium-, and high-income group countries while the long-run effect was negative and significant for the low- and high-income groups. While milex impaired economic growth whether or not countries were conflict-affected, contrary to expectations, the difference between these groups was not pronounced. However, milex had an insignificant effect in conflict-affected medium-income countries. The authors also found consistent results when they categorised countries with respect to their natural resource endowments, aid dependence and trade openness.

In another major study, Töngür and Elveren (2017) considered inequality in the nexus of milex and economic growth. They examined the effect of milex on economic growth for 82 countries for 1988–2008 by incorporating inequality along with its interaction with human capital in an augmented Solow growth model. Overall, the findings suggest that milex reduces economic growth across several model specifications and sensitivity analyses that include heterogeneity from different country groups (e.g. development level, arms trade, or fuel dependency). The findings also suggest that milex has a weaker effect on economic growth for arms-exporting and/or arms-importing countries than other countries. Unsurprisingly, human capital increases growth whereas income inequality decreases it. Considering human capital and income inequality together, income inequality hinders growth at lower levels of human capital but boosts it at higher levels.

Notes

1 See Halıcıoğlu (2004) for an application to Turkey and Atesoglu (2009) for the US.
2 See Dunne and Smith (2010) for a critical review of Granger causality studies and Emmanouilidis and Karpetis (2018) for other time-series methods used in researching the defence-growth nexus.

References

Alptekin, A. and Levine, P. (2012). Military expenditure and economic growth: A meta-analysis. *European Journal of Political Economy*, 28(4), pp. 636–650.

Atesoglu, H. S. (2002). Defence spending promotes aggregate output in the United States. *Defence and Peace Economics*, 13(1), pp. 55–60.

Atesoglu, H. S. (2009). Defence spending and aggregate output in the United States. *Defence and Peace Economics*, 20(1), pp. 21–26.

Barro, R. J. (1990). Government spending in a simple model of endogeneous growth. *Journal of Political Economy*, 98(S5), pp. S103–S126.

Benoit, E. (1973). *Defence and economic growth in developing countries*. Boston, MA: Lexington Books.

Benoit, E. (1978). Growth and defense in developing countries. *Economic Development and Cultural Change*, 26(2), pp. 271–280.

Biswas, B. and Ram, R. (1986). Military expenditures and economic growth in less developed countries: An augmented model and further evidence. *Economic Development and Cultural Change*, 34(2), pp. 361–372.

Churchill, S. A. and Yew, S. L. (2018). The effect of military expenditure on growth: An empirical synthesis. *Empirical Economics*, 5(3), pp. 1357–1387. doi:10.1007/s00181-017-1300-z

D'Agostino, G., Dunne, P. and Pieroni, P. (2018). Military expenditure, endogeneity and economic growth. *Defence and Peace Economics*. Available at: https://doi.org/10.1080/10242694.2017.1422314

Deger, S. (1986). Economic development and defense expenditure. *Economic Development and Cultural Change*, 35(1), pp. 179–196.

Deger, S. and Sen, S. (1995). Military expenditure and developing countries. In: K. Hartley and T. Sandler, eds., *Handbook of defense economics*. Amstrerdam, Netherlands: Elsevier, pp. 275–307.

Deger, S. and Smith, R. (1983). Military expenditure and growth in less developed countries. *The Journal of Conflict Resolution*, 27(2), pp. 335–353.

Dunne, J. P. (1996). Economic effects of military spending in LDCs: A survey. In: N. P. Gleditsch, A. Cappelen, O. Bjerkholt, R. Smith, and P. Dunne, eds., *The peace dividend*. Amsterdam: North Holland, pp. 439–464.

Dunne, P. and Smith, R. (2010). Military expenditure and Granger causality: A critical review. *Defence and Peace Economics*, 21(5–6), pp. 427–441.

Dunne, P., Smith, R. and Willenbockel, D. (2005). Models of military expenditure and growth: A critical review. *Defence and Peace Economics*, 16(6), pp. 449–461.

Dunne, P. and Tian, N. (2013). Military spending and economic growth: A survey. *The Economics of Peace and Security Journal*, 8(1), pp. 5–11.

Dunne, P. and Tian, N. (2015). Military expenditure, economic growth and heterogeneity. *Defence and Peace Economics*, 26(1), pp. 15–31.

Dunne, P. and Uye, M. (2010). Military spending and development. In: A. Tan, ed., *The global arms trade*. London: Routledge.

Emmanouilidis, K. and Karpetis, C. (2018). The defense – growth nexus: A review of time series methods and empirical results. doi:10.1080/10242694.2018.1428261

Feder, G. (1983). On exports and economic growth. *Journal of Development Economics*, 12(1–2), pp. 59–73.

Feder, G. (1986). Growth in semi-industrial countries: A statistical analysis. In: H. Chenery, S. Robinson, and M. Syrquin, eds., *Industrialization and growth: A comparative study*. New York: Oxford University Press, pp. 263–282.

Granger, C. W. J. (1969). Investigating causal relations by econometric models and cross-spectral methods. *Econometrica*, 37(3), pp. 424–438.

Halıcıoğlu, F. (2004). Defense spending and economic growth in Turkey: An empirical application of new macroeconomic theory. *Review of Middle East Economics and Finance*, 2(3), pp. 193–201.

Hou, N. and Chen, B. (2013). Military expenditure and economic growth in developing countries: Evidence from system GMM estimates. *Defence and Peace Economics*, 24(3), pp. 183–193.

Knight, M., Loayza, N. and Villanueva, D. (1996). *The peace dividend: Military spending cuts and economic growth*. IMF Staff Papers, No. 1577.

Mankiw, N. G., Romer, D. and Weil, D. N. (1992). A contribution to the empirics of economic growth. *The Quarterly Journal of Economics*, 107(2), pp. 407–437.

Mauro, P. (1998). Corruption and the composition of government expenditure. *Journal of Public Economics*, 69(2), pp. 263–279.

Pieroni, L. (2009). Military expenditure and economic growth. *Defence and Peace Economics*, 20(4), pp. 327–339.

Ram, R. (1986). Government size and economic growth: A new framework and some evidence from cross-section and time series data. *American Economic Review*, 76, pp. 191–203.

Ram, R. (1995). Defense expenditure and economic growth. In: K. Hartley and T. Sandler, eds., *Handbook of defense economics*. Amsterdam: Elsevier, pp. 251–273.

Romer, P. M. (2000). Keynesian macroeconomics without the LM Curve. *Journal of Economic Perspectives*, 14(2), pp. 149–170.

Sandler, T. and Hartley, K. (1995). *The economics of defense*. Cambridge: Cambridge University Press.

Smith, R. (1980). Military expenditures and investment in OECD countries, 1954–1973. *Journal of Comparative Economics*, 41(1), pp. 19–32.

Smith, R. (2000). Defence expenditure and economic growth. In: N. P. Gleditsch, G. Lindgren, N. Mouhleb, S. Smith, and I. de Soysa, eds., *Making peace pay: A bibliography on disarmament and conversion*. Laremont: Regina Books, pp. 15–24.

Smith, R. (forthcoming). *Military expenditure and growth*. In: R. Matthews, ed., *The Political Economy of Defence*. Cambridge: Cambridge University Press.

Taylor, J. B. (2000). Teaching modern macroeconomics at the principles level. *American Economic Review*, 90(2), pp. 90–94.

Töngür, Ü. and Elveren, A.Y. (2017). The nexus of economic growth, military expenditures, and income inequality. *Quality and Quantity*, 51(4), pp. 1821–1842.

Yakovlev, P. (2007). Arms trade, military spending, and economic growth. *Defence and Peace Economics*, 18(4), pp. 317–338.

Yesilyurt, M. E. and Yesilyurt, F. (2014). Introducing Literaturematic.com: Survey of defence economics. *Defence and Peace Economics*, 25(3), pp. 329–330.

3 Military Keynesianism and the military-industrial complex

Introduction

Military Keynesianism, which is the policy of using milex as a counter-cyclical economic tool, suffers from a lack of theoretical sophistication (Dunne, 2013). That is, it has no clear theory; rather, milex is simply considered as one component of government spending.

From a long-run perspective, the dynamics of milex is explained through military-industrial complex (MIC) theory. It is essential to understand the role of the U.S. in the current world, as it undertakes the great bulk of milex in the capitalist system. Therefore, below I attempt to provide a brief discussion of the MIC and Military Keynesianism.

The root of the term military-industrial complex goes back to the writings of C. Wright Mills (1956), although it first became popular with President Dwight Eisenhower's well-known farewell address in 1961, when he described a new kind of threat:

> [W]e can no longer risk emergency improvisation of national defense; we have been compelled to create a permanent armaments industry of vast proportions. Added to this, three and a half million men and women are directly engaged in the defense establishment. We annually spend on military security more than the net income of all United States corporations. *This conjunction of an immense military establishment and a large arms industry is new in the American experience*. . . . [W]e must not fail to comprehend its grave implications. Our toil, resources and livelihood are all involved; so is the very structure of our society. In the councils of government, we must guard against the acquisition of unwarranted influence, whether sought or unsought, by *the military industrial complex*. The potential for the disastrous rise of misplaced power exists and will persist. We must never let the weight of this combination endanger our liberties or democratic processes. . . . Only an alert and knowledgeable citizenry can compel the proper meshing of the huge industrial and military machinery of defense with our peaceful methods and goals, so that security and liberty may prosper together.
>
> (Eisenhower, 1961, emphasis added)

The speech did not provide a precise definition of the MIC; neither was there a common understanding among the authors of the liberal school of how it operated.[1] For John Kenneth Galbraith, the MIC (or *the military power* in his terms) is a symbiotic coalition between the military services and their industrial suppliers that promotes bureaucratic over national needs by increasing defence expenditure (Galbraith, 1967a, 1969a). Or, in longer, more explicit terms, it is

> a loose, informally defined collection of firms producing military products, senior military officers, and members of the executive and legislative branches of the federal government – all of them limited by the market relations of the military products network and having a common ideology as to the importance of maintaining or enlarging the armed forces of the United States and their role in American politics.
>
> (Melman, 1970, p. 10)

In other words, the MIC is a coalition of vested interests within the state and industry, promoting the interests of this symbiotic coalition in the name of 'national security', although this may not necessarily overlap with the interest of the general public. The MIC, in this sense, has established itself a sort of autonomous structure within the state, a structure of permanent pressure for increasing milex, justified by perceived or actual external threats.

The MIC, which arose during the dual crises of the Great Depression and WWII, became a massive network of expanded political power, arms producers, and increased state authority. It was a powerful and extended network serving the interests of unions, industry, the military, and politicians with jobs, high profits, large budgets, and votes, respectively (Duncan and Coyne, 2013). In this sense, milex not only benefits giant corporations in the arms industry but also benefits their subcontractors and supporting non-military firms to a certain degree.

For example, Roosevelt's Civilian Conservation Corps (CCC) programme provided jobs for men between 18 and 25 to reclaim the country's forests. Those recruits lived in government-built camps run by the army. This secured a massive budget for the army and was supported by war veterans with significant political power. The extension of the programme, and its immense political support made it impossible to reduce its size during the interwar period (ibid. p. 225). The CCC therefore earned the approval and support of both the military and the unions. To allay widespread fears that the programme was a way to train non-unionised labour to replace unionised workers, Roosevelt appointed the vice president of a major union as the programme's director, which gained the support of labour (ibid., p. 227).

The perception that Franklin D. Roosevelt's extensive civilian New Deal programmes were unable to achieve their desired outcomes – in contrast to how the war economy during WWII had boosted business and created full employment – led to the following ideological consensus (Baran and Sweezy, 1966; Melman, 1985): milex can be used not simply as "a time-limited economic effort to achieve a political goal (winning World War II)" but as a "means for governmental control of the economy" (Melman, 1985, p. 16). At a theoretical level, the era's economic success was explained by the "combined strands of Keynesianism and Marxism", through which the state had generated the desired aggregate demand through excessive milex, which would otherwise have been impossible within *the pure market system*, thereby creating "state capitalism". Hence, there was a broad political consensus by the 1950s that the war economy was not merely sustainable but also essential for economic growth. Melman describes this consensus succinctly: On the right, *U.S. News and World Report* (1950) stated that "[b]usiness won't go to pot so long as war is a threat; so long as every alarm can step up spending, lending for defense at home and aid abroad; cold war is almost a guarantee against a bad depression". In the liberal centre, an adviser to Presidents Kennedy and Johnson noted that "the armaments industry has provided a sort of automatic stabilizer for the whole economy". On the left, Herbert Gintis (1970), for example, argued that "the military industrial complex has eliminated the specter of secular stagnation" (quoted in Melman, 1986, p. 72).

During the post-war period, the MIC was quick to stress the 'danger' of the Soviet Union to sustain military mobilisation. During Eisenhower's administration, although some argued to abandon military Keynesianism, the composition of milex changed to increase the size of subsidised private-sector investment (Cypher, 2015, p. 461). Military Keynesianism experienced its heyday during the Kennedy and Johnson administrations. Although Carter campaigned to reduce milex, military Keynesianism rose in his era due to the revolution in Iran and the 1979 Soviet military operation in Afghanistan.

Many aspects of MIC theory have remained since the end of the Cold War (Dunne and Sköns, 2011). Major contractors continue to dominate the market and heavily influence government policy. Contractors are in turn dependent on domestic government support despite the internationalisation of the military industry, while new firms have been unable to displace incumbents in core areas of arms production (Dunne and Sköns, 2011). MIC theory therefore continues to be relevant today in explaining the impact of vested interests on the determination of milex.

As the Soviet Union collapsed, the U.S. military remained powerful, continuing to spend a relatively large percentage of the national budget on military interests, such as continued development of sophisticated new weapons (Dunne and Sköns, 2011). During this era, the main U.S. security concern shifted from communism toward global terrorism, sustaining the so-called international division of military labour, whereby the U.S. takes on the hard-power tasks of destruction by investing heavily in super-high-tech armaments, leaving the soft-power work of stabilisation and peacekeeping to its allies. Just like the shift in the post-war period – when the MIC highlighted the 'danger' of the Soviet Union to sustain military mobilisation – with the September 11 attacks, the MIC shifted the focus to the 'war on terror', so that a "'terrorism industry' consisting of consultants, counterterrorism experts, and pundits has emerged in the wake of the 9/11 attacks" (Mueller, 2006 cited in Duncan and Coyne, 2013, p. 234). The establishment of the Office of Homeland Security in 2001 had a similar effect to that of NASA in the 1950s in that the MIC was very capable of introducing new state apparatuses to increase milex (Cypher, 2016). A year later, the declaration of the Bush Doctrine, which included unilateralism and the use of preventative war as part of the national security strategy, broadened the space for the MIC.

Military Keynesianism and its effect

There are two main views regarding the economic effects of milex. According to the first view, known as Military Keynesianism, it has a positive effect by increasing aggregate demand. The other view is that the effect is negative because milex eventually reduces the economy's productive capacity by crowding out public and private investment.

Regarding the positive effect of milex, Marxist theories show how milex decisions are made and their economic effects. According to the Marxist view, the operation of the MIC and the pursuit of profit by individual corporations are determined by the laws of motion of the capitalist system and the interests of the capitalist class (Smith, 1977). There are two similar views in Marxist thought in this regard.

According to Baran and Sweezy's (1966) view of underconsumption, milex prevents the realisation crisis by absorbing the surplus in the economy, contrary to other types of government expenditure that increase the economy's productivity capacity. The other similar view is Michael Kidron's permanent arms economy approach, which suggests that milex prevents the economy overheating (Kidron, 1970).

These two Marxist theories offer five reasons why milex performs better than civilian government expenditure (Baran and Sweezy, 1966; Reich, 1972). First, milex is easily manipulated by the state. Second, weapons are either rapidly used or rendered obsolete, which guarantees endless demand. Third, high milex is supported by powerful ideological arguments regarding the Cold War and widespread insurgencies. Fourth, U.S. military power helps to reinforce American political and economic hegemony. Fifth, welfare state expenditure is not preferred because it expands the civilian state sector, redistributes income, and turns labour market regulations in favour of labour, all of which may reduce private-sector profit margins.

Joan Robinson also emphasised this convenience of milex:[2]

> When there is unemployment and low profits the government must spend on something. . . . [F]or twenty-five years serious recessions were avoided by following this policy. The most convenient thing for a government to spend on is armaments. . . . It was the so-called Keynesians who persuaded successive [U.S.] presidents that there is no harm in a budget deficit and left the military-industrial complex to take advantage of it.
>
> (Robinson, 1972, pp. 6–7, quoted in Cypher, 2015, p. 457)

Thus, James Tobin, for example, severely criticised the Eisenhower administration for not recognising the dual role of milex in terms of enhancing national security and boosting the economy (Tobin, 1958, cited in Gold, 2005).

Overall, these Marxist approaches consider that, because milex is wasteful, this inefficiency maintains high profit rates by absorbing surplus, thereby counteracting the economic crises inherent to the capitalist system. (See Chapter 5 for more detailed discussion.)

In contrast, the liberal school, led by Seymour Melman[3] (see also Kaldor, 1981; Dumas, 1986), claims that the impact of milex is negative because the military sector creates economic inefficiencies by crowding out productive civilian investment (Melman, 1970, 1985; Rosen, 1973; Kaldor, 1981; Dumas, 1986). Regarding liberal views on how milex decisions are made, Smith (1977) argued that "decisions emerge not from a consensus on some national interest, but from bargaining and compromises between a variety of special interests. Because the various interests have unequal power and information, the decisions tend to be biased in favour of the groups with the largest stakes in military expenditure, the military-industrial complex" (p. 64). Thus, since the liberal school's analysis is based on "class-free national interest", it concludes that the removal of politicians with a hardline agenda and right fiscal and monetary policies would be enough to promote civilian over military production (Smith, 1977; Georgiou, 1983).

Yet, although the liberal school consider militarism irrational and immoral, they naïvely argue that "closer monitoring of R&D" and "more public accountability" are sufficient to deal with it (Georgiou, 1983). Except for Melman, the liberal school in general tended to ignore milex's specific role in the economy.

Seymour Melman is a highly prolific author on the economic impact of the MIC. His critique of milex refers to the predatory behavior of the MIC – or "Pentagon Capitalism" as he describes it in a Veblenian sense.[4] As he clearly points out in the preface of *The Permanent War Economy*, "[i]ndustrial productivity, the foundation of every nation's economic growth, is eroded by the relentlessly predatory effects of the military economy" (Melman, 1985, p. 7). However, the key distinction here is that while, for Veblen, the state is the "auxiliary agent of the Interests", in Melman's depletion thesis, it is an "absolutely autonomous agent" (Cypher, 1987, p. 36).

Melman's criticisms are not based on a sophisticated theory but on the suggestive empirical relationship that milex has damaging effects on various macroeconomic indicators, such as labour productivity, balance of payments, and inflation. The liberal school in general argues that the state generally runs a deficit to finance milex, which increases interest rates. Because higher interest rates discourage investment, increasing milex crowds out investment (Cypher, 2015).

More specifically, milex wastes intellectual, financial, and material resources by diverting them away from civilian industries, where they could have been used more efficiently to increase the economy's long-term productive capacity and boost economic growth (Melman, 1965). Within the MIC, the defence department acts as a de facto planning ministry (Melman, 1970), transforming the economy into a military-based version of state capitalism (Melman, 1974).

In *Our Depleted Society* (1965), Melman explains the *depletion* process in terms of the concentration of civilian resources in the military sector, emphasising that more than two thirds of technical researchers work for the military, which has "siphoned off" a large proportion of the skilled population (p. 7). Thus, the cost of military power is "the depletion of American society, a process now well advanced in industry, civilian technology, management, education, medical care, and the quality of life" (p. 7). He dismisses the economic growth resulting from the excessive use of resources in the military sector as "parasitic growth" because military production "does not, by its very nature, contribute to economic health, or to further production" (p. 7). Melman argues that the belief, based on WWII, that the U.S. can produce both guns and butter, is no longer valid because military production overuses scientific and material resources and shapes corporate culture according to the needs of the Pentagon, which prevents the country from meeting civilian needs.

In *Pentagon Capitalism* (1970), Melman describes *the state-management* developed under the Secretary of Defense to increase military power and economic efficiency. This Pentagon-based system, Melman argues, transformed the federal government into a giant business controlling a substantial portion of the nation's resources, creating a military form of state capitalism. Because this "para-state" had both economic and political decision-making power for the first time in U.S. history, it became possible to build a military-industrial empire both domestically and globally (p. 5). Importantly, Melman rightly noted a crucial consequence of this development of this new form of management: that it "enhances the war-making capability of" the U.S., which in turn "increases the likelihood of recourse to 'solutions' based upon military power" (p. 6). In short, the new management system reinforces its own *raison d'être*. Melman argues that developments from 1965 to 1969 support his thesis in *Our Depleted Society*, that the concentration of resources and young, high-skilled labour in the military sector was detrimental to the productive civilian sector. Melman further discussed the MIC in *The Permanent War Economy* to show how this military form of state capitalism works by reducing individual liberty and productivity. He then reinforced his view that military production makes no economic contribution, but instead wastes productive resources and their outputs, which reduces the competitiveness of the U.S. economy.

John Kenneth Galbraith on the military-industrial complex

Below I analyse the MIC by focusing on the works of John Kenneth Galbraith for two equally important reasons. First, although he did not analyse militarism or the effects of milex *per se*, his theory of the power of giant corporations helps to understand the role of military corporations and thereby MIC. Second, Galbraith is an insider public intellectual who played a decisive role in American economic policy during World War II, the 1950s, 1960s, and the late 1970s and

1980s (in a somewhat diminished role), by serving in various major positions in the administrations of Roosevelt, Truman, Kennedy, and Johnson.

Galbraith contributed to policy making in the U.S. in two major areas during World War II. First, he was asked to take charge of controlling prices (with Chester Bowles), which he did with great success, not just in terms of controlling the prices of most U.S. goods but also "in creating the conditions under which saving in the form of government bonds became credible and macroeconomic balance could therefore be achieved" (James Galbraith, 2004, p. 295). Second, he was also asked to take charge of assessing the allies' strategic bombing campaign against Germany in the closing months of the war, leading a distinguished group of Nicholas Kaldor, E. F. Schumacher, Edward F. Denison, Paul Baran, and Tibor Scitovsky.[5] Galbraith also prepared a ten-point plan in 1946, which anticipated the Marshall Plan advocated by Secretary of State George Marshall in 1947 to rebuild Europe (Galbraith, 1946; Dunn and Pressman, 2005, p. 167).

Galbraith's influence on U.S. economic and warfare policies continued as an adviser to Presidents John F. Kennedy and Lyndon B. Johnson, and as the ambassador to India, from where he sent Kennedy telegrams and letters advising against increased U.S. involvement in Vietnam, the planned Bay of Pigs operation in Cuba, and secret CIA operations in India (Galbraith, 1969b, 1998b, cited in Dunn and Pressman, 2005). He was then appointed to the White House Task Force by President Johnson to fight against poverty. During this period, Galbraith became more concerned over increasing U.S. involvement in Vietnam under the new administration of Johnson while he was also "a strong and highly visible dissenter" from the mainstream view on the arms race with the Soviet Union during the Cold War (Galbraith, 1967a; Cypher, 2008, p. 39). First, he strongly raised his concerns that the Cold War had created a severe public-sector imbalance. Second, he rejected the general view of the time that the U.S. had to increase milex because the Soviet Union was spending at least as much on its military. Instead, he advocated negotiations over nuclear arms development.

Galbraith expanded his views of the MIC and the economic role of milex in *The New Industrial State* (1967a) and *How to Control the Military* (1969a), in several short articles published in *A View from the Stands* (1986), in commentaries in *Economics and the Public Purpose* (1973), through further discussion on the military nexus in *The Culture and Contentment* (1992), and in some interviews in Stanfield and Stanfield (2004). Galbraith took a strongly anti-war stance, both as an insider providing advice to Presidents Kennedy and Johnson and as a public intellectual, such as in *How to Get Out of Vietnam: A Workable Solution to the Worst Problem of Our Time* (Galbraith, 1969b cited in Dunn and Pressman, 2005, p. 168). His opposition to the Vietnam War is clear from his letters to President Kennedy (Galbraith, 1998a, 2017).

In *The Affluent Society* (1958), Galbraith makes a few short but major commentaries on the regulatory economic role of milex. More importantly, however, he argues that militarism "plays a deeply functional role in underwriting technology" (p. 257). He continues by noting that despite failing to generate security, the commitment to the arms race with the Soviet Union remains strong. This is because the race has a "deeply organic relation to economic performance" whereby a consumer goods economy cannot allocate enough resources to research and development whereas the military sector can "sustain such effort on a vastly greater scale". This enabled the development of major consumer goods, such as air transport and the computer, as well as the non-military use of nuclear energy, which would have been too expensive and risky for the private sector to have developed alone. He contends that such highly useful research at this scale could not have been achieved by any private-sector product. Consequently, milex "has done more to save us from the partial technological stagnation that is inherent in a consumer goods economy" (p. 259) because, without "military inspired and for this reason publicly supported research", technical progress in American industry would have been significantly slower. Nevertheless, he maintains that "this is a hideously inefficient way of subsidising general scientific and technical development" (p. 259).

Galbraith provides much more detailed discussion on the effects of milex in *The New Industrial State* (1967).[6] Here, he argues that the Marxian notion that a capitalist economy suffers from a chronic lack of aggregate demand is wrong because aggregate demand can be stimulated by different types of public spending. He contends that milex has a unique role in increasing aggregate demand, which makes his view on the role of milex similar to that of Baran and Sweezy, in that milex stimulates aggregate demand and plays a unique role because other types of public expenditure cannot match this large scale. Hence, military Keynesianism – a concept that he did not prefer to use – stabilises the economy (Cypher, 2008).

Galbraith argues that many economists tend to ignore the role of milex in regulating aggregate demand. Some ignore it because they argue that "the same effect could easily be obtained by shifting the outlays to civilian purposes or returning them to private use", citing Paul Samuelson[7] and noting that he once held the same view (Galbraith, 1967a, p. 230). He then explains why this view is simplistic: "Income released to or taken from private expenditure will only serve effectively to regulate demand if the public sector is large and the resources released or absorbed are large enough to count" (ibid. p. 203). In addition to this problem of insufficient volume, "there is also that of underwriting technology and therewith the planning of the industrial system" (ibid. p. 231). He argues that civilian public expenditure, such as on schools, parks, and the poor, do not have the same effect because they lack milex's relation to technology (ibid. p. 231). In addition to underwriting technology, Galbraith also claims that milex-mediated innovation may have civilian purposes, referring to a spillover effect (ibid. p. 339).

Thus, for Galbraith, "[i]f a large public sector of the economy, supported by personal and corporate income taxation, is the fulcrum for the regulation of demand, plainly military expenditures are the pivot on which the fulcrum rests" (p. 229). He emphasises that milex is strongly supported by businessmen because public expenditure in the form of defence and space exploration is considered as meeting international policy goals (pp. 228–229). That is, there is a symbiotic relationship between military corporations and the state.

Galbraith explains this symbiotic relationship – the dynamics of how the MIC operates – by analysing the role of a new class: *the technostructure*.[8] He argues that, with the rise of the modern corporation, "the emergence of the organization required by modern technology and planning and the divorce of the owner of the capital from control of the enterprise, the entrepreneur no longer exists as an individual person in the mature industrial enterprise" (Galbraith, 1967a, p. 71). According to Galbraith, decisions are not made by *management* but by the "the guiding intelligence – the brain – of the enterprise". He considers this new class, the new decision-making group, *the technostructure*, in a similar manner to Veblen's concept of *absentee ownership* and his distinction between *business* and *industry*. This is a very powerful tool to understand how power is exercised in society, particularly between the state and giant corporations.

In this sense, Galbraith's concept of *the revised sequence* is another key part of his theory: "[T]he accommodation of the market behavior of the individual, as well as social attitudes in general, to needs of producers and the goals of the technostructure is an inherent feature of the system" (ibid. p. 212). That is, rather than running from consumers to the products they demand, controls run the other way – in a *revised sequence*. Thus, he argues it is not true that defence requirements are purely a national policy, independent of the needs of the industrial system. Rather, the state, through its military and related procurements and policies, serves to accommodate the needs of the industrial system, which means that the industrial system is no longer an independent entity, but one that exerts a certain degree of control over public and national policy to accommodate it to its own interests (ibid. p. 232). Thus, "[t]he military power has reversed constitutional process in the United States – removed power from the public and Congress to the Pentagon" (Galbraith, 1969a, p. 61). Image building is the key part of this process because it provides a reason to justify or rationalise the continued high milex. The Cold War, Galbraith argues, played that role for about two decades (Galbraith, 1967a, p. 326) along with other interventions in Africa and Central America and in the Middle East against Iraq in 1991 (Galbraith, 1992, pp. 140–141).

Galbraith argues that the state guarantees corporations' largest capital commitments in developing highly advanced technology through military and related procurements (p. 308) because such investments entail the long-term, specialised allocation of capital and labour that has to be protected against cost increases (Galbraith, 1967a, p. 308). In contrast, entrepreneurial corporations do not need such long-term planning because they use simpler technology and make smaller capital commitments. It is giant corporations with the technostructure that require such protection, provided by regulating aggregate demand to eliminate planning uncertainties (ibid. p. 225). Government procurements thus stabilise demand for the industrial system because defence procurements provide long-term contracts with assurances against any demand change or risk of price fluctuations (pp. 309–310). According to Galbraith, this "leads the technostructure to identify itself closely with the goals of the armed services" (p. 310) by choosing those strategies that reinforce and sustain its existence. Moreover, this mechanism does not only operate within the Department of Defense but also in other major agencies, such as the National Space Agency, the Atomic Energy Commission, and the Federal Aviation Agency (p. 315), creating a symbiotic relationship between military corporations and the state. Galbraith discusses this relationship in *Economics & Public Purpose* (1973) in terms of how the roles are assigned between these two entities and how this symbiotic relationship functions.

> The public bureaucracy, in citing the need for new weapons, can seem to be speaking out of a disinterested concern for the public security. Its control over intelligence allows it, as necessary, to exploit public and congressional fears as to what the Soviets are doing or might be doing. . . . The private bureaucracy has freedom and financial resources not available to the public bureaucracy for making strategic political contributions, for mobilising union and community support, for lobbying, for advertising and for public and press relations.
>
> (Galbraith, 1973, p. 284)

At the personnel level, the weapons firms and the Department of Defense engage in reciprocal recruitment of top members of the technostructure (Galbraith, 1973, p. 143; also see Galbraith, 1969a, pp. 20–21). Similarly, at the organisational level, while the weapon firms developing and building aircraft achieve their "affirmative goal of growth with the concurrent reward to their technostructures", the public bureaucracy in charge of such contracts is "similarly rewarded by the development and possession of a new generation of planes" (Galbraith, 1973, p. 143).

Galbraith, as a firm advocate of a strong role for the state, persistently warned about the danger of the power of giant corporations over the state and argued for reforms to address the symbiotic relationship that generates inefficient outcomes for the general public through the inequitable distribution of public expenditure between arms and social infrastructure, health, and education. In this regard, paraphrasing Marx, he declared that "[t]he modern state . . . is not the executive committee of the bourgeoisie, but it is more nearly the executive committee of the technostructure". He suggested that the space competition might be an admirable substitute for weapons production (Galbraith, 1967a, p. 341). That is, while being the first to reach Saturn may not represent the ideal use of public resources, at least such a competition would not be extremely dangerous, in contrast to the conventional and nuclear arms races (Galbraith, 1967a, p. 341).

In *How to Control the Military* (1969a), Galbraith provides a deeper analysis of the MIC in which he contends that *the revised sequence* is more critical when power passes to the Pentagon or to giant corporations producing weapons than to General Motors (ibid. p. 5). Galbraith asks us to recognise that large military contractors that conduct almost all of their business with the Pentagon are not "private firms" but basically "public extensions of the Pentagon" (ibid. p. 7). This is the core of Galbraith's view on the MIC, which he prefers to call *the military power*. He contends that "the Services, not their industrial suppliers, are the prime wielders of this power" (ibid. p. 7). The military power, however, is more than the services and their contractors because it also includes the intelligence agencies, university scientists, defence-oriented research institutes, and "the organized voice of the military in the Congress" (ibid. pp. 23–24). According to Galbraith, the problem is "not conspiracy or corruption but unchecked rule" because being unchecked allows the MIC to serve bureaucratic rather than national needs to reinforce its own power (ibid. p. 24). Galbraith therefore advocates the nationalisation of top military corporations (Galbraith, 1969a, p. 7, 1969c, p. 162, 1973, pp. 284–285).

Galbraith lists the following main factors that enabled the MIC to gain the strength it had during the Cold War: increasing bureaucratisation, communism, secrecy regarding knowledge of Soviet weaponry, "the disciplining effect of personal fear" of being mislabelled, the economic effects of milex, and the absence of either liberal or conservative opposition to the MIC. Galbraith therefore argues that the military power is based on three beliefs (Galbraith, 1969a, p. 17). First, any danger caused by the arms race with the Soviets is less harmful than any agreement because they could exploit it. Therefore, it is safer to continue the arms race. Second, because the fight against communism is humanity's ultimate battle, the arms race must be pursued, no matter how dangerous it becomes. Third, the national interest is supreme, so not even the risk of Armageddon should prevent the development of new weapons because they serve this national interest (ibid. p. 18).

During World War II, "the military services and their industrial allies were given unprecedented authority" to keep up the Soviet Union's technological advances (ibid. p. 34). The Democrats were always careful not to question the excessive power of this symbiotic coalition between the military corporations and the military services because of the fear of being accused of being soft on communism, given that anyone who criticised the MIC was considered a disguised Marxist. Moreover, the economic situation also served to reinforce the MIC's power. Since milex helped to sustain employment, the danger of economic stagnation and unemployment made it impossible to criticise the military, particularly from an economic viewpoint (ibid. p. 38). Therefore, although liberal economists thought that spending on education, housing, welfare, and civilian public works would be a better alternative to milex, the lack of public support prevented them from promoting their ideas, which gave milex a clear run (ibid. p. 41).

In conclusion, as an insider public intellectual, Galbraith provides an important account to understand the MIC.[9] His core conclusion is that the military power should be returned from the Pentagon to the public and Congress. He outlined how to accomplish this task in *How to Control the Military* (Galbraith,

1969a, pp. 52–62). One way that Galbraith's views on the effects of milex appear to have developed is that he paid more attention in his early writings to the role of milex in underwriting technology, whereas he began to emphasise its detrimental role more by the late 1980s. For instance, whereas he argued that milex boosted the American economy during World War II, it later became a powerful restraining factor for economic development. In line with Melman, he emphasised the excessive allocation of resources and technical experts to the military sector (Galbraith, 1988, 1994).

Military-industrial complex today

Both in the U.S. and across Europe, MIC has changed with respect to economic developments and has become more global. State-industry relations in the military sector have changed remarkably due to mergers in the 1990s, transatlantic networks (e.g. U.S.-U.K.), the increased role of private contractors,[10] and expanded outsourcing to civil companies, both nationally and internationally (Dunne and Sköns, 2011). However, national governments still play the dominant role, and vested interests are still a powerful lobbying group (ibid. pp. 6–7).

History has proved that Galbraith's concern over *the revised sequence* was fully justified as the expanded control of MIC contributed to the U.S. becoming more totalitarian. First, it undertook 'new imperial ventures'. Second, during the 2000s, it experienced asymmetric guerrilla-type conflicts, which, together with the growth of 'homeland security', made communications and surveillance technologies increasingly important (Dunne and Sköns, 2011). This paved a way for what Foster and McChesney (2014) refer to as "surveillance capitalism". Third, civil liberties were curtailed. The dominance of bureaucratic interests over the public interest has expanded from the military to major areas of public life. The Trump presidency is one outcome of this authoritarian transformation (Boggs, 2018, p. 13), which is accelerating the ongoing process.

Regarding the 'new imperial ventures', the U.S. has pursued its main objective of protecting the "liberal world order" with about 800 military bases in more than 70 countries and territories, including in the major conflict regions of Iraq, Syria, and Afghanistan, where the U.S.'s longest war has already lasted 17 years.

The U.S. has involved itself in numerous wars and conflicts across the world. The presentation of the 1991 Gulf War as entertainment was designed to heal the Vietnam Syndrome (Cypher, 2007, p. 38), while the war in Kosovo in 1998–1999, in which U.S. (and NATO) air attacks on the former Yugoslavia were very successful, resulting in no U.S. casualties (Cypher, 2007, p. 38). These two wars refreshed the public's belief that the scale of the U.S. military build-up is legitimate, and that its overwhelming forces only fight just wars (Cypher, 2007, p. 38). In the case of Iraq[11] and Afghanistan, "the 'Pentagon propaganda machine' worked assiduously with the mass media to de-legitimate opposition to these interventions and promote a numbing, universal 'patriotic' discourse" (Cypher, 2016, p. 805). These military operations were also utilised by

Hollywood effectively through *disguised militarism*, yielding the heydays of *the Military-Industrial-Hollywood Complex*.

Homeland security became the top concern following the 9/11 attacks. The general understanding is that, especially at this point, U.S. security policies focused on the war against terrorism while leaving other NATO members to deal with 'soft' issues, such as human security and peacekeeping. However, according to Aguirre (2007) for example, the U.S. aimed to reinforce its dominant role through humanitarian assistance (cited in Cypher, 2016, p. 806). It sought to reduce the UN's role by promoting the concept that NATO is an extension of the U.S. military force, which in turn reinforces U.S. leadership in international crises.

Increasing financialisation and technology have generated new national security concerns, particularly a worry that cyberwarfare could cripple the U.S.'s financial and military systems. The MIC's reaction to this development was to collaborate with the private sector further. Due to financialisation and the so-called dot-com boom around the turn of the millennium, giant computer-internet corporations have become "the repressive arm of the state in the form of its military, intelligence, and police functions," while the secret national security state has made itself larger than the government to create a *military-digital complex* (McChesney, 2013; Foster and McChesney, 2014).

The root of this *totalitarian* collaboration between giant corporations and the state goes back to the very structure of *the planning system/industrial system* (Marcuse, 1964; Galbraith, 1967a). Marcuse (1964) argued that "[b]y virtue of the way it has organised its technological base, contemporary industrial society tends to be *totalitarian* . . . [which is] a non-terroristic economic-technical coordination [of society] which operates through *the manipulation of needs by vested interests*" (quoted in Boggs, 2018, p. 8, emphasis added). Galbraith (1958) argued that militarism "plays a deeply functional role in underwriting technology" (p. 257) in "the planning of the industrial system" (Galbraith, 1967a, p. 231), and milex-mediated innovation may have civilian purposes (ibid. p. 339). In other words, the nature of giant corporations requires the state to help build the technological base that ensures the smooth functioning of the industrial system. This collaboration may be manipulated by those corporations and the state, prioritising their vested interests above the public's general interest. An example given in Foster and McChesney (2014) fits this context perfectly:

> In 2012 DARPA Director Regina Dugan left her position to join Google. During her period as director, DARPA had been at the forefront of drone research. . . . However, the outgrowth of this in the deployment of General Atomic Aeronautical System's Predator drones in warfare did not occur until the late 1990s in the Kosovo War. . . . In the opening years of this century DARPA extended its research to developing drones that could be used for mobile wi-fi capabilities. . . . In 2014 Google announced that it was buying Titan Aerospace, a U.S.-based start-up company for building drones which cruise at the very edge of the atmosphere. Facebook meanwhile bought the

> U.K. corporation, Ascenta, which specializes in making high-altitude solar drones. Such drones would allow the spread of the Internet to new areas. The goal was to capitalize on a new military technology and create larger global Internet monopolies, while expanding the military-digital complex.

The expanded control of the MIC paved a way to curtailing civil liberties and imposing a more authoritarian regime. This authoritarian order has become more pronounced with the Trump presidency. Perhaps it is unnecessary to note that the rise of "strongman politics" is not particular to the U.S. but represents a new phase of neo-conservative ideology worldwide. In this contemporary politics, "class anger is routinely turned on its head, with populism manipulated to serve profoundly conservative interests" of "emotionally-charged" moral concerns, such as guns, immigration, foreign threats, gay sexuality, abortion, and 'family values' (Boggs, 2018, p. 3). In this context, mobilising the poor in defence of militarism is indispensable. Thus, strengthening the MIC was both a cause and consequence of this new phase of contemporary politics.

Although President Trump pursued a sort of anti-militaristic election campaign,[12] being against U.S. involvement in Iraq, after he took the office, he decided to delay the U.S. withdrawal from Syria, increased the U.S. forces in war zones, and proposed a Pentagon budget for 2018 and 2019 that exceeded even the Pentagon's own expansive expectations. In fact, the mixed policies of President Trump can be considered as the power struggle with the MIC. For instance, he has worked to defuse tensions and reduce the sense of insecurity that keeps the MIC going in North Korea, Russia, and China, which is contrary to his own early public statements in two of those cases. In Syria, he preferred to some clearly wholly symbolic interventions. In this sense, the U.S. under Trump has not seriously resisted the present drift of the war. However, in the case of Iran, he withdrew from the internationally supported denuclearisation agreement despite the opposition of his previous national security team, leading to a confrontation with Iran at the moment. In general, President Trump's national security strategy is simply the continuation of previous ones in that it calls for strengthening the U.S.'s role in the MENA region and South Asia, Europe, and Asia (Cordesman, 2018).

Overall, Trump's policies are a reiteration of Reaganism, in which taxes on corporations and the rich were reduced while milex was increased substantially, but with a remarkably more authoritarian touch in general. In conclusion, increasing authoritarianism and expanding the MIC have proceeded hand in hand, both in the U.S. and globally.

Notes

1 This speech had enormous influence by allowing people to agree with Eisenhower without fear of being labelled Marxists or soft on communism at the height of the Cold War. In reference to this, Galbraith notes that "[f]or many years thereafter anyone (myself included) who spoke to the problem of the military power [e.g. the MIC] took the thoughtful precaution of first quoting President Eisenhower" (Galbraith, 1969a, p. 37).

2 For Joan Robinson, military Keynesianism was the worst version of "bastard Keynesianism".
3 Both Cypher and Gold disagree with the main arguments of the liberal school. They argue that, first, the crowding out argument is not valid; second, there was no long-term trade-off between military and civilian R&D; third, there was no evidence of insufficient scientists and engineers in the civilian sector because of excessive recruitment by the military; fourth, it was not plausible that "military contractor 'cost-maximizing' practices had spread into the sphere of production of the civilian economy"; and finally, there was no evidence that other advanced countries had outperformed the U.S. since the late 1960s due to higher milex in the U.S. (Cypher, 1985; Adams and Gold, 1987; Gold, 1990 cited in Cypher, 2015, p. 465). See Chapter 2 for further discussion on the effects of milex on economic growth.
4 Cypher (1987) argues that milex "can be better understood within the context of the analytical construct known as State Monopoly Capitalism" in a similar manner to Thorstein Veblen's "absentee ownership" (page 34). Veblen argues that the new institutionalisation of capital accumulation involves two main capitalist groups. While the majority became a pure rentier class, a so-called *absentee owner*, a small group acted as a kind of executive committee both economically and politically, to promote the interests of the entire capitalist class. Veblen (1898) argued that there are two incommensurate groups of human instincts: 'workmanship' and 'predatorship'. The former, which Veblen also describes as the "parental instinct" or "instinct of idle curiosity", motivates people to do useful work, whereas the latter motivates conflict and exploitation. As long as human social development remained primitive and only weakly productive, work was essential for survival, so social relations were characterised by workmanship. Conversely, once human social development produced more advanced methods and knowledge, predatorship became dominant, enabling private property to appear. Private property and the predator instinct created a predatory, class-ridden society, in which "the forces of workmanship and the predatory forces of exploitation had become locked in a struggle" (Hunt, 2002, p. 328). This struggle is the conflict between business and industry or between salesmanship and workmanship. While the former includes the predatory instinct, the latter includes the instinct of workmanship. Thus, through the development of capitalist production, absentee owners left control over production processes to a "professional class of 'efficiency engineers'" (Veblen, 1914; Hunt, 2002). However, the driving motivation of this managerial class was profit rather than serving the interest of the community at large. That is, the control of business over industry led to the "sabotage" of business, as Veblen puts it (Hunt, 2002, p. 330).
5 They found that the bombing, in contrast to their initial expectations, had not damaged the German economy because it had primarily destroyed civilian businesses in major cities, which generally did not contain military factories. Ironically, bombing the cities created a surplus of unemployed urban labour that became available for military production (Galbraith, 1981, pp. 199–205 cited in Dunn and Pressman, 2005). The survey yielded two basic principles: substitution and induced innovation (Galbraith, 2004). First, there was limited substitution between the civilian and military use of infrastructure, so bombing the civilian economy had little impact on military production. Secondly, a way can always be found to reorganise industrial production if the need is sufficiently great. As James Galbraith has argued, "the validity of these principles was demonstrated again in Vietnam, in Kosovo, and twice in recent years in Iraq" (ibid. p. 296).
6 Galbraith was given a two-term sabbatical when he was at Harvard University to continue to develop his ideas in *The Affluent Society*. He finally published this in 1967 because he was serving as an adviser during Kennedy's presidential election, after which Kennedy appointed him as Ambassador to India (Galbraith, 1969b cited in Dunn and Pressman, 2005, p. 167).
7 "There is nothing about [government] spending on jet bombers, intercontinental missiles and moon rockets that leads to a larger multiplier support of the economy than

would other kinds of expenditure (as on pollution control, poverty relief and urban blight) . . . America's potential and actual growth rate, far from depending upon war preparations, would be markedly *increased* by an end of the cold war" (emphasis in original in Samuelson, 1970, p. 804 cited in Galbraith, 1973, p. 185).

8 Galbraith's principal theoretical contribution can be traced in his trilogy *The Affluent Society* (1958), *The New Industrial State* (1967a) and *Economics and the Public Purpose* (1973). One major contribution he made is the analysis of economic power of large corporations to understand the actual functioning and evolution of economies.

9 Cypher (2008) argues that Galbraith's interpretation of the MIC was "vague and seemingly contradictory" (p. 39). By comparing *How to Control the Military* (1969a) and *Economics & the Public Purpose* (1973), Cypher argues that "instead of the military bureaucracy performing the dominating role within the military-industrial complex, he insisted that the military contracting firms and the military bureaucracy were equally powerful" (p. 40). In my opinion, although it is true that Galbraith did not provide a very explicit definition of the MIC, his position is not contradictory. Rather, his seemingly contradictory remark results from his "vague" definition. For instance, in *How to Control the Military*, he acknowledged this vague structure of the MIC, which shows that his view had not shifted, contrary to what Cypher argues. Regarding decisions on weapons or weapon systems, he notes that "[n]o one can tell where the action originates – whether the Services or the contractors initiate decisions on weapons – nor can the two be sharply *distinguished*" (Galbraith, 1969a, p. 26, emphasis added). In addition, regarding the symbiotic relationship between the Department of Defense and the weapon firms, he notes that "no conclusion can or should be reached as to where the initiative lies" (Galbraith, 1973, p. 144).

10 One consequence of the neo-liberal paradigm, which promotes the a priori belief that the private sector is more efficient than the public sector, was the extension of the MIC, with private contractors operating an unofficial army (Cypher, 2007, p. 44). This predatory behaviour became the mainstream model for U.S. military forces, especially since the Iraq War, generating new opportunities for private-sector profit.

11 A worryingly high proportion of the U.S. public kept believing the claims that Iraq had weapons of mass destruction, which totally contradicted the facts known at that time and acknowledged by U.S. policymakers. Among other dimensions, one key element of this "mass cognitive dissonance" was the U.S. public's "very long and deep, and largely positive, association with things military", a relationship rooted in WWII (Cypher, 2007, p. 37).

12 It is not easy to disregard the extremely similar strategies of President Trump and his fellow authoritarian, Recep Tayyip Erdoğan of Turkey. Perhaps one key difference is that Erdoğan had to reduce the role of the military in politics and promoted and funded law enforcement and intelligence aggressively to overcome the military's threat until he gained total control over the military. Finally, he created his 'own' MIC with his inner circle in the military industry.

References

Adams, G. and Gold, D. (1987). *Defense spending and the economy*. Washington, DC: Center on Budget and Policy Priorities.

Aguirre, M. (2007). Humanitarian intervention and US hegemony: A reconceptualization. In: A. Vanaik, ed., *Selling US wars*. Northampton, MA: Olive Branch Press, pp. 183–206.

Baran, P. and Sweezy, P. (1966). *Monopoly capital: An essay on the American economic and social order*. New York: Monthly Review Press.

Boggs, C. (2018). *Fascism old and new: American politics at the crossroads*. New York and London: Routledge.

Cordesman, A. H. (2018). *U.S. National security strategy in the MENA region*. Washington, DC: Center for Strategic & International Studies.

Cypher, J. M. (1985). A review of Robert Degrasse, military expansion, economic decline. *Journal of Economic Issues*, 19(1), pp. 227–233.
Cypher, J. M. (1987). Military spending, technical change, and economic growth: A disguised form of industrial policy? *Journal of Economic Issues*, 21(1), pp. 33–59.
Cypher, J. M. (2007). From military Keynesianism to global-neoliberal militarism. *Monthly Review*, 59(2), pp. 37–55.
Cypher, J. M. (2008). Economic consequences of armaments production: Institutional perspectives of J.K. Galbraith and T.B.Veblen. *Journal of Economics Issues*, XLII(1), pp. 37–47.
Cypher, J. M. (2015). The origins and evolution of military Keynesianism in the United States. *Journal of Post Keynesian Economics*, 38(3), pp. 449–476.
Cypher, J. M. (2016). Hegemony, military power projection and US structural economic interests in the periphery. *Third World Quarterly*, 37(5), pp. 800–817.
Dumas, L. J. (1986). *The overburdened economy*. Berkeley and Los Angeles: University of California Press.
Duncan, T. K. and Coyne, C. J. (2013). The origins of the permanent war economy. *The Independent Review*, 18(2), pp. 219–240.
Dunn, S. P. and Pressman, S. (2005). The economic contributions of John Kenneth Galbraith. *Review of Political Economy*, 17(2), pp. 161–209.
Dunne, P. (2013). Military Keynesianism. In: M. Chatterji and C. Bo, eds., *Cooperation for a peaceful & sustainable world – part 2*. Bingley: Emerald.
Dunne, P. and Sköns, E. (2011). *The changing military industrial complex*. Available at: http://ideas.repec.org/p/uwe/wpaper/1104.html
Eisenhower, D. D. (1961). *Military-industrial complex speech*. Available at: http://avalon.law.yale.edu/20th_century/eisenhower001.asp
Foster, J. B. and McChesney, R. W. (2014). Surveillance capitalism monopoly-finance capital, the military-industrial complex, and the digital age. *Monthly Review*, 66(3). Available at: https://monthlyreview.org/2014/07/01/surveillance-capitalism/#fn61
Galbraith, J. K. (1946). *Recovery in Europe*. Washington, DC: National Planning Association.
Galbraith, J. K. (1967a). *The new industrial state*. Boston, MA: Houghton Mifflin Company.
Galbraith, J. K. (1967b). *How to get out of Vietnam: A workable solution to the worst problem of our time*. New York: New American Library.
Galbraith, J. K. (1969a). *How to control the military*. New York: Doubleday and Company.
Galbraith, J. K. (1969b). *Ambassador's journal: A personal account of the Kennedy years*. London: Hamilton.
Galbraith, J. K. (1969c). The big defense firms are really public firms and should be nationalized. *New York Times* (16 November 1969).
Galbraith, J. K. (1973). *Economics & the public purpose*. Boston, MA: Houghton Mifflin Company.
Galbraith, J. K. (1981). *A life in our times: Memoirs*. Boston, MA: Houghton Mifflin.
Galbraith, J. K. (1988). The political asymmetry of economic policy. *Eastern Economic Journal*, 14(2), pp. 125–128.
Galbraith, J. K. (1992). *The culture of contentment*. Boston, MA, New York and London: Houghton Mifflin Company.
Galbraith, J. K. (1994). *A journey through economic time a firsthand view*. Boston, MA and New York: Houghton Mifflin Company.
Galbraith, J. K. (1998) [1958]. *The affluent society*. Boston, MA and New York: Houghton Mifflin Company.
Galbraith, J. K. (1998a). *Letters to Kennedy*. (Edited by J. Goodman). Cambridge, MA and London: Harvard University Press.
Galbraith, J. K. (1998b). More than vague dinner conversation. *New Statesman*, 127, pp. 25–26.

Galbraith, J. K. (2004). The worldly philosophers and the war economy. *Social Research*, 71(2), pp. 293–304.

Galbraith, J. K. (2017). *The selected letters of John Kenneth Galbraith* (Edited by Richard P. F. Holt). New York: Cambridge University Press.

Georgiou, G. (1983). The political economy of military expenditures. *Capital & Class*, 7, pp. 183–205.

Gintis, H. (1970). American Keynesianism and the war machine. In: D. Mermelstein, ed., *Economics-mainstream readings and radical critiques*. New York: Random House.

Gold, D. (1990). *The impact of defense spending on investment, productivity and economic growth*. Washington, DC: Center on Budget and Policy Priorities.

Gold, D. (2005). *Does military spending stimulate or retard economic performance? Revisiting an old debate*. International Affairs at the New School Working Paper 2005–01.

Hunt, E. K. (2002). *History of economic thought: A critical perspective*. New York and London: M.E. Sharpe.

Kaldor, M. (1981). *The baroque arsenal*. New York: Hill and Wang.

Kidron, M. (1970). *Western capitalism since the war revised edition*. Harmondsworth: Pelican Books.

Marcuse, H. (1964). *One-dimensional man*. Boston, MA: Beacon Press.

McChesney, R. W. (2013). *Digital disconnect: How capitalism is turning the internet against democracy*. New York: The New Press.

Melman, S. (1965). *Our depleted society*. New York: Holt, Rinehart and Winston.

Melman, S. (1970). *Pentagon capitalism: The political economy of war*. New York: McGraw-Hill.

Melman, S. (1974) [1985]. *The permanent war economy: American capitalism in decline*. New York: Simon & Schuster.

Melman, S. (1986). Limits of military power: Economic and other. *International Security*, 11(1), pp. 72–87.

Mills, C. W. (1956). *The power elite*. New York: Oxford University Press.

Mueller, J. (2006). *Overblown: How politicians and the terrorism industry inflate national security threats, and why we believe them*. New York: Free Press.

Reich, M. (1972). Does the US economy require military spending? *American Economic Review*, 62(1/2), pp. 296–303.

Robinson, J. (1972). The second crisis of economic theory. *American Economic Review*, 62(1/2), pp. 1–10.

Rosen, S. (1973). *Testing the theory of the military-industrial complex*. Lexington, MA: Lexington Books.

Samuelson, P. A. (1970). *Economics*. 8th ed. New York: McGraw-Hill.

Smith, R. (1977). Military expenditure and capitalism. *Cambridge Journal of Economics*, 1(1), pp. 61–76.

Stanfield, J. R. and Stanfield, J. B. (2004). *Interviews with John Kenneth Galbraith*. Jackson: University Press of Mississippi.

Tobin, J. (1958). Defense, dollars and deficits. *The Yale Review*, 47, pp. 321–334.

U.S. News and World Report, May 19, 1950.

Veblen, T. (1898). The instinct of workmanship and the irksomeness of labor. *American Journal of Sociology*, 4(2), pp. 187–201.

Veblen, T. (1914). *The instinct of workmanship: And the state of industrial arts*. New York: Macmillan Company.

William, A. D. (1986). *John Kenneth Galbraith a view from the stands*. Boston, MA: Houghton Mifflin Company.

4 Marxist crisis theories

Introduction

Although crisis is a core aspect of Marxist thought, there is no common theory of it. Rather, the theory of crisis is regarded as one of the weakest parts of Marxist theorising. Marxist crisis theories deal with the long-term economic crisis caused by the internal contradictions of the capitalist production system, not with business cycles or other short-term fluctuations resulting from various economic shocks. In this sense, Marx associates crises with various phenomena, such as the tendency for the profit rate to fall and the potential for overproduction or underconsumption (Clarke, 1994).

Marxist scholars have categorised crisis theories differently, based on their methodological approaches that emphasise different sources of crisis. For example, Sweezy (1942) describes four kinds of crises under two main categories: those 'associated with the falling tendency of the rate of profit' and 'realization crises', resulting from capitalists' inability to sell commodities at their values (Howard and King, 1992, p. 11). Regarding the tendency of profit rates to decline, this may occur either when the organic composition of capital increases more than the rate of exploitation because of mechanisation or when increasing capital accumulation uses up the reserve army of the unemployed, increasing wages, thereby reducing the rate of exploitation. Regarding realisation crises, this may occur either because of 'disproportionalities' between different production sectors or because of 'underconsumption' – that is, lack of aggregate demand.

While Clarke (1994) preferred three main categories of crisis theories, 'underconsumptionism', 'falling rate of profit theories', and 'disproportionality theories', Shaikh (1978a, 1978b) emphasised two general types: 'possibility theories' and 'necessity theories'. According to possibility theories, crises occur when certain historically determined factors are encountered "based on the notion of law as the resultant of conflicting tendencies". Necessity theories, on the other hand, suggest that crises are inevitable because the inherently dominant tendency subordinates countervailing ones. According to Shaikh, while underconsumption or stagnation and a wage squeeze are *possibilities*, the falling rate of profit is a *necessity*. In this chapter, we follow Shaikh's classification to discuss underconsumption/stagnation and profit/wage squeeze theories before focusing on the law of the tendency for the rate of profit to fall.

Underconsumption/stagnation theories

The price of a commodity in the capitalist system is the sum of the wages paid to workers and the profit the capitalist acquires. This very simple identity generates the system's key internal contradiction: the tendency of stagnation, if either the workers or the capitalists (or both) fail to spend all of what they have made. The workers cannot consume all of the products they produce as they are paid less than the total value of the commodities they produce. Capitalists, on the other hand, have two types of spending: their own consumption of goods and new investment. Their spending on commodities is limited by the requirement for new investment to make more profit. However, their new investment is also subject to the availability of 'new markets'. Here, 'new markets' refer to growing international trade, new products, new technologies, or milex. If this is the case, then all value produced is consumed by the workers and capitalists. However, the capitalists may prefer to hold part of their profits (e.g. savings – or 'leakages' in a Keynesian view), causing a crisis of underconsumption or overproduction. Obviously, saving by workers is also a possibility and would have the same effect of underconsumption.

Against this background, the common principle of theories of underconsumption/stagnation is that if increases in wages fall below the rate of expansion of output, then this causes insufficient aggregate demand, leading to stagnation, if demand from the capitalists, in the form of consumption and investment, cannot absorb the increase.

Engels rejected underconsumptionism theory in favour of the overproduction theory of crisis. The difference between these is that, according to the former, accumulation is unsustainable due to the suppression of wages, whereby production inevitably outstrips demand.

For Engels, overproduction was not inevitable but was one possibility due to the circumstances that could arise from the 'anarchy of production' (Clarke, 1994). The anarchy of production is the core aspect of Engels's theory of crisis. Engels argued that

> the ever increasing perfectibility of modern machinery is, by the anarchy of social production, turned into a compulsory law that forces the individual industrial capitalist always to improve his machinery, always to increase its productive force. The bare possibility of extending the field of production is transformed for him into a similar compulsory law. The enormous expansive force of modern industry, compared with which that of gases is mere child's play, appears to us now as a necessity for expansion, both qualitative and quantitative, that laughs at all resistance. Such resistance is offered by consumption, by sales, by the markets for the products of modern industry. But the capacity for extension, extensive and intensive, of the markets

> is primarily governed by quite different laws that work much less energetically. The extension of the markets cannot keep pace with the extension of production. The collision becomes inevitable, and as this cannot produce any real solution so long as it does not break in pieces the capitalist mode of production, the collisions become periodic. Capitalist production has begotten another 'vicious circle'.
>
> (Part III: Socialism, Anti-Dühring, Engels, 1878)

In other words, the anarchy of production is that investment/production decisions are made by numerous profit-seeking individual enterprises without central coordination, which causes overproduction because production and consumption are determined by different laws (Engels, 1878). Thus, for Engels, the capitalist system has an inherent tendency to overproduction.

Karl Kautsky viewed capitalism as causing the creation of the proletariat class and the class struggle, exacerbated by the mechanisation of production, which reduced the value of both existing machinery and workers while the constant development of mechanisation rendered entire industries redundant (Kautsky, 1910). Kautsky argued for secular rather than cyclical tendencies and did not connect the secular tendency for the rate of profit to fall to economic crisis (Clarke, 1994). Instead, he argued that the fall in the rate of profit merely results in a "narrowing of the capitalist class".

Kautsky argued that the capitalist system inherently tends to overproduction because of a fundamental contradiction between production and consumption. On the one hand, there is continuous development and expansion in production due to the pressure of competition; on the other hand, a persistent decline in the consumption side results from the decline in the value of labour power. Kautsky argued that since there is a limit for markets to expand, "capitalist large production digs its own grave. . . . The capitalist system begins to suffocate in its own surplus" (Kautsky, 1910). Kautsky thought that overproduction in a single branch inevitably spreads through the economy at large.

Kautsky's theory of crisis is based on 'anarchy of the market'. Clarke (1994) notes the difference between his 'anarchy of the market' and Engels's 'anarchy of production'. The difference is that while Kautsky focused on 'the markets' to explain the 'anarchic system', Engels stressed that this fragmenting of decision-making power ran throughout the whole system of capitalist production.

In fact, Kautsky's theory crisis, Clarke (1994) argues, has a significant "Keynesian character" in that the theory emphasises imbalance between supply and demand in one branch of production due to each individual capitalist having to estimate demand for his/her product. This imbalance in one branch is then prone to diffuse through the whole economy because of the interdependence between these small production units. The likelihood of crisis may be increased by credit since it is more "sensitive than commerce to any disturbance".

Overall, Clarke (1994, p. 27) argues that "Kautsky offers neither an under-consumptionist nor an overproduction theory of crisis, but a 'proto-Keynesian' theory of the business cycle, which has no distinctively Marxist features".

An alternative version of the realisation crisis occurs due to unevenness or 'disproportionality' in various branches of production. The difference of disproportionality from overproduction is that while some branches in the economy produce more output than what is demanded, other branches produce less. That is, overproduction and underproduction occur in different branches at the same time, which does not necessarily lead to overproduction in total, but to disproportionality. The breakdown in the relation between production and consumption can be seen from the accumulation of unsold stocks, leading to economic crisis. This disproportionality version of realisation crises was developed by Rudolf Hilferding in 1910, who considered underconsumptionism as a special case of disproportionality.

Hilferding contributed to the discussion on disproportionality significantly with his sophisticated analysis of 'finance capital', defined as a new stage of capitalism whereby banks and industrial capital control the economy to maximise profits. In this sense, his analysis is based on 'imperfect competition' rather than the capitalist mode of production in the orthodox Marxist tradition. The disproportionality that creates a surplus of capital is basically due to fixed capital, which leads to 'imperfect competition' among individual capitalists in an unorganised business environment.

Hilferding argues that the immobility resulting from increasing fixed capital, cartels, and banking capital prevent the equalisation of profit rates between branches of production. While orthodox economists assume that discrepancies between profit rates are eliminated by (perfect) competition, and Engels holds that real capitalist competition creates disproportionality, for Hilferding it is the lack of competition or imperfect competition that causes disproportionality. For Hilferding, disproportionalities in specific branches are not simply a temporary result of the anarchy of the market but of systematic decline in profit rates. However, Clarke (1994) argues that, according to Hilferding, rate of profit does not decline because of Marx's 'law'. Rather, he claims that branches of production with high fixed capital and slow turnover are prone to cyclical overproduction. From this, he concludes that the investment cycle rather than the capitalist system itself inherently produces crises. While for Engels and Kautsky, overinvestment is a rational decision for capitalists facing capitalist competition, for Hilferding it represents a miscalculation by capitalists.

Rosa Luxemburg's *The Accumulation of Capital* (1913) is regarded as the foundation of the theory of underconsumption. Her major argument was that capitalism needs non-capitalist systems to expand, based on Marx's reproduction schema:

> Capitalism arises and develops historically amidst a non-capitalist society. In Western Europe it is found at first in a feudal environment from which it in fact sprang . . . and later, after having swallowed up the feudal system. . . . European capitalism is further surrounded by vast territories of non-European civilisation ranging over all levels of development, from the

> primitive communist hordes of nomad herdsmen, hunters and gatherers to commodity production by peasants and artisans. This is the setting for the accumulation of capital.
>
> (Luxemburg, 1913, p. 368)

Against this background, Luxemburg successfully explained the limits of capitalism. However, she mistakenly thought that the driving force of capitalist production is consumption: that capitalists only invest if there is already an increase in consumption. Thus, the problem of the capitalist system that Luxemburg discussed is the source of that increase in demand to absorb increased surplus value. Luxemburg argues that surplus value cannot be absorbed by those whose income is based on wages or surplus value itself. Foreign trade does not help either because it simply transfers surplus value. She therefore argued that capitalism expands toward pre-capitalist regions via imperialism; that is, force and the state play major roles in primitive accumulation (Rowthorn, 1980; Clarke, 1994; Brewer, 2001, p. 72). In this sense, she paid special attention to the role of the military. (See Chapter 5.)

Overall, although Luxemburg was mistaken to consider consumption rather than the tendency to expand production without regard to the limits of the market as the driving force of capitalist production, she provided a rigorous foundation of an underconsumption theory of crisis (Clarke, 1994).

Sweezy (1942) provided the most articulated theory of stagnation, relying on Keynes, Alvin Hansen, Marx, and Luxemburg's underconsumptionism (Howard and King, 1992). For Sweezy, overaccumulation and underconsumption are the two core causes of stagnation. He argued that capitalism is prone to rely on unproductive expenditure to survive. In 1966, along with Paul Baran in *Monopoly Capital*, he emphasised the role of milex. (See Chapter 5.) Sweezy's underconsumption analysis was severely criticised because his argument of 'rising surplus' contradicted the profit squeeze in the late 1960s, his theory of investment was inconsistent with his general framework of *Monopoly Capital*, and his narrative of inflation was not satisfactory to explain the more comprehensive dynamics of money and inflation[1] (Howard and King, 1992, pp. 314–315).

Both disproportionality and underconsumption theories imply that economic crises can be prevented through the coordination of decision making by individual firms or the state or by raising real wages (Clarke, 1994; Howard and King, 1992).

Profit/wage squeeze theories

Both Sweezy and Dobb argue that a core element of Marxist crisis theories is rising real wages due to prosperity or workers' resistance reduce the rate of exploitation and profit rate (Shaikh, 1978a, 1978b).

The profit/wage squeeze approach was introduced by Glyn and Sutcliffe (1972), who argued that the main cause of the decline in the rate of profits in the U.K. was the decline in profit share resulting from increasing union militancy.[2] The same argument was put forward by Boddy and Crotty (1975) for the U.S. Glyn and Sutcliffe's argument is based on empirical observation of the linkage between the rate of surplus value and the general rate of profit in that a rise in real wages and/or a decline in the rate of exploitation (e.g. a decline in the length and intensity of work) reduces the profit rate. That is, this theory explains the crisis in terms of real wages increasing faster than productivity.

Shaikh (1978a) notes two versions of this theory. In one, the rising profit rate boosts investment; in the other, as the theory of underconsumption/stagnation dictates, the increasing profit rate along with monopoly capital intensifies the demand gap in the economy.

Some Marxists have argued that the profit/wage squeeze theory is non-Marxist as it deals with distribution rather than production and attributes a voluntaristic character to the class struggle (Clarke, 1994). The theory implies that economic crises can be prevented if the state facilitates conciliation between capitalists and workers (Shaikh, 1978a, 1978b). The theory also failed to establish itself as a valid approach to explaining the current crisis empirically as real wages have stagnated since the 1980s.

Tendency for the rate of profit to fall

The tendency for the rate of profit to fall is a very controversial issue in Marxist thought, which has generated a sizeable theoretical and empirical literature. The studies referred to in this section are just representative rather than exhaustive. That is, this section is not a 'survey' of this literature but merely an attempt to highlight the main issues in three layers of this debate. First, at the core level, there is a debate on what role the tendency for the falling rate of profit played in Marx's thinking. Second, there are different views on how to measure the rate of profit. Perhaps this is a relatively less controversial part, as there are some issues on which a large majority of scholars have reached consensus. Third, the outer layer concerns alternative accounts for the sources of change in the rate of profit in recent empirical work.

The rate of profit is the key indicator of the health of a capitalist economy. The law of the tendency for the rate of profit to fall is highly significant in Marx's theory, which Marx developed based on the works of Adam Smith and David Ricardo. While for Smith the fall in the rate of profit was due to competition between capitalists, pushing up prices and thereby profits down, for Ricardo, who criticised Smith's argument, it was due to an increase in wages. Ricardo's argument, based on Malthus's thesis of the falling marginal productivity of land, was that a rising population drives agricultural production into less fertile lands, leading to a rise in the price of grain, so wages must rise to cover the increased costs of the reproduction of the labour force. Marx rejected Ricardo's argument by considering the possibility of increase in agricultural productivity and argued that the fall in the rate of profit is due to the inner mechanism of capitalist production.

In *Das Kapital* Volume III, Marx stresses the role of the tendency for the rate of profit to fall in capitalist production as follows:

> The rate of profit is the compelling power of capitalist production, and only such things are produced as yield a profit. . . . The development of the productive forces of social labor is the historical task and privilege of capital. It is precisely in this way that it unconsciously creates the material requirements of a higher mode of production. What worries Ricardo is the fact that the rate of profit, the stimulating principle of capitalist production, the fundamental premise and driving force of accumulation, should be endangered by the development of production itself. . . . It is here demonstrated in a purely economic way, that is from a bourgeois point of view, within the confines of capitalist understanding, from the standpoint of capitalist production itself, that it has a barrier, that it is relative, that it is not an absolute but only a historical mode of production corresponding to a definite and limited epoch in the development of the material conditions of production.

Marx's writings up to an including the early 1860s, when he wrote and rewrote his numerous drafts of *Das Kapital*, clearly indicate that he held the view that capitalism would progress from one cyclical fall in the rate of profit to the next, each tendentially more severe. This was a view that was held then nearly universally among political economists, notwithstanding their different explanations for these decreases. These profit rate declines would be accompanied by economic and social crises that were likewise tendentially intensifying, until they caused a collapse of capitalism. It was broadly held among Marxists until the late 20th century that this was Marx's view on the tendency of the rate of profit to fall and crises. A current reading of the now much more extensive available writings of Marx has given rise to a more nuanced interpretation of his views on these (see for example Heinrich 2013a). From the mid-1860s Marx ceased to talk of a law of the tendency for the rate of profit to fall. The argument is that the failure of the economic downturns from 1857 onward to clearly manifest either a tendency for ever- deeper profit rate declines or linked intensified economic and social crises caused him to come to consider it as an empirical question whether it would fall or not. Already in his notes in the early 1860s that were later published by Engels as Volume III of *Das Kapital* he listed numerous countertendencies that would work against the tendency of the rate of profit to fall, notwithstanding that at that time he did consider the "tendency" would dominate the "countertendencies". Section 4.4.1 briefly discusses this further. Then partly because less attention is given to Marx's writings in the 1870s, along with the problematic description of "the three drafts of *Das Kapital*", which falsely implies the "seamless continuity" of Marx's analysis, and partly due to Engel's problematic editing and arrangement of Marx's notes (ibid. p. 25), most Marxists misunderstood his "law" of the tendency of the rate of profit to fall as the single key to the crisis nature of capitalism and from that the inevitability of humans transcending it. Against this background, Section 4.4.2 focuses on some major debates and measurement issues on which now a large majority of scholars have reached consensus. Finally, since as noted above, for the elder Marx in this interpretation, "the law of the tendency *for* the rate of profit to fall" (not "the law of the fall *in* the rate of profit"[3]) was an empirical question, Section 4.4.4 considers this issue by highlighting some of the major findings of empirical studies.

Marx's law of the tendency for the rate of profit to fall

As the expansion of the capitalist economy is based on the general rate of profit, the rate of profit is the focal point of the capitalist system. One of Marx's major claims in Volume III of *Das Kapital* was that there is a tendency for the general rate of profit to fall.

> The progressive tendency of the general rate of profit to fall is, therefore, just an expression peculiar to the capitalist mode of production of the progressive development of the social productivity of labor. This does not mean to say that the rate of profit may not fall temporarily for other reasons. But proceeding from the nature of the capitalist mode of production, it is thereby proved a logical necessity that in its development the general average rate of surplus value must express itself in a falling general rate of profit. Since the mass of the employed living labor is continually on the decline as compared to the mass of materialised labour set in motion by it, i.e., to the productively consumed means of production, it follows that the portion of living labour, unpaid and congealed in surplus value, must also be continually on the decrease compared to the amount of value represented by the invested total capital. Since the ratio of the mass of surplus value to the value of the invested total capital forms the rate of profit, this rate must constantly fall.
>
> (Marx, 1894: Ch. 13)

For the younger Marx, "the composition of capital and the changes it undergoes in the course of the process of accumulation" was one of the "most important factors" in his theory (Marx, 1867), and therefore, the law of the tendency for the rate of profit to fall was "the most important law of political economy" (Marx, 1894: Ch. 13). However, Marx's view on the tendency for the rate of profit gradually changed, as argued above.

Marx's analysis in Volume II of *Das Kapital* considers money value stock-flow relations for capital (Marx, 1885). Marx represents the three stages of capital with the formula of M-C . . . P . . . C'-M', in which M, C, and P refer to money, commodity, and production processes, respectively, where money purchases the means of production and the labour power used to create a new commodity that will be sold at a markup (Marx, 1885). During the production process, workers use plants and equipment to transform materials into finished products (from C to C'). The process ends with M', which is bigger than M – the difference between them being surplus value.

The total labour time required for the finished product therefore has two parts. The first is the labour time implicit in the means of production (e. g. materials, plants, and equipment) used up, namely *constant capital* (*C*). The second is the current labour time expended by workers in the labour process itself, namely *value added by living labour* (*L*). *L* is composed of two parts: the labour value of the workers' consumption requirements (*V*) and the labour value of the surplus product (*S*). Therefore, value added by living labour has two components: *necessary labour* (*V*), the labour time necessary for workers to reproduce themselves, and *surplus labour* (*S*), the labour time during which workers create *surplus* for capitalist *exploitation*.

Marx defines S/V as *the rate of surplus value* or *the rate of exploitation* and C/V as *the organic composition of capital* (and, in a similar manner, *the technical composition of capital*, which is defined as the mass of means of production per worker). This means there are two ways to increase the rate of surplus value, S/V: increasing the numerator or decreasing the denominator. That is, a capitalist can increase surplus value by lengthening the working day and/or by shortening the required labour time, either reducing real wages and/or increasing labour productivity. Since there are limits to lengthening the working day and lowering real wages, increasing labour productivity is the main tool for capitalists.

Marx indicates that the driving force of capitalism is the relentless search for surplus value because there is a constant fierce competition among capitalists for higher rates of profit. Marx defines this as $r = S/(C + V)$. However, Marx argues that the capitalist production system faces certain internal contradictions to its own unlimited expansion. The accumulation of capital is accompanied by mechanisation of the production process. This 'progressive' process generates, on the one hand, increasing productivity of labour as workers use more sophisticated tools and machinery and increasing organic composition of capital increases on the other hand. This leads to one key contradiction of capitalism: rising labour productivity reduces the profitability of capital. Thus, the young Marx wanted to prove that that the tendency for the organic composition of capital to rise due to mechanisation leads to a fall in the rate of profit despite the continued rise in the mass of profit.

However, Marx also notes some countertendencies that mitigate the tendency for the rate of profit to fall.[4] These include raising the intensity of exploitation, depression of wages below their value, cheapening of the elements of constant capital, and foreign trade. First, a capitalist can increase the length of the working day and the intensity of labour to increase the rate of surplus value. Second, a capitalist can pursue an aggressive wage policy while an increase in the reserve army of the unemployed also depresses wages. Third, increasing mechanisation reduces the value of constant capital per unit by raising labour productivity. That is, although the material volume of constant capital grows, its increase in value per unit is not so large. This counteract, Marx notes, can be so substantial that it may totally offset the initial increase. Fourth, foreign trade may have a few counter effects on the falling rate of profit. Investment in foreign trade may yield a higher rate of profit. It also makes acquiring cheap raw materials possible. It also increases the rate of surplus value.[5]

Therefore, there are two different aspects to the proof of "the law". First, showing why the tendency must outweigh all the counteracting tendencies. Second, showing why in $r = S/(C + V)$, when both the numerator and the denominator increase, the latter grows faster than the former in the long run, so that the fraction – the rate of profit – declines. Heinrich (2013a) claims that Marx was unable to prove either of these. Regarding the former, Marx nowhere tries to argue why what he calls the tendency should have a stronger effect than the sum of all the effects he calls countertendencies. Regarding the latter, he does make arguments but, in the end, does not show the necessity. Marx rewrites the rate of profit as

$$r = \frac{S}{C+V} = \frac{S/V}{(C+V)/V} = \frac{S/V}{(C/V)+1}$$

To address the general case where both the numerator and denominator are increasing over time, he drops his initial simplification of the constant rate of surplus value, S/V, arguing that in general an increase in C will cause an increase in S/V. That is, when C increases, both the numerator and the denominator increase. Then to "prove" the "law", one must show that, in the long run, the denominator must grow faster than the numerator. Marx argued that technical progress will generally involve a decrease in the number of workers relative to C, so C/V will go up. But the argument gets no further than that. We have S/V going up and C/V going up and so $C/V + 1$ going up, but no reason $C/V + 1$ should go up faster than S/V. In fact, the "+1" tends to make the denominator increase proportionally less, but again the point is that Marx gave no economic reason the denominator should increase faster than the numerator (ibid. p. 24).

Marx certainly considered capitalism to be a crisis-prone system to the day he died, but in his argument the heart of the crisis-prone nature of capitalism was not an inevitable fall in the rate of profit. Rather, for him, capitalism's crisis resulted from "a fundamental contradiction between the tendency towards an unlimited production of surplus value, and the tendency toward a limited realization of it, based upon the 'antagonistic conditions of distribution'" (ibid. p. 26).

A brief overview of the debates

The "law of the tendency of the rate of profit to fall" has become one of the most debated parts of Marx's analysis. The debate on the law of the tendency expanded in the late 1960s when some Marxists pursued the law to explain the economic crisis in terms of the decline in the rate of profit. (One explanation for the falling rate of profit was linked to rising real wages. See above: *Profit/Wage Squeeze Theories*.) The origin of the falling rate of profit theory of crisis is

Paul Mattick's *Marx and Keynes: The Limits of the Mixed Economy* (1969), whose argument was further developed by Yaffe (1972) and Cogoy (1972, 1973).

One early criticism of the falling rate of profit theory was that Marx had underestimated the effects of technical progress on the productivity of labour. The criticism argued that since mechanisation reduces the value of constant capital and increases the rate of exploitation, it is likely that the rate of profit would increase instead of fall (Howard and King, 1992, p. 131). Dobb (1937) and Sweezy (1942) argued that technical change is the capitalist's reaction to increasing real wages resulting from worker resistance, which has two counter effects. While increasing productivity increases the rate of profit, rising real wages reduce the rate of profit. Therefore, the ultimate effect is contingent on these two forces. Shaik (1978a, p. 234), however, notes that in Marx's analysis "the rising real wages are themselves made possible by a prior cause, namely the mechanization arising from the battle of production. Thus, the effect that Sweezy and Dobb analyse is a secondary one, superimposed on (and indeed only possible because of) the primary one. Given that they ignore the primary cause, it is not surprising that they can find no particular reason for the rate of profit to fall".

Another criticism was initiated by the Okishio Theorem. Nobuo Okishio (1961) argued that the rate of profit is not reduced by any change in technology that would actually be adopted under capitalism, leading some to then claim that Marx's theories of value and the falling rate of profit are internally inconsistent. According to the Okishio Theorem, if the real wage was fixed, any cost reducing changes would increase profits. In other words, according to Samuelson and Okishio, technical change can only reduce the rate of profit if it is accompanied by an increase in real wages (Howard and King, 1992, p. 140). However, Salvadori (1981) showed that the Okishio Theorem could be invalid[6] in the case of joint production, in which technical progress can reduce the rate of profit while reducing the real wage due to rising unemployment. In short, the claim that technological change cannot cause a decline in the rate of profit because a capitalist would never adopt a new method that would reduce profits is not plausible.

Most recently, Michael Heinrich's (2013a) work has led to further debates (Heinrich, 2013b; Carchedi and Roberts, 2013; Mage, 2013; Moseley, 2013; Samol, 2013; Kliman et al., 2013; Harvey, 2016). His argument, based on a vigilant review of Marx's original draft manuscripts, is that Marx did not propose the falling rate of profit theory of crisis and that although he held the tendency for the rate of profit to fall to be a logical result of capitalist production when he was young, he began to see the tendency of the rate of profit to fall as an empirical question in his later years (ibid. p. 28).

Heinrich (2013a) was criticised with respect to the 'indeterminacy' of Marx's law (Carchedi and Roberts, 2013; Kliman et al., 2013; Samol, 2013; Mage, 2013), problems in proving the law (Carchedi and Roberts, 2013; Mage, 2013), his argument of Marx's abandonment of the distinction between 'capital in general' and 'competition of the many capitals' *in Das Kapital* (Moseley, 2013), his argument about Engels's editorial distortion, and his assumptions about Marx's probable abandonment of the law (Carchedi and Roberts, 2013; Kliman et al., 2013).

Regarding the 'indeterminacy' of Marx's law, the key controversy is whether a rising rate of surplus value is part of the law itself or a counteracting factor. Heinrich considers a rising rate of surplus value as part of the law. For Kliman et al (2013) and Carchedi and Roberts (2013), on the other hand, rising organic composition (the movement of the rate of exploitation) and rising surplus value are separate, and the latter is a counteracting factor. Heinrich (2013b) argues that an increase in productivity leads simultaneously to a rising organic composition of capital and a rising rate of surplus value, which have opposite effects on the rate of profit. Thus, one cannot dismiss either one of these two interconnected forces without leading to a misconstruction of the law. Heinrich's argument seems plausible, and he notes that it is also how Marx treated rising surplus value, as part of the law. Needless to say, the plausibility of Heinrich's reasoning is independent of Marx's own view.

Regarding problems in proving the law, there are two objections to Heinrich. First, Mage attempts to prove the law of the tendency for the rate of profit to fall with a different profit rate. Rather than maintaining Marx's original profit rate formula, $r = S/(C + V)$, he drops V by pointing out that V becomes negligible over time. Leaving aside the plausibility of such an exercise, Heinrich shows that Mage's profit rate is also subject to the same problem: that the direction of the fraction depends on relative changes in the numerator and denominator.

Seemingly, the real challenge to Heinrich's proof is the objection to his treatment of the constant capital. Reworking Marx's example of a downsizing of labour power from 24 workers to 2 workers, Heinrich argues that the rising productivity of labour eventually makes the constant capital (and the means of subsistence) cheaper. Therefore, the constant capital necessary to employ a worker can also fall, causing a further downward impact on the denominator, which increases the whole fraction, the rate of profit. Both Carchedi and Roberts (2013) and Kliman et al. (2013) argue that the point is not the change of constant capital, but the change in the organic composition of capital. Kliman et al. (2013) argue that once one explicitly assumes that 2 workers are employed for the same amount of capital required to employ 24 workers, then Heinrich's assertion that the constant capital could also drop is no longer plausible because it would mean that the organic composition of capital did not rise as fast as assumed in the example. That is, Heinrich's assertion apparently needs to be proved.

Regarding Heinrich's (2013a) argument that Engel's editing and arrangement of Marx's notes was somewhat problematic and his assumption that Marx had abandoned the falling rate of profit theory of crisis were found to be unjustified by Kliman et al. (2013) and Carchedi and Roberts (2013). Whether Engels' editing caused some distortions or whether Marx actually would have abandoned it are less important in terms of the validity of the law of the tendency for the rate of profit to fall. However, it is still worth noting that Heinrich maintained (and strengthened) his argument that Marx abandoned the tendency by further arguing that although Marx discussed crises several time in the 1870s, he did not mention the tendency in letters, manuscripts or in excerpts[7] (Heinrich, 2013b).

Issues on the measurement of the rate of profit

There is no common understanding among Marxist scholars of how to measure profit and capital precisely to calculate the rate of profit. The distinction between "unproductive" and "productive" is one of the most controversial issues since Joseph Gillman and Paul Baran's books in 1957 (Gillman, 1957; Baran, 1957 cited in Hunt, 1979), and it is important in terms of proper measurement of surplus value and the rate of profit. (See Gough, 1972; Fine, 1973; Fine and Harris, 1976, 1979; Hunt, 1979; Moseley, 1983, 1994; Mohun, 1994, 1996, 1998, 2012; Harvie, 2005; Olsen, 2017 for a detailed discussion.)

Mohun (1996) argues that "[i]f the distinction between productive and unproductive labor is rejected, then other fundamental categories of Marx's theory lose their theoretical coherence. It is not possible both to maintain the labor theory of value and to dispense with its fundamental building blocks" (p. 31). While some Marxists claim that the distinction matters (e.g. Mohun, 1996, 2002; Fine, 1973; Fine and Harris, 1976, 1979; Shaikh and Tonak, 1994), others reject this because all wage labour is subject to exploitation regardless of whether they are employed by capital or not (e.g. Gough, 1972; Houston, 1997; Laibman, 1992, 1999; Harvie, 2005), and these scholars reject that this invalidates Marx's labour theory of value.

In Chapter IV of *Theories of Surplus Value*, Marx defines productive labour (and repeats this basic aspect of productive labour several times in other works):

> Productive labour, in its meaning for capitalist production, is wage-labour which, exchanged against the variable part of capital (the part of the capital that is spent on wages), reproduces not only this part of the capital (or the value of its own labour-power), but in addition produces surplus-value for the capitalist. It is only thereby that commodity or money is transformed into capital, is produced as capital. Only that wage-labour is productive which produces capital.
>
> (Marx, 1863)

Furthermore, unproductive labour is "labour which is not exchanged with capital, but directly with revenue, that is, with wages or profit (including of course the various categories of those who share as copartners in the capitalist's profit, such as interest and rent)" (Marx, 1863).

So the key aspect of the distinction is not whether the labour is necessary or not but whether it produces surplus value or not. Therefore, state employees are paid out of taxes (or government borrowing) rather than from sales of a commodity, so they are unproductive[8] (Shaikh and Tonak, 1994; Savran and Tonak, 1999). Empirical analysis commonly indicates that the share of unproductive labour has increased in the U.S. Since unproductive labour is ultimately paid out of surplus value, its amount is an important indicator of how much profit is actually available (Mohun, 2012a, p. 282).

Several studies have investigated the effect of unproductive labour on economic performance in general or the rate of profit specifically. Olsen, 2017 provides a precise summary of this part of the literature. Although some Marxist scholars argue that unproductive activities hinder economic growth because they consume surplus value and reduce profits (Gillman, 1957; Moseley, 1991; Shaikh and Tonak, 1994; Paitaridis and Tsoulfidis, 2012 cited in Olsen, 2017), Baran (1957) and Baran and Sweezy (1966) consider unproductive activities the key tool for absorbing surplus value, helping to prevent stagnation due to a lack of effective demand. (See the more detailed discussion in Chapter 5.) While Duménil and Lévy (2003, 2011b) argued that the function of unproductive labour is to maximise profits, Resnick and Wolff (1987) and Olsen (2015) showed that the ultimate effect on economic performance is contingent on different factors, such as whether expenditure on unproductive labour reduces the total cost (cited in Olsen, 2017). Vasudevan (2016), on the other hand, discussed the effect of inequality on profitability in a model that included the 'unproductive' labour of the managerial class. She shows that the increase in inequality from rising managerial power reduces accumulation in a regime where consumer borrowing is exogenous.

In addition to the debate on the distinction between productive and unproductive labour, there are other issues regarding the precise measurement of the rate of profit. One debate is how to valorise capital at current prices (i.e. replacement costs) as carried out in most work, including Shaikh (1999), Duménil and Lévy (2011a), Kotz (2009, 2013), Bakir and Campbell (2006, 2009, 2010, 2013), and Basu and Vasudevan (2013), or at historic cost, as preferred by only Kliman and Freeman (see Kliman and McGlone, 1988; Freeman and Carchedi, 1996; Kliman, 2011) within the Temporal Single System Interpretation of Marx's theory of value.

Two other concerns are treatment of corporate income taxes (pre- or post-tax profits) and capital stock measurement (gross or net terms). Regarding the former, Duménil and Lévy (2011a) claim that profit tax deductions are necessary to realistically reflect profit flows. Regarding the latter, it is noted that net stock measures overstate profit rates since net stocks decline over time (Shaikh, 1999; Basu and Vasudevan, 2013). Although gross stocks could be an alternative measure, there is no available data. It is also unclear how best to measure depreciation since gross stocks could be calculated inaccurately using geometric depreciation because some assets continue to be useful.

Empirical literature

There is an immense literature on the 'law of the tendential fall of profit rates', leading to an inconclusive debate on the issue (Basu and Vasudevan, 2013).

While some scholars have argued in favour of the validity of tendency of the profit rate to fall (Carchedi and Roberts, 2018; Glyn and Sutcliffe, 1972; Glyn, 2006; Kliman, 2007, 2015; Shaikh, 1978a, 1987, 1992; Rosdolsky, 1977), others either simply reject it[9] (Roemer, 1981; Bowles, 1985), or argue that neither upward nor downward tendency can be a priori in the capitalist development (Foley, 1986; Michl, 1988; Moseley, 1991; Duménil and Lévy, 1993, 2003; Duménil et al., 1987; Foley and Michl, 1999 cited in Basu and Manolakos, 2013; Heinrich, 2013a).

Weisskopf's seminal work in 1979 has stimulated numerous studies analysing the secular and cyclical dynamic of the rate of profit (Weisskopf, 1979). Weisskopf suggested the following profit rate equation:

$$r = \frac{\pi}{K} = \frac{Y}{Y^*}\frac{Y^*}{K}\frac{\pi}{Y}$$

where r is the rate of profit, π is the net profit, K is the net capital stock, Y is the net output and Y^* is the net potential output, the maximum level of output that can be produced when capital stock is fully utilised. Weisskopf decomposes the profit rate into three theoretical concepts: the rate of capacity utilisation $(\frac{Y}{Y^*})$, potential output-capital ratio

$(\frac{Y^*}{K})$ and profit share $(\frac{\pi}{Y})$.

This decomposition allows one to investigate three alternative Marxist crisis theories. First, the impact of 'underconsumption' (or 'overinvestment') can be considered as the realisation problem (capitalists' inability to sell commodities at their full values) decreases the rate of capacity utilisation, which in turn reduces the rate of profit. An increase in the organic composition of capital due to capital accumulation and technical change reduces the rate of profit by reducing the potential output-capital ratio. Finally, the profit/wage squeeze problem, which is a decline in profit share (or an increase in real wages) resulting from the increasing strength of labour, shows its effect through the profit share. While most studies that have adopted Weisskopf's method (e.g. Michl, 1988; Duménil and Lévy, 2002a, 2002b; Bakir and Campbell, 2006, 2009, 2010; Shaikh, 2011; Basu and Vasudevan, 2013) have used the standard rate of profit, Duménil and Lévy (2004), Bakir and Campbell (2013) and Bakir (2015) incorporated the financial sector in their analyses.

Profit rates rose in the post–WWII era up until the mid-1960s, during the so-called Golden Age. This was followed by a fall until 1982 and another rise during the neo-liberal period, which peaked in 1997. After another fall from 1997 to 2001, profit rates recovered in the credit boom up to 2005–6 in the U.S. and for other major economies to some extent (Wolff, 1979, 2001, 2003; Duménil and Lévy, 2011a; Roberts, 2009, 2012; Li et al., 2007; Basu and Vasudevan, 2013; Bakir and Campbell, 2009; Bakir, 2015).

Calculating profit rates using different measures provides similar results. For example, Basu and Vasudevan (2013) found similar trends, including a break in the decline of the profit rate in the early 1980s, followed by a trendless or slowly rising profit rate. The only variation to this trend is based on data that uses the historical cost valuation of the capital stock and before tax and interest profits. Once this data is used, the profit rate shows a declining trend over the entire post–WWII period.

However, there are alternative accounts of the fall of profit rates (see Basu and Vasudevan, 2013). For example, according to Bellamy-Foster and Magdoff (2009), monopoly capitalism not only increases wealth and income inequality but also suppresses competition and innovation. This in turn limits consumption demand, which widens the disconnection between economic surplus and profitable investment. When the credit-debt system expands dramatically under 'monopoly finance capital', then demand increases, and the economic surplus can be absorbed. On the other hand, Brenner (2009) suggests overinvestment results from globalisation and intensified competition, which has reduced the rate of return of capital since the 1970s. According to Kotz (2009), however, higher demand leads to overinvestment, which becomes excessive due to asset price bubbles. For Shaikh (1987, 1999, 2011), capital-intensive production lowers profit rates, which increases the composition of capital. Finally, Moseley (1991) argues that the growth of the ratio of unproductive to productive labour leads to the fall in profits. (See also Mohun, 1996, 1998.)

Basu and Vasudevan (2013) noted a rise in capital productivity in 1946–1968, followed by a fall between 1968 and 1982, a gradual rise in 1982–2000 and a sharp drop after 2000. The first decline from 1966 to 1982 reflected a 'Marx-biased technological change' as labour productivity rose and capital productivity fell (Foley and Michl, 1999). From 1982 to 2000, productivity grew for both labour and capital, which contradicts the 'Marx-biased technological change' theory. Since 2000, it has returned to the Marx-biased technological change pattern.

Using an advanced econometric model, with special attention to non-stationary, Basu and Manolakos (2012, p. 93) analysed the tendency for the rate of profit to fall in the U.S., controlling for countertendencies, namely the intensity of exploitation, the relative cheapening of the elements of constant capital, the deviation of the wage rate from the value of labour power, the existence of relative overpopulation in the labour market, and a deterministic time trend. They found that the rate of profit declined at a rate of approximately 0.2 percent per annum for 1948–2007. They concluded that this happened because the long-run labour-saving bias of technological change dominated countertendencies. However, their findings also showed that, when the counteracting tendencies were strong enough, the rate of profit rose during 1982–2000.

Bakir and Campbell (2010) showed a structural change in the 1970s and substantial transfer of profit from the non-financial to financial sector in the US, leaving less profit available for accumulation in the non-financial sector. This gap also widened in the 1980s and early 1990s under the full neo-liberal paradigm.

Bakir (2015) and Bakir and Campbell (2013), drawing on methodology introduced by Duménil and Lévy, 2004, analysed the pattern of profit rates in the U.S. in more detail. Bakir (2015, p. 405) found that while the standard rate of profit increased during the neo-liberal era, the augmented profit rate, which includes the impact of financial relations, declined substantially despite the increase in net adjusted financial income. In other words, once the important financial factors under neoliberalism are taken into account, "the profit rate once again becomes explanatory for the crisis". Bakir (2015, p. 405) concludes that "the true cause of the crisis is the breakdown in the interrelated process of the super-exploitation of labor through suppression of real wage growth and higher debt, financialization, and sluggish capital accumulation".

Notes

1 See Chapter 5 for more discussion on *Monopoly Capital*.
2 Rowthorn (1976), Roemer (1979) and Bowles (1981) were other major opponents of this theory.
3 Note that the title of Section III of Volume III is "The law of the tendency of the rate of profit to fall".
4 Marx originally noted six counteracting factors. One of these deals with the calculation of the rate of profit. One of those five causes, 'relative overpopulation', via its effect on the reserve army, apparently concerns the depression of wages as well.
5 In this context, Marx stressed the importance of the expansion of foreign trade as capital production needs expanding markets. See the discussion on Rosa Luxemburg in Chapter 5.
6 Okishio himself accepted that the key assumption of his theorem – constant real wages – was not realistic (Okishio, 1961, cited in Basu and Manolakos, 2013).
7 In this context, Harvey's (2016) view is parallel to Heinrich's.
8 Shaikh and Tonak (1994)'s methodology has established itself as the common methodology of productive and unproductive labour, which was updated by Mohun (2005, 2014).
9 Elveren and Hsu (2016), a study that investigates the effect of milex on the rate of profits for 24 OECD countries for 1963–2008, found a highly significant positive impact of the time trend in most model specifications to argue that the results suggest no tendency for the profit rate to fall, providing some evidence indirectly for a large group of countries for a relatively long period.

References

Bakir, E. (2015). Capital accumulation, profitability, and crisis: Neoliberalism in the United States. *Review of Radical Political Economics*, 47(3), pp. 389–411.

Bakir, E. and Campbell, A. (2006). The effect of neoliberalism on the fall in the rate of profit in business cycles. *Review of Radical Political Economics*, 38(3), pp. 365–373.

Bakir, E. and Campbell, A. (2009). The bush business cycle profit rate: Support in a theoretical debate and implications for the future. *Review of Radical Political Economics*, 41(3), pp. 335–342.

Bakir, E. and Campbell, A. (2010). Neoliberalism, the rate of profit and the rate of accumulation. *Science & Society*, 74(3), pp. 323–342.

Bakir, E. and Campbell, A. (2013). The financial rate of profit: What is it, and how has it behaved in the United States? *Review of Radical Political Economics*, 45(3), pp. 295–304.

Baran, P. (1957). *The political economy of growth*. New York: Monthly Review Press.
Baran, P. and Sweezy, P. (1966). *Monopoly capital: An essay on the American economic and social order*. New York: Monthly Review Press.
Basu, D. and Manolakos, P. (2013). Is there a tendency for the rate of profit to fall? Econometric evidence for the U.S. economy, 1948–2007. *Review of Radical Political Economics*, 45(1), pp. 76–95.
Basu, D. and Vasudevan, R. (2013). Technology, distribution and the rate of profit in the US economy: Understanding the current crisis. *Cambridge Journal of Economics*, 37, pp. 57–89.
Bellamy-Foster, J. and Magdoff, H. (2009). *The great financial crisis: Causes and consequences*. New York: Monthly Review Press.
Boddy, R. and Crotty, J. (1975). Class conflict and macro policy: The political business cycle. *Review of Radical Political Economics*, 7(1), pp. 1–19.
Bowles, S. (1981). Technical change and profit rate: A simple proof of the Okishio Theorem. *Cambridge Journal of Economics*, 5(2), pp. 183–186.
Bowles, S. (1985). The production process in a competitive economy: Walrasian, Neo-Hobbesian, and Marxian Models. *The American Economic Review*, 75(1), pp. 16–36.
Brenner, R. (2009). *What is good for Goldman Sachs is good for America: The origins of the current crisis*. Available at: www.sscnet.ucla.edu/issr/cstch/papers/BrennerCrisisTodayOctober2009.pdf
Brewer, A. (2001). *Marxist theories of imperialism a critical survey*. 2nd ed. London and New York: Routledge.
Carchedi, G. and Roberts, M. (2013). A critique of Heinrich's, 'crisis theory, the law of the tendency of the profit rate to fall, and Marx's studies in the 1870s'. *Monthly Review* Available at: https://monthlyreview.org/features/exchange-with-heinrich-on-crisis-theory/
Carchedi, G. and Roberts, M. (eds.) (2018). *World in crisis: A global analysis of Marx's law of profitability*. Chicago, IL: Haymarket Books.
Clarke, S. (1994). *Marx's theory of crisis*. New York: St. Martin's Press.
Cogoy, M. (1972). Les théories néo-Marxistes, Marx et l'accumulation du Capital. *Les Temps Modernes*, pp. 314–315.
Cogoy, M. (1973). The fall in the rate of profit and the theory of accumulation. *Bulletin of the Conference of Socialist Economists*, Winter 1973.
Dobb, M. (1937). *Political economy and capitalism*. London: Routledge & Kegan Paul.
Duménil, G., Glick, M. and Rangel, J. (1987). The rate of profit in the United States. *Cambridge Journal of Economics*, 11(4), pp. 331–359.
Duménil, G. and Lévy, D. (1993). *The economics of the profit rate: Competition, crises and historical tendencies in capitalism*. Aldershot: Edward Elgar.
Duménil, G. and Lévy, D. (2002a). The field of capital mobility and the gravitation of profit rates (USA 1948–2000). *Review of Radical Political Economics*, 34(4), pp. 417–436.
Duménil, G. and Lévy, D. (2002b). The profit rate: Where and how much did it fall? Did it recover? USA 1948–2000. *Review of Radical Political Economics*, 34(4), pp. 437–461.
Duménil, G. and Lévy, D. (2003). Production and management: Marx's dual theory of labor. In: R. Westra and A. Zuege, eds., *Value and the world economy today*. New York and Basingstoke: Palgrave Macmillan.
Duménil, G. and Lévy, D. (2004). *Capital resurgent*. Cambridge, MA: Harvard University Press.
Duménil, G. and Lévy, D. (2011a). *The crisis of the early 21st century: A critical review of alternative interpretations*. Available at: www.jourdan.ens.fr/levy/dle2011e.pdf
Duménil, G. and Lévy, D. (2011b). Unproductive labor a profit-rate-maximizing labor. *Rethinking Marxism*, 23(2), pp. 216–225.

Elveren, A. Y. and Hsu, S. (2016). Military expenditures and profit rates: Evidence from OECD countries. *Metroeconomica*, 67(3), pp. 551–577.

Engels, F. (1878). *Anti-duhring*. Available at: www.marxists.org/archive/marx/works/1877/anti-duhring/ch15.htm#061

Fine, B. (1973). A note on productive and unproductive labour. *Bulletin of the Conference of Socialist Economists*, Autumn, pp. 99–102.

Fine, B. and Harris, L. (1976). Controversial issues in Marxist economic theory. In: R. Miliband and J. Saville, eds., *The Socialist register: A survey of movements and ideas*, vol. 13, pp. 141–178. Available at: https://socialistregister.com/index.php/srv/article/view/5390

Fine, B. and Harris, L. (1979). *Rereading capital*. London: Macmillan.

Foley, D. K. (1986). *Understanding capital: Marx's economic theory*. Cambridge, MA: Harvard University Press.

Foley, D. K. and Michl, T. R. (1999). *Growth and distribution*. Cambridge, MA: Harvard University Press.

Freeman, A. and Carchedi, G. (eds.) (1996). *Marx and non-equilibrium economics*. Aldershot: Edward Elgar.

Gillman, J. (1957). *The falling rate of profit: Marx's law and its significance to twentieth-century capitalism*. London: D. Dobson.

Glyn, A. (2006). *Capitalism unleashed, finance, globalization, and welfare*. Oxford and New York: Oxford University Press.

Glyn, A. and Sutcliffe, B. (1972). *British capitalism, workers and the profits Squeeze*. Harmondsworth: Penguin.

Gough, I. (1972). Marx's theory of productive and unproductive labour. *New Left Review*, 76, pp. 47–72.

Harvie, D. (2005). All labour produces value for capital and we all struggle against value. *The Commoner*, 10, pp. 132–171.

Harvey, D. (2016). Crises theory and the falling rate of profit. In: T. Subasat, ed. *The great financial meltdown systemic, conjunctural or policy created?* Cheltenham, UK and Northampton, MA: Edward Elgar, pp. 37–54.

Heinrich, M. (2013a). Crisis theory, the law of the tendency of the profit rate to fall, and Marx's studies in the 1870s. *Monthly Review*, 64(11), pp. 15–31.

Heinrich, M. (2013b). Heinrich answers critics. *Monthly Review*. Available at: https://monthlyreview.org/features/exchange-with-heinrich-on-crisis-theory/

Hilferding, R. (1910) [1981]. *Finance capital*. London: Routledge and Kegan Paul.

Houston, D. (1997). Productive – unproductive labor: Rest in peace. *Review of Radical Political Economics*, 29(1), pp. 131–139.

Howard, M. C. and King, J. E. (1992). *A history of Marxian economics*. London: Palgrave Macmillan.

Hunt, E. K. (1979). The categories of productive and unproductive labor in Marxist economic theory. *Science and Society*, 43(3), pp. 303–325.

Hunt, E. K. (2002). *History of economic thought: A critical perspective updated second edition*. New York and London: M.E. Sharpe.

Kautsky, K. (1910). *The class struggle* (1892) (Translated by William E. Bohn). Charles H. Kerr & Co. Chicago. Available at: www.marxists.org/archive/kautsky/1892/erfurt/index.htm

Kliman, A. (2007). *Reclaiming Marx's capital: A refutation of the myth of inconsistency*. Plymouth: Lexington Books.

Kliman, A. (2011). *The failure of capitalist production: Underlying causes of the great recession*. London: Pluto Press.

Kliman, A. (2015). The great recession and Marx's crisis theory. *American Journal of Economics and Sociology*, 74(2), pp. 236–277.

Kliman, A., Freeman, A., Potts, N., Gusev, A. and Cooney, B. (2013). *The unmaking of Marx's capital: Heinrich's attempt to eliminate Marx's crisis theory*. Available at: http://papers.ssrn.com/sol3/papers.cfm?abstract_id=2294134

Kliman, A. and McGlone, T. (1988). The transformation non-problem and the non-transformation problem. *Capital and Class*, 12(2), pp. 56–84. https://doi.org/10.1177/030981688803500106

Kotz, D. (2009). The financial and economic crisis of 2008: A systemic crisis of neoliberal capitalism. *Review of Radical Political Economics*, 41(3), pp. 305–317.

Kotz, D. (2013). The current economic crisis in the United States: A crisis of over-investment. *Review of Radical Political Economics*, 45(3), pp. 284–294.

Laibman, D. (1992). *Value, technical change and crisis: Explorations in Marxist economic theory*. Armonk, NY: M. E. Sharpe.

Laibman, D. (1999). Productive and unproductive labor: A comment. *Review of Radical Political Economics*, 31(2), pp. 61–73.

Li, M., Xiao, F. and Zhu, A. (2007). Long waves, institutional changes and historical trends: A study of the long-term movement of the profit rate in the capitalist world economy. *Journal of World-System Research*, 13(1), pp. 33–54.

Luxemburg, R. (1951) [1913]. *The accumulation of capital*. London: Routledge and Kegan Paul.

Mage, S. (2013). Response to Heinrich – in defense of Marx's law. *Monthly Review*. Available at: https://monthlyreview.org/features/exchange-with-heinrich-on-crisis-theory/

Marx, K. (1863). *Theories of surplus value, part 1*. Available at: www.marxists.org/archive/marx/works/1863/theories-surplus-value/

Marx, K. (1867). *Capital: A critique of political economy*, Vol. I. New York: Vintage Books.

Marx, K. (1885). *Capital: A critique of political economy*, Vol. II. https://libcom.org/files/Capital-Volume-II.pdf

Marx, K. (1894). *Capital: A critique of political economy*, Vol. III. https://www.marxists.org/archive/marx/works/download/pdf/Capital-Volume-III.pdf

Mattick, P. (1969). *Marx and Keynes*. London: Merlin.

Michl, T. (1988). The two-stage decline in U.S. nonfinancial corporate profitability, 1948–1986. *Review of Radical Political Economics*, 20(4), pp. 1–22.

Mohun, S. (1994). A re(in)statement of the labour theory of value. *Cambridge Journal of Economics*, 18, pp. 391–412.

Mohun, S. (1996). Productive and unproductive labor in the labor theory of value. *Review of Radical Political Economics*, 28(4), pp. 30–54.

Mohun, S. (1998). Unproductive labor and the rate of profit in Australia 1966/67–1991/92. In: R. Bellofiore, ed., *Marxian economics: A reappraisal*, Vol. II. Basingstoke: Palgrave Macmillan.

Mohun, S. (2002). Productive and unproductive labor: A reply to Houston and Laibman. *Review of Radical Political Economics*, 34(2), pp. 203–220.

Mohun, S. (2005). On measuring the wealth of nations: The US economy, 1964–2001. *Cambridge Journal of Economics*, 29(5), pp. 799–815.

Mohun, S. (2012). Productive and unproductive labour. In: B. Fine and A. Saad-Filho, eds., *The Elgar companion to Marxist economics*. Cheltenham, UK and Northampton, MA: Edward Elgar, pp. 277–282.

Mohun, S. (2014). Unproductive labor in the U.S. economy 1964–2010. *Review of Radical Political Economics*, 46(3), pp. 355–379.

Moseley, F. (1983). Marx's concepts of productive labor and unproductive labor: An application to the postwar U.S. economy. *Eastern Economics Journal*, 9(3), pp. 180–189.

Moseley, F. (1991). *The falling rate of profit in the postwar United States economy*. New York: St. Martin's Press.

Moseley, F. (1994). Unproductive labor and the rate of profit: A reply. *Science and Society*, 58(2), pp. 84–92.

Moseley, F. (2013). Critique of Heinrich: Marx did not abandon the logical structure. *Monthly Review*. Available at: https://monthlyreview.org/features/exchange-with-heinrich-on-crisis-theory/

Okishio, N. (1961). Technical changes and the rate of profit. *Kobe University Economic Review*, 7, pp. 85–99.

Olsen, E. K. (2015). Unproductive activity and endogenous technological change in a Marxian model of economic reproduction and growth. *Review of Radical Political Economics*, 47(1), pp. 34–55.

Olsen, E. K. (2017). Productive and unproductive labour. In: D. M. Brennan, D. Kristjanson-Gural, C. P. Mulder, and E. K. Olsen, eds., *Routledge handbook of Marxian economics*. London: Routledge.

Paitaridis, D. and Tsoufidis, L. (2012). The growth of unproductive activities, the rate of profit, and the phase-change of the U.S. economy. *Review of Radical Political Economics*, 44(2), pp. 213–233.

Resnick, S. A. and Wolff, R. D. (1987). *Knowledge and class*. Chicago: University of Chicago Press.

Roberts, M. (2009). *The great recession profit cycles, economic crisis a Marxist view*. Available at https://archive.org/details/TheGreatRecession.ProfitCyclesEconomicCrisisAMarxistView/page/n1

Roberts, M. (2012). *A world of profit*. Available at: http://thenextrecession.files.wordpress.com/2012/09/a-world-rate-of-profit.pdf

Roemer, J. E. (1979). Continuing controversy on the falling rate of profit: Fixed capital and other issues. *Cambridge Journal of Economics*, 3(4), pp. 379–398.

Roemer, J. E. (1981). *Analytical foundations of Marxian economic theory*. Cambridge: Cambridge University Press.

Rosdolsky, R. (1977). *The making of Marx's capital*. London: Pluto Press.

Rowthorn, R. (1976). Mandel's late capitalism. *New Left Review*, 98.

Rowthorn, R. (1980). *Capitalism conflict & inflation essays in political economy*. London: Lawrence and Wishart.

Salvadori, N. (1981). Falling rate of profit with a constant real wage an example. *Cambridge Journal of Economics*, 5(1), pp. 59–66.

Samol, P. (2013). Michael Heinrichs Fehlkalkulation der Profitrate. *Krisis 1*. Available at http://www.krisis.org/wp-content/data/peter-samol-michael-heinrichs-fehlkalkulationen-2013-1.pdf

Savran, S. and Tonak, E. A. (1999). Productive and unproductive labour: An attempt at clarification and classification. *Capital and Class*, 68, 113–152.

Shaikh, A. (1978a). An introduction to the history of crisis theories. In: *U.S. Capitalism in crisis*. New York: URPE.

Shaikh, A. (1978b). Political economy and capitalism: Notes on Dobb's theory of crisis. *Cambridge Journal of Economics*, 2, pp. 233–251.

Shaikh, A. (1984). The transformation from Marx to Sraffa. In: E. Mandel and A. Freeman, eds., *Ricardo, Marx, Sraffa: The Langston memorial volume*. London: Verso.

Shaikh, A. (1987). Falling rate of profit and the economic crisis in the US. In: R Cherry, C. D'Onofrio, C. Kurdas, T. R. Michl, F. Mosley, and M. I. Naples, eds., *The imperiled economy, book I: Macroeconomics from a left perspective*. New York: Monthly Review Press.

Shaikh, A. (1992). The falling rate of profit as the cause of long waves: Theory and empirical Evidence. In: A. Kleinknecht, E. Mandel, and I. Wallersten, eds., *New findings in long-wave research*. London: Palgrave Macmillan.

Shaikh, A. (1999). Explaining the global economic crisis. *Historical Materialism*, 5(1), pp. 103–144.

Shaikh, A. (2011). The first great depression of the 21st century. In: L. Panitch, G. Albo, and V. Chibber, eds., *The crisis this time: Socialist register 2011*. New York: Monthly Review Press, pp. 44–63.

Shaikh, A. M. and Tonak, E. A. (1994). *Measuring the wealth of nations: The political economy of national accounts*. Cambridge: Cambridge University Press.

Sweezy, P. (1942). *The theory of capitalist development principles of Marxian political economy*. New York: Oxford University Press.

Vasudevan, R. (2016). Financialization, distribution and accumulation: A circuit of capital model with a managerial class. *Metroeconomica*, 67, pp. 397–428. doi:10.1111/meca.12106

Weisskopf, T. E. (1979). Marxian crisis theory and the rate of profit in the postwar U.S. economy. *Cambridge Journal of Economics*, 3(4), pp. 341–378.

Wolff, E. (1979). The rate of surplus value, the organic composition, and the general rate of profit in the U.S. economy, 1947–67. *American Economic Review*, 69(30), pp. 329–341.

Wolff, E. (2001). The recent rise of profits in the United States. *Review of Radical Political Economics*, 33(3), pp. 314–324.

Wolff, E. (2003). What's behind the rise in profitability in the US in the 1980s and 1990s? *Cambridge Journal of Economics*, 27(4), pp. 479–499.

Yaffe, D. (1972). The Marxian theory of crisis, capital and the state. *Bulletin of the Conference of Socialist Economists*, Winter.

5 The effect of military expenditure on profitability in Marxist theories

Within the Marxist literature, milex is thought to impact the profit rate via capital productivity and the organic composition of capital. Milex therefore plays a contradictory role in the economy, as has been discussed extensively in the Marxian literature. (See *inter alia* Georgiou, 1983; Kollias and Maniatis, 2003; Coulomb, 2004; Dunne et al., 2013; Elveren and Hsu, 2016, 2018.) Although a Marxist theory of militarism has not been developed, Marxist scholars do discuss linkages between milex and the profit rate. These may include various linkages. First, milex may include a surplus that can be realised as profit, or it may remove capital from the non-military sector, thereby reducing the increase in the organic composition of capital in that area while cheapening constant capital in the military sector. Alternatively, military spending may ideologically alter the class structure, allowing capitalists to exploit workers even more, thereby increasing their profit rates (Smith, 1977, 1983).

The following review of the role of milex in a capitalist economy has five main parts: i) Marx and Engels, ii) Rosa Luxemburg, iii) Baran and Sweezy and other underconsumptionists, iv) debates on the role of milex, and v) empirical works on profit rates.

Marx and Engels on military expenditure

Although Marx and Engels wrote during a time of revolts, characterised by civilian and military conflicts, neither of them attempted to examine the economic aspects of war or conflict from a coherent theoretical perspective (Coulomb, 2004). Rather, militarism for them was simply a result of the socio-political structure. They did not discuss the effect of military production on the economy, even though Marx pointed out that this explanation was lacking, and he might have intended to discuss this in another volume of *Das Kapital* regarding the role of the state. However, he was unable to complete this work. Instead, Marx's remarks on war and conflict appeared in his *Manifesto of the Communist Party*, co-authored with Engels (1848); *Discourse on Free Trade* (1848); various articles, particularly in *the Neue Rheinische Zeitung*; and some important annotations in his correspondence with Engels (Coulomb and Bellais, 2008). In those articles, Marx noted that capitalism has to locate overseas outlets in order to counteract the tendency of profit rates to fall. Thus, for Marx, wars and conflicts are symptoms rather than causes of economic crisis, so he did not consider the potential surplus-absorbing role of the military.

It was Engels who examined militarism in a more extended manner in *Anti-Dühring* (1878) and *Can Europe Disarm*? (1893). Engels (1878) believed that militarism would bring about its own destruction by forcing states to compete and build up their armies because, although armies and navies can win wars if they have the best technology, they are, as he noted in the chapter on the theory of force, "devilishly expensive". Engels continued: "[f]orce, however, cannot make any money; at most it can take away money that has already been made . . . money must be provided through the medium of economic production . . . [n]othing is more dependent on economic prerequisites than precisely army and navy" (Engels, 1878). Later, Engels (1893) emphasised again that milex has no direct or indirect positive effect on the economy; on the contrary, it increases financial difficulties.

Overall, neither Marx nor Engels dealt explicitly with the effect of milex on the economy, leaving this task for their followers to take on. Among them, Rosa Luxemburg was one of the early thinkers who provided a comprehensive framework to examine the role of milex in a capitalist economy.

Rosa Luxemburg

Rosa Luxemburg was a close follower of Marx's writings. She contributed to Marxist thought by revealing that force and state power were key mechanisms of primitive accumulation in the history of capitalism (Rowthorn, 1980; Brewer, 2001, p. 72). In fact, she was the first Marxist thinker who examined this issue explicitly, arguing that milex allows economies to extend into external markets, which is a key means for realising surplus value.[1]

One of her major arguments was that capitalism needs non-capitalist systems to expand. Against this background, she argued that milex helps the capitalist system to expand. For example, in *The Accumulation of Capital* (1913) she asserted that militarism "plays a decisive part in the first stages of European capitalism, in the period of the so-called 'primitive accumulation', as a means of conquering the New World and the spice-producing countries of India" (p. 454). Luxemburg also notes that milex, in addition to its direct role in primitive accumulation of capital, "destroys the social organisations of primitive societies so that their means of production may be appropriated, forcibly to introduce commodity trade in countries where the social structure had been unfavourable to it" to build a political, social, and economic hegemony in the colonies (p. 454).

Milex may also help the accumulation of capital by creating a new and growing sector for capitalists. Finally, militarism serves the interests of capitalists by increasing the exploitation and suppression of the working class. According to Luxemburg, militarism, "[f]rom the purely economic point of view" is "a preeminent means for the realisation of surplus value; it is in itself a province of accumulation" (p. 454).

Luxemburg also stresses the important distinction between arms spending and other state spending in *The Militia and Militarism* in 1899[2]: "The State's demand is distinguished by the fact that it is certain, that it orders in enormous quantities, and that its pricing is favourable to the supplier . . . which makes the State the most desirable customer and makes supplying it the most alluring business for capitalism".

Then she continues

> But what makes supplying the military in particular essentially more profitable than, for example, State expenditures on cultural ends (schools, roads, etc.), is the incessant technical innovations of the military and the incessant increase in its expenditures. Militarism thus represents an inexhaustible, and indeed increasingly lucrative, source of capitalist gain, and raises capital to a social power of the magnitude confronting the worker in, for example, the enterprises of Krupp and Stumm. Militarism – which to society as a whole represents a completely absurd economic waste of enormous productive forces – and which for the working class means a lowering of its standard of living with the objective of enslaving it socially – is for the capitalist class economically the most alluring, irreplaceable kind of investment and politically and socially the best support for their class rule.
>
> (Luxemburg, 1899)

Thus, Luxemburg's views on the military's effects on the economy involve both short-term problems of Keynesian effective demand – as interpreted by *inter alia* Dobb (1955), Sweezy (1942), Robinson (1951), and Kalecki (1971), cited in Rowthorn (1980) – and the long-term dynamics of capital accumulation (Rowthorn, 1980).

She argued that social capital can remain stable if taxes on the working class are used to pay government officials and army personnel, resulting in a constant level of demand and profit rates. If, however, taxes are used to pay for weapons production, this can increase the average profit rate, as the indirect tax on the working class reduces wages. This happens because, according to Luxemburg, indirect taxes reduce v (variable capital), such that, if s (surplus value) remains constant, $r = (s/v)/c/v + 1$ increases (where r is the profit rate and c is the constant capital), assuming that an increase in s/v will be larger than the actual increase in c/v. Because Luxemburg's reasoning implies that workers in civil sectors do not create surplus value, her analysis has been criticised as being unable to make a distinction between use-value and value, and between surplus product and surplus value, and as mistakenly treating workers who create constant and variable capital and aggregate surplus separately[3] (Rowthorn, 1980; Cypher, 1985). Joan Robinson, in her introduction to the English translation of Luxemburg's book in 1951, considers the taxation of workers as the main source of finance. She argues that the most important economic significance of militarism is its ability to "provide an outlet for the investment of surplus (over and above any contribution there may be from forced saving out of wages), which, unlike other kinds of investment, creates no further problem by increasing productive capacity". She then notes "the huge new investment opportunities created by reconstruction after the capitalist nations have turned their weapons against each other" (Robinson, 1951, pp. 27–28).

Overall, Rowthorn (1980) argued that, although Luxemburg's mathematical approach has some defects, the core of her argument – that militarism helps to redistribute income in favour of capital – is sound.

Some scholars have interpreted Luxemburg's theory as an 'underconsumptionist theory', in which milex helps to absorb the surplus of the capitalist production system without increasing productive capacity. While Sweezy and Mandel (and orthodox Oskar Lange) considered Luxemburg as 'underconsumptionist', Bleaney (1976) argues that this is due to their vague definition of underconsumption, as noted by Robinson and Kalecki, and concludes that "Luxemburg cannot be classified as an underconsumptionist, because at no stage is it specifically consumption demand that is lacking, and indeed she quite explicitly states that demand for means of production is equally as good" (p. 200). Others view the theory as claiming that such spending boosts technological development while reducing the internal contradictions of capitalist expansion, thereby increasing capital accumulation (Rowthorn, 1980).

Baran and Sweezy, and other underconsumptionists

Paul Baran and Paul Sweezy's *Monopoly Capital*, published in 1966, is a major contribution to Marxist thought and translated into several languages. The book is the product of their collaboration that began in the mid-1950s but was only published two years after Baran died in 1964.

Baran and Sweezy analyse a key characteristic of the capitalist system: a chronic lack of aggregate demand, or *underconsumption* (Baran and Sweezy, 1966). They assert that capitalist development causes capital to become concentrated in increasingly fewer giant firms, which restrict output, investment, and workers' purchasing power to earn higher profits. However, the workers' limited purchasing power causes a shortage of demand and leads to stagnation. In other words, huge corporations become so successful at maximising profits that they create a strong and systematic tendency for surplus value to rise. However, this 'success' generates its own problem in that the created surplus must be absorbed. Therefore, following Bleaney (1976), one can note two characteristics of Baran and Sweezy's underconsumption theory: first, "a very unequal distribution of income is inherent in capitalist production"; second, "capitalists cannot find ways to consume or invest all of their share and are 'forced' to save it" (p. 211).

Baran and Sweezy therefore analysed the roles of the capitalists' consumption and investment, sales efforts, civilian government expenditure, and militarism in absorbing the surplus. Among them, they argued, capitalist investment and civilian government spending are not effective mechanisms because they either increase wages or capital, thereby either reducing profit rates or further increasing surplus in the long term. They also disagreed with Lenin's remark that capital exports to underdeveloped countries would absorb the surplus by stressing that more capital flowed into the U.S. from underdeveloped countries than what the U.S. invested in them (Howard and King, 1992, p. 118). Baran and Sweezy therefore pay special attention to the role of sales efforts, militarism, and imperialism. In this regard, capitalism is not just prone to stagnation but also is forced to spend more resources on irrational uses.

In *The Theory of Capitalist Development*, Paul Sweezy notes the economic consequences of rising militarism:

> In the first place, it fosters the development of a group of specially favored monopolists in those industries, like steel and shipbuilding, which are most important to the production of armaments. The munitions magnates have a direct interest in the maximum expansion of military production; not only do they benefit in the form of state orders but also they are afforded safe and lucrative outlets for their accumulated profits. . . . In the second place, since military expenditures perform the same economic function as consumption expenditures, the expansion of armies and navies constitutes an increasingly important offsetting force to the tendency to underconsumption. . . . Finally, to the extent that production of armaments utilizes labor power and means of production for which there would otherwise be no demand, militarism actually provides the capitalist class as a whole with increased opportunities for profitable investment of capital.
>
> (Sweezy, 1942, pp. 309–310)

The above excerpt is all about the economic impact of milex that Sweezy covered in his comprehensive book. Paul Baran did not analyse milex extensively either until they together placed milex at the centre of their theory in *Monopoly Capital* (Howard and King, 1992).

Baran and Sweezy (1966) suggest an underconsumptionist theory of milex: through milex, capitalists can obtain higher profit rates and lower levels of competition, reducing the economic surplus of the economy. From this perspective, milex, including military aid to allies, is an important component of the monopolistic post-war capitalist system by increasing aggregate demand and absorbing surplus. Milex, unlike other forms of state spending, is useful in that it absorbs the surplus without harming the interests of any powerful fraction of the ruling class and without raising wages or capital.

Against this theoretical background, Baran and Sweezy argue that high milex in the 1940s and 1950s became a key element in the development of U.S. power and helped to preserve monopolistic capitalism, which reduced unemployment and staved off stagnation. In *Monopoly Capital*, they devote one chapter to militarism as a means to absorb surplus in order to explain why "the United States oligarchy need and maintain such a huge military machine" (p. 178). They emphasise the military's role in capitalism as a hierarchical international system that facilitates or sustains the exploitative relations between the metropolises and colonies. The military also serves to "dispossess, repress, and otherwise control the domestic labor", although they argue that this was of negligible importance in the case of the U.S. (p. 179). They suggest that the U.S. maintained its leadership in the West through high milex while its growing military was justified by the 'threat' of the rival socialist system.

At the same time, they also identify the limitations in the effectiveness of milex because of the very nature of arms production. That is, milex's ability to boost employment gradually declines as fewer employees with greater skills are required to maintain military production. Indeed, they argue that huge military outlays may even help increase unemployment as "military research and development are also applicable to civilian production, where they are quite likely to have the effect of raising productivity and reducing the demand for labor" (ibid. p. 215).

Baran and Sweezy also assert that milex can harm economic activity because, as arms production becomes more capital intensive, it becomes more difficult to prevent a decline in the profit rate because high levels of milex result in increased taxation, which dampens economic activity. Conversely, a tax cut due to lower milex can cause a crisis of overproduction.

Baran and Sweezy's analysis has been extensively criticised (Georgiou, 1983; Howard and King, 1992) for various reasons.[4] First, the most fundamental criticism was that contemporary capitalism was competitive, contrary to Baran and Sweezy's view. Second, Baran and Sweezy assume a passive working class, even though the size of the economic surplus is contingent on the state of the class struggle. Third, their analysis repudiated some basic elements of traditional Marxian economics, particularly the theory of the falling rate of profit. Fourth, they do not specify the method of financing milex, which has differing impacts on profit rates. Fifth, Cypher (1985) argues that Baran and Sweezy neglect technology. Cypher argues that, although Paul Baran dealt with the connection between milex and technological dynamism in his early work, this important issue was neglected in *Monopoly Capital* in order to sustain the argument because otherwise they "would have needed a new theory of the State and they (seemingly) would have been forced to drop the structuralist approach to monopoly capitalism" (Cypher, 1985, p. 275). Finally, they use a more general definition of economic surplus than the Marxist definition, which is not specific to capitalism.[5] A key criticism was that Baran and Sweezy treated all state spending as unproductive or surplus-absorbing and did not pay attention to the productive necessity of state functions (O'Connor, 1973; Stanfield, 1974; Cypher, 1985; Howard and King, 1992, p. 122).

O'Connor (1973) and Gough (1979) emphasised this productive role of non-military government spending in that the state contributes to the accumulation of capital in the form of the welfare state, which is an interventionist state that protects minimum standards of income, nutrition, health, housing, and education for every citizen to ensure some equality concerning social services. The expansion of social security and the provision of education and health care were in line with a growing need for the skilled, mobile labour force demanded by growing capital.

According to orthodox Marxist theory, the welfare state is an instrument of capitalist oppression because the state is not a neutral but merely an extension of the capitalist class. Therefore, the welfare state is regarded as "an attempt to deal with specific problems of capitalist development, class conflict, and recurring economic crises", and an entity that makes "an effort to integrate the working classes without fundamental challenge to the institution and distribution of private property" (Flora and Heidenheimer, 1981, p. 23). Therefore, orthodox Marxist state theory argues that public policy is formed according to the interests of capital. The state has no independence.

O'Connor revisited the Marxist state theory to argue that the state is not a mere instrument of the capitalist class but has independence to a certain degree. In O'Connor's analysis, the capitalist economy consists of three distinct sectors: the state and two parts of the capitalist entity – the monopoly sector and the competitive sector. The monopoly sector refers to the dominant, innovative sector in a capitalist economy, with well-paid, mostly secure jobs, while the competitive sector refers to the remainder of this core part of the economy, associated with small-scale capital and insecure jobs for the reserve army of unemployed. In this picture, the state has a double (and contradictory) role: to help the monopoly sector in capital accumulation (accumulator) while legitimising this role for the rest of the society (legitimator).

Welfare state expenditure contributes to profitability both by lowering the employers' costs of maintaining a healthy and skilled labour force and by improving infrastructure, providing subsidies, and promoting R&D. However, legitimation supported by welfare expenditures contradicts the process of capital accumulation because the state must provide and sustain the conditions for the whole society to maintain a minimum standard of living. This requires that capital surpluses belonging to the richest strata of society should be transferred to the lower strata of society that face a capital deficit. In this way, the government has to justify transferring capital from the sector of society that would otherwise build on capital (O'Connor, 1973). The contradiction in this mechanism is that, as the monopoly sector switches to more capital-intensive production, it increases the number of unemployed in the competitive sector, thereby increasing the need for more capital transfer to the competitive sector in terms of unemployment benefits and other social aid. In other words, as Standing (2003) suggests, economic stratification creates three strata: the well-paid elites detaching themselves from any type of state-based social protection, atypical workers detached from conventional state-based social protections, and those between these top and bottom strata that the welfare state was formed to serve. However, since this third stratum has shrunk due to the capitalist production system, it has created a legitimisation problem for the welfare state – its 'fiscal' crisis.[6]

This structuralist view of the state suggested by O'Connor thus allows one to consider some milex, such as procurement, R&D and arms exports, as part of the process of capital accumulation, and other milex as part of legitimisation, such as military bases in non-strategic areas, veteran benefits and other military personnel payments (Cypher, 1985, p. 276). However, Cypher (1985) contends that this framework fails to answer crucial questions regarding the dynamics of milex. For example, why and how far it rises and falls, how autonomous the state is in this process, and whether milex is both a solution and a problem.

The theory of the permanent arms economy

Baran and Sweezy's analysis was subsequently revisited by other scholars, including Reich and Finkelhor (1970), Kidron (1970), Magdoff (1970), Reich (1972), Cypher (1974) and Mandel (1978). Among these, a major revision was made by Kidron.

Kidron's theory of the permanent arms economy asserts that militarism stabilises the capitalist system[7] (Kidron, 1970). That is, according to Kidron, milex counteracts the "permanent threat of overproduction".

Kidron argues that milex, rather than other forms of government spending, serves this purpose efficiently because it is not productive investment. Therefore, it prevents the rise of the organic composition of capital in civil activities, thereby counteracting the fall in the profit rate (Kidron, 1970, pp. 55–56). In this regard, Kidron argues that military production – as opposed to civilian production – "has a 'domino effect': starting in one country, it proliferates inexorably through the system, compelling the other major economies to enter a competitive arms race, and so pulling them into the stabilizer's sphere of operations" (ibid. p. 56). Kidron argues that, since arms are a 'luxury' in the sense that they are neither instruments of production nor means of subsistence, "arms production is the key, and seemingly permanent, offset to the 'tendency of the rate of profit to fall'" (p. 56). However, he also noted that, in the long run, "military technology is becoming so specialist as to lose some of its economically stabilizing features" (p. 64). Finally, military research and development benefits the civil sector through a technological spin-off effect. Kidron notes that "[m]ilitary research has been crucial in developing civilian products like air navigation systems, transport aircraft, computers, drugs, diesel locomotives (from submarine diesels), reinforced glass, and so on" (Kidron, 1970, p. 52). The state finances research and development in the military sector; these new technologies and products then spread through the civilian sector, which helps to reinforce profit rates in competitive civilian markets. This so-called spin-off effect has been discussed further by Mandel (1978).[8,9]

Ernest Mandel is another classical Marxist who discussed the role of milex in capitalism.[10] He argued that the military sector is isolated from competition, thereby allowing capitalists to enjoy more than the general rate of profit (Mandel, 1962 cited in Coulomb and Bellais, 2008). Mandel argued that so long as the costs of military production are shouldered by the working class, milex can indirectly increase the level of exploitation of the working class, thereby preventing the rate of profit from falling.

Mandel (1978) also showed that arms spending is economically unproductive since armaments are neither production nor consumption goods. Milex can therefore be used to reduce excess capital and prevent the decline in the rate of profit by eliminating unproductive capital. Additionally, defence firms can obtain a higher profit rate because prices and profits are negotiated between the state and the industry.[11] Finally, milex is dependent on neither peoples' purchasing power nor economic fluctuations (Mandel, 1978).

The theory of the permanent arms economy has been challenged both empirically and theoretically (Smith, 1977; Kaldor, 1977; Mandel, 1978; Cypher, 1985; Howard and King, 1992). Kaldor (1977), for example, makes the case that milex is in fact unproductive, and that there is an inverse relationship between milex as a percentage of GNP and capital investment as a share of GNP. Kaldor also notes that countries that spend less on military research and development end up spending more on civil research and development (further empirical challenges to the theory will be discussed later in this chapter).

At a theoretical level, Purdy (1973) argues that this theory is ahistorical, like that of Baran and Sweezy (cited in Smith, 1977). Mandel also noted some negative impacts of arms production, which challenged the permanent arms economy theory (Mandel, 1978; Cypher, 1985; Coulomb and Bellais, 2008). For instance, regarding who shoulders the costs of arms production, Mandel (1978) argues that if the burden of arms production is taken over by capitalists then arms production does not prevent the fall in profit rates. Moreover, increasing the organic composition of capital due to military production accelerates the fall in the rate of profit, which destabilises the economy in the long run (Coulomb, 2004).

Finally, Cypher (1985) points out the contradictory mechanisms in Kidron's analysis in that milex, on the one hand, permanently offsets overaccumulation, yet on the other hand, generates technical innovation. According to Cypher, "[a]t best Kidron refers to anecdotes from the literature on arms production, but no data is presented, either macro or micro, to buttress his *aprioristic* statements, assertions, and insights" (page 278, emphasis in original).

Debates on the role of milex on the economy

Sweezy versus Szymanski

The validity of Baran and Sweezy's theory has also been challenged by Szymanski (1973a). He tested their argument that higher milex in monopoly capitalist countries leads to lower unemployment and higher growth rates for 18 major countries during the period of 1950–1968. Finding that higher milex is associated with lower rates of both unemployment and economic growth, he concludes that Baran and Sweezy's theory does not hold.

In response, Sweezy (1973) noted that Szymanski's methodology rather than the specific empirical method he used prevented him from evaluating Baran and Sweezy's theory appropriately. First, Sweezy notes that the 18 countries examined cannot be treated as independent entities because they are "interrelated parts of a single world capitalist system" with very unequal weights (p. 709). Second, he argues that Szymanski's model has "problems of theory and of the uses of theory in the interpretation of history" (p. 710).

Szymanski's work was also criticised by other scholars. Friedman (1974) raises two criticisms: that the model ignores the international context of the permanent arms economy and that it does not consider the analytical interconnections between politics and economics. He also argues that the model omits some important variables – as pointed out by Stevenson (1974) as well, causing a robustness problem. Similarly, Zeitlin (1974) argues that Szymanski's test is irrelevant for Baran and Sweezy's theory in that it does not reflect the "monopoly" structure, and that the data used does not reflect "time-order relationships" (p. 1453). This is because, in Baran and Sweezy's theory, milex, along with other indicators, is one mode of surplus; other indicators may include the sales interest and financial interest, which help monopoly capitalism to function, as it is a system within the specific sociohistorical context of post-war America (pp. 1453–1455).[12] Furthermore, Zeitlin rightly points out that Baran and Sweezy believed that, as the composition of milex changes, fewer people are employed. Finally, Stevenson (1974), in addition to the previous criticism and in line with Zeitlin (1974), argues that Szymanski's use of milex data for only 1968 is problematic and that his analysis ignores the Marxist law of uneven development, thereby suffering from a non-dialectical approach.

In his replies to Sweezy, Friedman, Stevenson, and Zeitlin, Szymanski (1973b, p. 74) rejects their criticisms of his use of the comparative method and defends his conclusion that there is no empirical relationship between milex and economic prosperity in wealthy countries, which suffices to confirm Baran and Sweezy's basic argument that milex is the major factor preventing economic stagnation. Szymanski (1974) also deals with other critiques in detail, providing further empirical analysis to suggest additional control variables, such as 'deliberate prohibitions against military spending', 'external hostility', 'the role of labor parties', and 'the effect of the destruction of WWII'. He concludes that these new findings confirm his original results.

Smith versus Hartley and McLean and Chester

Another debate occurred between Smith (1977, 1978) and Hartley and McLean (1978) and Chester (1978). Ron Smith's (1977) article, published in the first issue of *Cambridge Journal of Economics*, is a seminal contribution to the analysis of milex and its role in capitalism. Smith noted that, as a capitalist country grows, its inherently created surplus increases more than can be covered by consumption and investment. This surplus must be absorbed by increasing aggregate demand. One 'good' way to do this is to use milex because it is wasteful in the sense that it helps the economy to operate at near full capacity without raising its productive capacity. Smith (1977) therefore argued that the association of lower milex with a high rate of unemployment during the interwar years compared with higher milex and relatively full employment during the post-war era at first sight seems evidence of the permanent arms economy in that high milex in the post-war period generated an economic boom by absorbing surplus and maintaining effective demand. However, he argued, for the underconsumptionist argument to be valid it is necessary to show two things: first, not just milex should increase over time but also, as countries get richer, their milex should rise to keep up with increasing surplus; second, milex should be used by governments primarily to stabilise the economy while there are no effective substitutes to create demand to maintain full employment to absorb the surplus (Smith, 1977, p. 65; D'Agostino et al., 2016).

Smith (1977) investigated the effect of milex on the major economic indicators of 15 major NATO countries for 1960–1970. He concluded that, by crowding out investment that could have increased productivity otherwise, milex reduced economic growth and raised unemployment. Smith's findings of no positive relation between the military burden (i.e. milex as a share of GDP) and GDP per capita but a positive relationship between the military burden and unemployment rate challenged the underconsumptionist view. However, he emphasised that, although his results did not confirm the permanent arms economy argument, milex plays a crucial role in maintaining capitalism for strategic reasons.

Hartley and McLean (1978), from a liberal perspective, evaluated the theoretical framework of Smith (1977) and presented an alternative theoretical structure to test the determinants of milex in the case of the U.K. for 1948–1973. They used a model incorporating strategic (i.e. U.S. and U.S.S.R. milex), economic (unemployment rate, balance of payments and per capita income), and political variables (e.g. a dummy variable for the ruling party). Their findings support Smith's (1977) surplus absorption and underconsumptionist argument (ibid. p. 290).

Smith's work was also criticised from Marxist perspectives. Chester (1978), alas in a problematic empirical setting, argued that his own findings did not confirm any of Smith's findings.

Regarding Hartley and McLean's criticisms and their suggested model, Smith, based on a careful reinvestigation of their proposed model and data set, concluded that, although strategic variables significantly explained the U.K.'s pattern of milex, economic and political variables were not significant. Regarding Chester's findings, Smith accepts that there is no clear relationship between milex and unemployment, contrary to his earlier results in Smith (1977). However, he notes that this absence by no means supports the underconsumptionist view, concluding that this complex relationship between milex and unemployment needs further analysis. Regarding his other major findings, his careful revisit clearly refutes Chester's initial findings.

Thus, overall, Smith (1978)'s new and extended analyses in response to Hartley and McLean (1978), Chester (1978), and Green and Higgins (1977), who wrote on the Soviet Union (cited in Smith, 1978), confirmed and strengthened the findings against the underconsumptionist view. In addition, for 14 major OECD countries for 1954–1973, Smith (1980) found that high milex as a share of GDP is associated with a lower share of investment in GDP. The stable share of public and private consumption in GDP demonstrated the trade-off between milex and investment in that savings could be used to finance either milex or investment within the Bretton Woods system (Smith, forthcoming). That was further evidence against the underconsumptionist view.

Gottheil versus Riddell and Cypher

According to Gottheil (1986a), analyses by Perlo (1963), Baran and Sweezy (1966), Magdoff (1970), Kalecki (1972), Hunt (1972), Reich (1972), Reich and Finkelhor (1970), O'Connor (1973) and Weisskopf (1972, 1976) all fail to acknowledge the issue of who ultimately pays for military production (the taxpayer). This means that there is no discussion of the impact of milex on the after-tax profit rate. Gottheil (1986a) emphasises that military production is more capital intensive, which raises the organic composition of capital, resulting in a decline in the average rate of profit, arguing that their theses are incompatible with Marx's analytic framework.

Riddell (1986) claims that Gottheil's analysis "suffers from an unsophisticated Marxism and an oversimplification of the economics of military spending" (p. 574). Riddell notes that, while some arms companies are capital intensive, many of them employ scientific personnel and skilled workers, creating fewer jobs than an equivalent amount of money spent in other industries. Riddell also rejects Gottheil's narrow definition of military sector spending. He notes that it is not just spending for 'military production', as Gottheil defines it, but also spending on personnel, military construction, R&D, and the operations and maintenance costs of national defence, which are all more likely to be labour intensive than arms production. He also argues that there is no evidence for Gottheil's claim that profit rates are lower in military production than in the rest of the economy. Riddell suggests that military spending may be more important in certain periods, such as aggregated demand increasing the role of milex in the 1950s or Reagan's desire to revive U.S. power against the Soviet threat in the early 1980s. Overall, Riddell emphasises the contradictory role of milex on rates of profit and the capitalist system, arguing that Gottheil's arguments fail to address such a complex relationship.

In response to Riddell, Gottheil reemphasises the connection between profit rates and capital intensity, arguing that that is what Marx refers to over and over again, in contrast to what Riddell claims (Gottheil, 1986b). He also strongly (but falsely) rejects the argument that the capital intensity of the military may be lower than that of civilian production. In fact, Riddell clearly differentiates between possibly capital-intensive military production (e.g. weapons) and other sorts of military spending that is likely to be labour intensive.

In his evaluation of the debate between on Gottheil and Riddell, Miller (1987–88) stresses that Gottheil's remark on the falling profit rates is only one interpretation of economic crises in Marxist literature. According to this supply-side view, profit rates tend to decline because of "endangered profitability at the point of production, a relative lack of surplus value, or a rising organic composition of capital (p. 311)". The other interpretation is that a crisis occurs in the demand side of the economy, in terms of a realisation crisis, rising surplus, or underconsumption. He argues that military spending promotes capital accumulation by absorbing surplus value through taxation of productive labour. However, spending these state revenues on "unreproductive" expenditures (e.g. that do not reproduce labour power or capital) reduces the economy's productive capacity in the long run. This is because milex diverts intellectual, financial, and material resources away from civilian industries, which can translate into a reduction of industrial productivity (Melman, 1965). This is reinforced by Hunt (1972), who notes that "military spending keeps the capital-goods industry operating at near full capacity without raising the economy's productive capacity as rapidly as it would be the case if they provided capital goods for industry" (p. 141).

In response to Gottheil (1986a), Cypher (1987–88) argues that the military sector can have a positive impact on the profit rate in three ways. First, military research and development enhance the technology of major constant capital categories, such as computers or jets, thereby lowering production costs in major civilian sectors. Second, these military technologies can generate spill-over effects. Third, research and development in the military sector generally improve labour productivity so that milex actually prevents an increase in the organic composition of capital and a consequent fall in the rate of profit (Cypher, 1987–88).

Cypher (1987–88) also emphasises that Gottheil's focus on arms production to prove his case that the military sector has a higher capital-to-labour ratio is wrong because one cannot ignore the substantial part of the military budget devoted to high labour-capital ratio operations and maintenance. Cypher argues that Gottheil fails to consider the counteracting factors to the tendency of profit rate to fall in that, although technological progress increases the organic composition of capital and hence reduces profit rates, more productive methods used in both constant and variable capital can reduce the value of the composition of capital, thereby counteracting the decline in profit rates.

Dunne and Smith versus Pivetti

The most recent debate occurred between Pivetti (1992, 1994), and Dunne (1990) and Smith and Dunne (1994). Pivetti (1992, 1989) argued that, contrary to what Smith (1977, 1980), Dunne (1990), Dunne and Smith (1990) and Abell (1990) propose, high military spending from 1947 to the late 1960s kept effective demand high, leading to lower unemployment and a high growth rate in the U.S. Pivetti (1992) did not accept the general view of the negative impact of milex on economic growth. Instead, he defended the theoretical view that milex boosts economic growth because it absorbs excess savings that are not automatically absorbed by investment by not improving the productive capacity of the economy and by not crowding out private investment. Milex is also continuously renewable, boosting economic growth via the technological spin-off effect.

In their reply, Smith and Dunne (1994) strongly argue that both their work and that of others provide counter evidence to the underconsumptionist view. Smith and Dunne showed there was no evidence of a systematic relationship between unemployment and the military burden in the U.S. for 1948–1988, including its subperiods.

Pivetti (1994) restated, without providing any empirical analysis, that the low level of unemployment from 1947 to the end of the 1960s, coinciding with high milex and increasing unemployment, and the lower milex from the 1960s to the end of 1970s, as well as declining unemployment during Reagan's military build-up, contradict Smith and Dunne's 'military burden' argument.

Finally, D'Agostino et al. (2016), by revisiting Smith's (1977) analysis for 1960–2014, confirmed and strengthened his early findings. Using the Granger causality method, they found no significant evidence of a causal relationship between milex and GDP per capita, or between milex and unemployment in either the U.S. or U.K. They subsequently extended their analysis with a Keynesian structural model, following Dunne and Nikolaidou (2005) and Dunne (2013), to confirm that there was no evidence to support military Keynesian or underconsumptionist arguments.

Empirical work on the effect on the profit rate

More recently, some scholars have focused on the effect of milex on the profit rate rather than economic growth, bringing a new empirical approach to the issue. To the best of our knowledge, there are only four time-series studies: Georgiou (1992), Kollias and Maniatis (2003), Dunne et al. (2013), and Elveren and Özgür (2018) and two panel studies: Elveren and Hsu (2016; 2018).

Georgiou (1992) used an ordinary least squares (OLS) methodology to examine the effect of milex on profit rates in the U.K., the U.S., and the former West Germany for 1958–1987 to test Luxemburg's and Mandel's arguments. Georgiou found a positive significant effect of milex on profit rates in the case of the U.S. but insignificant effects for the other two countries. Kollias and Maniatis (2003) employed the autoregressive distributed lag model (ARDL) to show in the case of Greece during 1962–1994 that milex has a positive effect on the profit rate in the short run but an inverse relationship in the long run. Dunne et al. (2013) examined the case of the U.S. for 1959–2010. Using OLS and ARDL methods, they provide some evidence on the positive long-run relationship between the military burden and the profit rate. Finally, Elveren and Özgür (2018) examined the case of Turkey during 1950–2008 using ARDL and Markov-Switching to show that military spending reduces profit rates further during economic downturns, whereas it boosts profitability during regular periods.

Elveren and Hsu (2016) employed a panel ARDL model to analyse 24 OECD countries for the period of 1963–2008. Their findings suggest that, while there is positive linkage between milex and profit rates for the whole period, the impact of milex is negative in the post-1980 era. They also found weak evidence that there is positive relationship between milex and profit rates for arms-exporting countries but a negative one for countries that do not export arms.

Elveren and Hsu (2018) examined 32 major countries for 1963–2008. In addition to confirming and strengthening the early findings, the study also provides some new evidence on the relationship in question through a Granger causality analysis. It shows that bidirectional causality exists only for one third of the countries; however, there is a clear distinction between country groups in that profit rates Granger cause milex in arms-importing countries, whereas milex causes profit rates in arms-exporting countries.

Conclusion

There are three positions on the underconsumptionists (Bleaney, 1976, pp. 2402–2441). First, milex is necessary to maintain full employment and economic growth because of its surplus-absorbing function. Bleaney argues that this implies that the state is aware of the underconsumptionist tendency in the economy and consciously uses milex to counteract it. Second, although milex is necessary to keep the economy at full employment, it is used for political reasons. This implies that the state implements the right policy but for the wrong reason. In *Monopoly Capital*, Baran and Sweezy argue that the state's position is like the first interpretation (Bleaney, 1976). Third, similar growth and employment performance could be reached without such high milex. Therefore, high milex is simply political, such as fighting against socialism. Milex has economic drawbacks because the same money could be used in productive investment or for increasing working-class consumption. Ron Smith's view can be considered the first representative of this position.

The effect of milex in absorbing surplus value, and thereby profit rates, is contingent on the historical context, the prevailing conditions (Georgiou, 1983). However, the general problem with underconsumption theories is that they tend to stress one single defect in capitalist production, which inevitably reduces the significance of other historical and theoretical factors (Bleaney, 1976). Specifically, underconsumptionists have paid insufficient attention to crisis tendencies and the role of technology (Cypher, 1985). It is important to keep in mind in assessing theories that they are also the product of their specific time periods, shaped by the theorists' backgrounds. That is, they carry on the particular 'problematique' of their time. The view of post-war economists Baran and Sweezy and Kidron, that milex is a key tool to maintain full employment, was substantially influenced by their youth spent during the Great Depression. Similarly, Ron Smith's view that, although milex does not create demand to maintain full employment to absorb the surplus, it plays a crucial role in maintaining capitalism for strategic reasons was profoundly influenced by the particular Cold War confrontation of capitalism and communism.

The underconsumptionists emphasised various variables in their analysis of milex. As noted above, neither Marx nor Engels had an articulated theory of milex; however, Marx recognised that capitalism has to expand into non-capitalist areas to counteract the tendency of profit rates to fall. Here, although

Marx did not make a direct linkage with the milex, his followers, such as Lenin and Luxemburg, developed this idea of imperialism. Thus, I argue that by describing the basic character of armies and navies as "devilishly expensive", Engels points out the negative effect of the military in terms of capital accumulation/investment.

Rosa Luxemburg focused on the military's critical role in primitive accumulation, stressing the increasing role of milex in the rate of exploitation and the rate of profit. Baran and Sweezy comprehensively analysed milex, emphasising capital accumulation/investment, rate of profit, and the reserve army/unemployment. First, in line with Lenin and Luxemburg, they stressed the military's role in capital accumulation/investment through imperialism by arguing that militarism provides the capitalist class with more opportunities for profitable investment of capital (Sweezy, 1942, p. 310). They also strongly argued that the capitalist can obtain higher profit rates through milex and that higher milex kept the rate of unemployment rate low during the 1940s and 1950s in the U.S. In line with Luxemburg, the school of the permanent arms economy, within which Mandel's view can be included, takes the rate of profit as the central element of their analysis.

Milex can operate in three main ways (Smith, 1977, 1983): first, by means of production and realisation – the direct economic channel – operating through the organic composition of capital, underconsumption, cost, or production; second, through class struggle, either through the military's direct coercive power or the ideological influence of militarism; third, through the military's international role, through both expanding capitalism and conflict between capitalist powers.

Regarding the direct economic channel, it can be argued that all the scholars reviewed here have dealt with it to various extents while emphasising different aspects. For instance, Engels stressed the cost of arms production, albeit negatively. In his comprehensive and empirical framework, Ron Smith also dealt with the 'cost' of milex, namely the crowding out of investment that would otherwise increase the economy's productive capacity. Luxemburg, Baran and Sweezy, and Pivetti all stressed the realisation problem through underconsumption (e.g. the role of milex in offsetting lack of aggregate demand). Similarly, Kidron argued that milex counteracts the permanent threat of overproduction. His analysis (along with Cypher and Reich to a certain degree), differed from Baran and Sweezy in directly focusing on the effect of milex on the organic composition of capital through cheapening constant capital and the spin-off effect. Mandel, however, considered the negative impact of an increasing organic composition of capital on the rate of profit.

Second, milex can operate through class struggle and government use of an external threat to justify the need for stronger military forces. According to Luxemburg, the direct coercive power provided by the military or the ideological influence of militarism were key mechanisms of primitive accumulation in the history of capitalism (Rowthorn, 1980). Although Baran and Sweezy also note that the military serves to "dispossess, repress, and otherwise control the domestic labor", they argue that this did not have a major effect in the U.S.

(Baran and Sweezy, 1966, p. 179), whereas this was obviously significant in the case of most developing countries.

Third, milex also operates through the military's international role. This has two parts: expansion of the capitalist system into non-capitalist systems and conflict between capitalist powers. This is the imperialism discussed by Lenin and Luxemburg while Baran and Sweezy also emphasised this function of milex. They argued that capitalism is a hierarchical international system within which imperial power influences the social order of underdeveloped countries, facilitating and sustaining exploitative relations. They argued that Britain's hegemony was replaced after World War II by U.S. leadership. The U.S. then required high milex, not just for world domination but also due to the Soviet Bloc, whose threat – which they argue was illusory – served very well to sustain high milex. Magdoff also emphasised the military's critical function of easing the exploitation of underdeveloped regions, thereby helping prevent the falling rate of profit by reducing the organic composition of capital.

Overall, the Marxist literature regarding the effect of milex on the economy reports diverse linkages based on different crisis theories with different underlying assumptions while the empirical studies remain inconclusive.

References

Abell, J. D. (1990). Defence spending and unemployment rates: An empirical analysis disaggregated by race. *Cambridge Journal of Economics*, 14, pp. 405–419.

Baran, P. and Sweezy, P. (1966). *Monopoly capital: An essay on the American economic and social order*. New York: Monthly Review Press.

Barkan, J. (1997). A blast from the past Paul A. Baran and Paul M. Sweezy's *Monopoly Capital*. *Dissent*, 44, pp. 95–101.

Basu, D. (2014). Comparative growth dynamics in a discrete-time Marxian circuit of capital model. *Review of Radical Political Economics*, 46(2), pp. 162–183.

Bleaney, M. F. (1976). *Underconsumption theories*. London: Lawrence and Wishart.

Brewer, A. (2001). *Marxist theories of imperialism a critical survey*. 2nd ed. London and New York: Routledge.

Chester, E. (1978). Military spending and capitalist stability. *Cambridge Journal of Economics*, 2, pp. 293–298.

Coulomb, F. (2004). *Economic theories of peace and war*. London and New York: Routledge.

Coulomb, F. and Bellais, R. (2008). The Marxist analysis of war and military expenditures, between certainty and uncertainty. *Defence and Peace Economics*, 19(5), pp. 351–359.

Cypher, J. M. (1974). Capitalist planning and military expenditures. *Review of Radical Political Economics*, 6(3), pp. 1–19.

Cypher, J. M. (1985). Critical analyses of military spending and capitalism. *Eastern Economic Journal*, XI(3), pp. 273–282.

Cypher, J. M. (1987–88). Military production and capital accumulation: A comment. *Journal of Post-Keynesian Economics*, 10(2), pp. 304–309.

D'Agostiono, G., Dunne, P. and Pieroni, L. (2016). *Military spending and contemporary capitalism*. Available at: www.cpes.org.uk/dev/wp-content/uploads/2016/06/Agostino_Dunne_Pieroni_Milex_and_Contemporary_Capitalism.pdf

Dobb, M. H. (1955) [2012]. The accumulation of capital. In *On economic theory and socialism.* London: Routledge.

Dunne, P. (1990). The political economy of military expenditure: An introduction. *Cambridge Journal of Economics*, 14, pp. 395–404.

Dunne, P. (2013). Military Keynesianism. In: M. Chatterji and C. Bo, eds., *Cooperation for a peaceful & sustainable world – part 2.* Bingley, UK: Emerald.

Dunne, P. and Nikolaidou, E. (2005). Military spending and growth in Greece, Portugal and Spain. *Frontiers in Finance and Economics*, 2(1).

Dunne, P., Pieroni, L. and D'Agostino, G. (2013). *Military spending and the falling rate of profit in the US.* Available at: www.sipri.org/research/armaments/milex/ICES2013/papers/archive/dunne-pieroni-agostino-milex-falling-rate-of-profit-in-usa

Dunne, P. and Sköns, E. (2011). *The changing military industrial complex.* Available at: http://ideas.repec.org/p/uwe/wpaper/1104.html

Dunne, P. and Smith, R. (1990). Military expenditure and unemployment in the OECD. *Defence Economics*, 1, pp. 57–73.

Elveren, A. Y. and Hsu, S. (2016). Military expenditures and profit rates: Evidence from OECD countries. *Metroeconomica*, 67(3), pp. 551–577.

Elveren, A.Y. and Hsu, S. (2018). The effect of military expenditure on profit rates: Evidence from major countries. *World Journal of Applied Economics*, 4(2), pp. 75–94.

Elveren, A. Y. and Özgür, G. (2018). The effect of military expenditures on the profit rates in Turkey. MPRA No: 88848. Available at: https://mpra.ub.uni-muenchen.de/88848/1/MPRA_paper_88848.pdf

Engels, F. (1878). *Anti duhring.* Available at: www.marxists.org/archive/marx/works/1877/anti-duhring/ch15.htm#061

Engels, F. (1893). *Can Europe disarm?* Available at: https://marxists.catbull.com/archive/marx/works/cw/volume27/index.htm

Finkelhor, D. and Reich, M. (1970). Capitalism and the military-industrial complex: The obstacles to conversion. *Review of Radical Political Economics*, 2(4), pp. 1–25.

Flora, P. and Heidenheimer, A. J. (1981). The historical core and changing boundaries of the welfare state. In: P. Flora and A. J. Heidenheimer, eds., *The development of welfare states in Europe and America.* New Brunswick and London: Transactions Books, pp. 17–36.

Foley, D. K. (1982). Realization and accumulation in a Marxian model of the circuit of capital. *Journal of Economic Theory*, 28, pp. 300–319.

Foley, D. K. (1986). *Money, accumulation, and crisis.* London, Paris and New York: Harwood Academic Publishers.

Friedman, S. R. (1974). An alternative model to Szymanski's. *American Journal of Sociology*, 79(6), pp. 1459–1462.

Georgiou, G. (1983). The political economy of military expenditures. *Capital & Class*, 7, pp. 183–205.

Georgiou, G. (1992). Military expenditure and the rate of profit: Some empirical results. *International Review of Applied Economics*, 16(3), pp. 344–361.

Gottheil, F. M. (1986a). Marx versus Marxists on the role of military production in capitalist economies. *Journal of Post-Keynesian Economics*, 8(2), pp. 563–573.

Gottheil, F. M. (1986b). Marxism and military spending: A reply. *Journal of Post Keynesian Economics*, 8(4), pp. 581–584.

Gough, I. (1979). *The political economy of the welfare state.* London: Palgrave Macmillan.

Green, D. W. and Higgins, C. I. (1977). *SOVMOD I: A macro-econometric model of the Soviet Union.* London: Academic Press.

Hartley, K. and McLean, P. (1978). Military expenditure and capitalism: A comment. *Cambridge Journal of Economics*, 2, pp. 287–292.

Howard, M. C. and King, J. E. (1992). *A history of Marxian economics*. London: Palgrave Macmillan.

Hunt, E. K. (1972). *Property and prophets*. New York: Harper and Row.

Kaldor, M. (1977). The role of arms in capitalist economies: The process of overdevelopment and underdevelopment. In: D. Carleton and C. Schaerf, eds., *Arms control and technological innovation*. London: Croom Helm.

Kalecki, M. (1971). The problem of effective demand with Tugan-Baranowski and Rosa Luxemburg. In *Selected essays on the dynamics of the capitalist economy*. Cambridge: Cambridge University Press.

Kalecki, M. (1972). *The last phase in the transformation of capitalism*. New York: Monthly Review Press.

Kidron, M. (1970). *Western capitalism since the war revised edition*. Harmondsworth: Pelican Books.

Kollias, C. and Maniatis, T. (2003). Military expenditure and the profit rate in Greece. *Defence and Peace Economics*, 14(2), pp. 117–127.

Luxemburg, R. (1951) [1913]. *The accumulation of capital*. London: Routledge and Kegan Paul.

Luxemburg, R. (1899). *The militia and militarism*. Available at: www.marxists.org/archive/luxemburg/1899/02/26.htm

Magdoff, H. (1970). Militarism and imperialism. *The American Economic Review*, 60(2), pp. 237–242.

Mandel, E. (1962). *Traité d'économie Marxiste*. Paris: Editions 10/18.

Mandel, E. (1978). *Late capitalism*. New York: Verso.

Marx, K. (1848). *The discourse on free trade*. Available at www.marxists.org/archive/marx/works/1848/free-trade/.

Marx, K. (1885) [1992]. *Capital*, Vol. II. New York: Penguin Books.

Marx, K. and Engels, F. (1848). *The manifesto of the communist party*. Available at: www.marxists.org/archive/marx/works/download/pdf/Manifesto.pdf

Mazzucato, M. (2013). *The entrepreneurial state*. London: Anthem Press.

Melman, S. (1965). *Our depleted society*. New York: Holt, Rinehart and Winston.

Miller, J. (1987–88). Military spending and economic crises: A comment on Gottheil and Riddell. *Journal of Post-Keynesian Economics*, 10(2), pp. 310–318.

O'Connor, J. (1973). *The fiscal crisis of the state*. New York: St Martin's Press.

Perlo, V. (1963). *Militarism and industry*. New York: International Publishers.

Pivetti, M. (1989). Military expenditure and economic analysis: A review article. *Contribution to Political Economy*, 8, pp. 55–67.

Pivetti, M. (1992). Military spending as a burden on growth: An 'underconsumptionist' critique. *Cambridge Journal of Economics*, 16, pp. 373–384.

Pivetti, M. (1994). Effective demand, 'Marxo-marginalism' and the economics of military spending: A rejoinder. *Cambridge Journal of Economics*, 18, pp. 523–527.

Purdy, D. (1973). The theory of the permanent arms economy – a critique and an alternative. *Bulletin of the Conference of Socialist Economists*, 5, pp. 12–33.

Reich, M. (1972). Does the us economy require military spending? *American Economic Review*, 62(1/2), pp. 296–303.

Reich, M. and Finkelhor, D. (1970). Capitalism and the "military-industrial complex": The obstacles to "conversion". *Review of Radical Political Economics*, 2(4), pp. 1–25. Available at: https://journals.sagepub.com/doi/10.1177/048661347000200402

Riddell, T. (1986). Marxism and military spending. *Journal of Post Keynesian Economics*, 8(4), pp. 574–580.

Robinson, J. (1951) [1913]. Introduction. In: R. Luxemburg, ed., *The accumulation of capital*. London: Routledge and Kegan Paul.

Rowthorn, R. (1980). *Capitalism conflict & inflation essays in political economy*. London: Lawrence and Wishart.

Shaikh, A. (2003). Who pays for the 'Welfare' in the welfare state? A multicountry study. *Social Research*, 70(2), pp. 531–550.

Smith, R. (1977). Military expenditure and capitalism. *Cambridge Journal of Economics*, 1(1), pp. 61–76.

Smith, R. (1978). Military expenditure and capitalism: A reply. *Cambridge Journal of Economics*, 2, pp. 299–304.

Smith, R. (1980). Military expenditure and investment in OECD countries. *Journal of Comparative Economics*, 4(1), pp. 19–32.

Smith, R. (1983). Aspects of militarism. *Capital & Class*, 7, pp. 17–30.

Smith, R. (2009). *Military economics the interaction of power and money*. New York: Palgrave Macmillan.

Smith, R. (forthcoming). *Military expenditure and growth*. In: R. Matthews, ed., *The Political Economy of Defence*. Cambridge: Cambridge University Press.

Smith, R. and Dunne, P. (1994). Is military spending a burden? A 'Marxo-marginalist' response to Pivetti. *Cambridge Journal of Economics*, 18, pp. 515–521.

Standing, G. (2003). Globalization: Eight crises of social protection. In: L. Beneria and S. Bisnath, eds., *Global tensions, challenges and opportunities in the world economy*. Abingdon: Routledge, pp. 111–136.

Stanfield, R. (1974). A revision of the economic surplus concept. *Review of Radical Political Economics*, 6(3), pp. 69–74.

Stevenson, P. (1974). A defense of Baran and Sweezy. *American Journal of Sociology*, 79(6), pp. 1456–1459.

Sweezy, P. (1942). *The theory of capitalist development principles of Marxian political economy*. New York: Oxford University Press.

Sweezy, P. (1973). Comments on Szymanski's paper 'military spending and economic stagnation'. *The American Journal of Sociology*, 79(3), pp. 709–710.

Szymanski, A. (1973a). Military spending and economic stagnation. *The American Journal of Sociology*, 79(1), pp. 1–14.

Szymanski, A. (1973b). Reply to Sweezy. *The American Journal of Sociology*, 79(3), pp. 710–711.

Szymanski, A. (1974). A reply to Friedman, Stevenson, and Zeitlin. *The American Journal of Sociology*, 79(6), pp. 1462–1477.

Weisskopf, T. (1972). The problem of surplus absorption. In: R. Edwars, M. Reich, and T. Weisskopf, eds., *The capitalist system*. Englewood, NJ: Prentice-Hall.

Weisskopf, T. (1976). Theories of American imperialism: A critical evaluation. *Review of Radical Political Economics*, 6(3). https://doi.org/10.1177/048661347400600303

Zeitlin, M. (1974). On "military spending and economic stagnation". *American Journal of Sociology*, 79(6), pp. 1452–1456.

Appendix: A circuit of capital model with a military sector

This section presents an altered version of the circuit of capital model introduced by Foley (1982) to specify the impact of milex on the rates of profit. Foley's model is an appropriate one for this purpose for two reasons. First, the model yields the dynamics of Keynes's general argument that economic activity relies on effective aggregate demand. This aspect of the model allows one to extend this discussion into the view of 'military Keynesianism'. Second, the model explicitly represents the parameters for which an increase in the share of milex would have a direct effect. Changes in milex impact the parameters and therefore the whole model. Below is a contour of the model introduced by Foley (1982) and substantially benefiting from Basu (2014). The model below is just a practical attempt to show the effect of milex to encourage further research with a comprehensive approach to modify the model in this specific direction.

The circuit of capital model in Marx's analysis in Volume II of *Das Kapital* represents the money value stock-flow relations for capital (Marx, 1885). Marx represents the three stages of capital with the formula of M-C ... P ... C'-M', in which M, C, and P refer to money, commodity, and production process, respectively, where money purchases the means of production, and labour power is used to create a new commodity that will be sold at a markup (Marx, 1992).

The circuit of capital model incorporates three flow variables, three stock variables, and five parameters. The three flow variables include: C_t, the flow of capital outlays; P_t, the flow of finished products; and S_t, the flow of sales. The three stock variables include: N_t, the stock of productive capital; X_t, the stock of commercial (or commodity) capital; and F_t, the stock of financial capital. Finally, the five parameters include: p_t, the proportion of surplus value recommitted to production; q_t, the markup over costs; and T^P, T^R, and T^F, the production, realisation, and finance lags, respectively.

When embarking upon a steady-state growth path, all flow and stock variables grow at the same rate, g, while the parameters remain constant. This means that on a steady-state growth path

$$p_t = p, \; q_t = q \tag{4}$$

After a production lag of T^P periods, the flow of finished products in any period is equal to the flow of capital outlays T^P periods ago:

$$P_t = C_{t-T^P} \tag{5}$$

After the realisation lag, the flow of sales in any period is equal to the flow of finished products T^R periods ago:

$$S_t = (1+q)P_{t-T^R} \tag{6}$$

where q is the markup over cost that comes from the exploitation of labour by capital. Markup over cost is defined as the product of the rate of exploitation, e, and the share of capital outlays devoted to variable capital, k: $q_t = ek$ is the markup of sales price with $e = \frac{s}{v}$ as the rate of surplus value, $k = \frac{v}{c+v}$ is the ratio of variable capital to total capital outlays.

We can separate the flow of sales into two parts:

$$S_t = (1+q)P_{t-T^R} = S_t^{'} + S_t^{''} = \frac{S_t}{1+q} + \frac{qS_t}{1+q}$$

Where $S_t^{'}$ is the flow of sales due to the recovery of capital outlays, and $S_t^{''}$ is the part of sales flow coming from the realisation of surplus value. Capital outlays are financed by the flow of past sales after a time lag, the finance lag, T^F; therefore, we can say

$$C_t = S_{t-T^F}^{'} + pS_{t-T^F}^{''} \tag{7}$$

where T^F is the finance lag (the number of periods required for realised sales flows to be recommitted to production), and p is the fraction of surplus value that is reapplied to production, the rest being consumed by capitalist households, unproductive labour households, and the state.

Positive production, realisation, and finance lags result in a build-up of stocks of value at any point in time. If N_t represents the stock of productive capital in period t, then the accumulation (or decumulation) of the stock of productive capital can be stated as

$$\Delta N_{t+1} \equiv N_{t+1} - N_t = C_t - P_t \tag{8}$$

Allowing X_t to denote the stock of commercial capital, we have

$$\Delta X_{t+1} \equiv X_{t+1} - X_t = P_t - \frac{S_t}{1+q} = P_t - S_t^{'} \tag{9}$$

If F_t denotes the stock of financial capital in period t, then

$$\Delta F_{t+1} \equiv F_{t+1} - F_t = S_t^{'} + pS_t^{''} - C_t \tag{10}$$

The basic circuit of capital model can be represented by the six equations, (5) through (10), with q, p, and the three lags T^P, T^R, and T^F acting as parameters.

$P_t = C_{t-T^P}$ so on the steady-state growth path

$$P_0 (1+g)^t = C_0 (1+g)^{t-T^P} \text{ so } P_0 = \frac{C_0}{(1+g)^{T^P}} = \frac{1}{(1+g)^{T^P}}$$

In addition, $S_t = (1+q) P_{t-T^R}$

$$S_0 = (1+q)\frac{C_0}{(1+g)^{T^P+T^R}} = \frac{1+q}{(1+g)^{T^P+T^R}}$$

Which means that

$$S_0^{'} = \frac{1}{(1+g)^{T^P+T^R}} \text{ and } S_0^{''} = \frac{q}{(1+g)^{T^P+T^R}}$$

Adding aggregate demand

In a capitalist economy that is closed to trade and missing credit for workers and capitalists, there are four sources of aggregate demand that come from expenditures of capitalist enterprises: (a) the portion of capital outlays that finances the purchase of the non-labour inputs to production, such as raw materials and long-lived fixed assets, (b) the consumption expenditure by households out of wages, (c) the consumption expenditure of capitalist households, unproductive labour households, and the state out of surplus value, and (d) the government sector, G_t. We can separate the government sector into military, V_t and non-military, Z_t, sectors as follows:

$$V_t = \varphi G_t \text{ and } Z_t = (1-\varphi) G_t \;\; where\, 0 < \varphi < 1$$

Therefore, if D_t represents aggregate demand in period t, then

$$D_t = (1-k) C_t + E_t^W + E_t^S + V_t + Z_t \tag{11}$$

where E_t^W represents consumption expenditure out of wages, E_t^S represents consumption expenditure out of surplus value, V_t represents milex by government out of total taxes, Z_t represents non-milex by government out of total taxes, and C_t represents capital outlays (as before).

If τ represents the tax ratio, then the total tax, $\mp_{t,}$ is

$$\mp_t = \tau k C_t + \tau(1-p)S''_t \tag{12}$$

The finance lag (T^F), consumption expenditure out of wages, and surplus value all occur with a time lag. If T^W represents the time lag of expenditure out of wages, then

$$E_t^W = (1-\tau)kC_{t-T^W}. \tag{13}$$

In addition, if T^S represents the time lag of expenditure out of surplus value, then

$$E_t^S = (1-\tau)(1-p)S''_{t-T^S} \tag{14}$$

Similarly, milex out of total tax and non-milex out of total tax occur with time lags, T^V and T^Z, respectively. Therefore,

$$V_t = \varphi \mp_{t-T^V} \tag{15}$$

$$Z_t = (1-\varphi)\mp_{t-T^Z} \tag{16}$$

The five spending lags, T^F, T^W, T^S, T^V, and T^Z are highly important variables of the system. When the system is not in a steady state, an increase in any of the spending lags means that the amount of aggregate demand is falling relative to supply. This means that the ability of capitalist enterprises to sell finished products falls, and as a result, the opposite is implied. Thus, these spending lags can be understood as parameters that capture the state of aggregate demand in the system (Foley, 1986, p. 24).

After bringing in the spending lags, the aggregate demand equation becomes

$$\begin{aligned} D_t = {} & (1-k)C_t + (1-\tau)kC_{t-T^W} + (1-\tau)(1-p)S''_{t-T^S} \\ & + \varphi \mp_{t-T^V} + (1-\varphi)\mp_{t-T^Z} \end{aligned} \tag{17}$$

Using equations 12–16 and normalising by the capital outlay in the initial period, C_0, on a steady-state path with growth rate g we have

$$\begin{aligned} D_t = {} & (1-k)C_t + (1-\tau)kC_{t-T^W} + (1-\tau)(1-p)S''_{t-T^S} \\ & + \varphi\left(\tau k C_{t-T^V} + \tau(1-p)S''_{t-T^V}\right) \\ & + (1-\varphi)\left(\tau k C_{t-T^Z} + \tau(1-p)S''_{t-T^Z}\right) \end{aligned} \tag{18}$$

$$D_0 = (1-k) + \frac{(1-\tau)k}{(1+g)^{T^W}} + \frac{(1-\tau)(1-p)q}{(1+g)^{T^S+T^P+T^R}}$$
$$+\varphi\left[\frac{\tau k}{(1+g)^{T^V}} + \frac{q\tau(1-p)}{(1+g)^{T^V+T^P+T^R}}\right] \tag{19}$$
$$+(1-\varphi)+\left[\frac{\tau k}{(1+g)^{T^Z}} + \frac{q\tau(1-p)}{(1+g)^{T^Z+T^P+T^R}}\right]$$

Recalling that $D_0 < S_0 = \dfrac{1+q}{(1+g)^{T^P+T^R}}$, in equation (19), the gap will be lower (e.g. profit will be higher) as the share of military sector, ϕ, increases because $T^V < T^Z$, and p, k, ϕ, τ are between 0 and 1, and q, g, and all lags are positive.

The effect of military expenditure on the realisation lag

According to Foley (1986, p. 24), in Keynesian models, aggregate demand's impact on production is related to the relation between sales and production, as well as the movements of inventories. In the model, this is presented by the realisation lag, T^R. Increasing T^R refers to capitalists having difficulty selling their products. Keynes states that in a static equilibrium framework, the parameters that determine aggregate demand have a close relationship with the state of realisation in the economy.

According to first-in first-out reasoning and equation (17), we have the following relations:

$$\frac{dT^R}{dt} = 1 - \frac{S_t}{P_{t-T^R}} \tag{20}$$

$$\frac{dT^W}{dt} = 1 - \frac{E_t^W}{(1-\tau)kC_{t-T^W}} \tag{21}$$

$$\frac{dT^S}{dt} = 1 - \frac{E_t^W}{(1-\tau)(1-p)S''_{t-T^S}} \tag{22}$$

$$\frac{dT^V}{dt} = 1 - \frac{V_t}{\varphi \text{Ŧ}_{t-T^V}} \tag{23}$$

$$\frac{dT^Z}{dt} = 1 - \frac{Z_t}{(1-\varphi)\text{Ŧ}_{t-T^Z}} \tag{24}$$

Assuming an economy with the basic circuit capital relation presented earlier, we have the following:

$$S_t = D_t = (1-k)C_t + E_t^W + E_t^S + V_t + Z_t \tag{25}$$

Substituting (20)–(24) into (25),

$$\begin{aligned}\left(1-\frac{dT^R}{dt}\right)P_{t-T^R} &= (1-k)C_t + \left(1-\frac{dT^W}{dt}\right)(1-\tau)kC_{t-T^W} \\ &+ \left(1-\frac{dT^S}{dt}\right)(1-\tau)(1-p)S''_{t-T^S} \\ &+ \left(1-\frac{dT^V}{dt}\right)\varphi \mp_{t-T^V} + \left(1-\frac{dT^Z}{dt}\right)(1-\varphi)\mp_{t-T^Z}\end{aligned} \tag{26}$$

$$\frac{dT^R}{dt} = 1 - \left[\begin{aligned}&(1-k)C_t + \left(1-\frac{dT^W}{dt}\right)(1-\tau)kC_{t-T^W} \\ &+ \left(1-\frac{dT^S}{dt}\right)(1-\tau)(1-p)S''_{t-T^S} \\ &+ \left(1-\frac{dT^V}{dt}\right)\varphi \mp_{t-T^V} \\ &+ \left(1-\frac{dT^Z}{dt}\right)(1-\varphi)\mp_{t-T^Z}\end{aligned}\right] / P_{t-T^R} \tag{27}$$

As a result, T^R will increase as the five spending lags, T^F, T^W, T^S, T^V, and T^Z, rise because the derivatives of the spending lags are negative. The key implication of this model is that since $T^V < T^Z$ for the higher share of military sector, ϕ, an increase in the realisation lag and therefore the rate of profit will be lower. The key presumption of the model that $T^V < T^Z$ is plausible. For example, in countries like the U.S., the Congress is much more willing to fund milex even by borrowing than many other categories of expenditure. In fact, such willingness is observed in many countries as well. As discussed earlier in this chapter, in fact, it can be argued that, *de facto*, there is no spending lag for the military sector.

It is worth noting again that this specific set up of circuit of capital model is just a practical attempt to show the effect of milex. In fact, the steady-state growth paths are only one part of the whole circuit of capital, which continues to constrain capital accumulation whether an economy is close to or far from a steady-state path. It would be more informative to expand this extension of the circuit of capital model to consider the non-steady-state capital accumulation.

For example, the economic dynamics of demobilisation in the post-war period of 1946–48 would present non-steady-state dynamics.[13]

Notes

1 See Bleaney (1976), Rowthorn (1980), Howard and King (1992), and Brewer (2001) for critical reviews of Luxemburg's analysis.

2 Cypher (1987–88) argues that, although Luxemburg did not express it explicitly, her remark of "incessant technical innovations" induced by arms spending boost the accumulation of capital and the rate of profit in three ways: milex generates major product technologies, which in turn creates spill-over effects, and military R&D generates new process technologies (p. 305).

3 Luxemburg's *The Accumulation of Capital* was heavily criticised, which led her to write a reply, two years after its publication in 1915, which was published in 1921 (Bleaney, 1976; Brewer, 2001, p. 58).

4 Although the argument of Baran and Sweezy addressed specifically the post-war U.S. economy some scholars such as Massimo Pivetti and James Cypher defended it in a more generalised way (D'Agostino et al., 2016).

5 In fact, the vagueness of the concept of surplus became a common critique of *Monopoly Capital* (Barkan, 1997). The meaning of the authors' definition of the concept, "The economic surplus, in the briefest possible definition, is the difference between what a society produces and the cost of producing it" (Baran and Sweezy, 1966, p. 9), depends on the interpretation of 'cost of production'. Bleaney (1976) argues that Baran and Sweezy's surplus value covers Marxist surplus value and all other costs that can be attributed to the wasteful and irrational nature of monopoly capitalism. However, in this sense, the concept is not specific to monopoly capitalism or capitalism in general, but rather can be applied to any economy (p. 226–227).

6 In fact, as Shaikh (2003) shows, although there was a rise in government expenditure between 1960 and 1988 in major countries, taxes rose in accordance. That is, the increase in the share of taxes in GDP was enough to compensate for rising social expenditure. Thus, there was no fiscal crisis; rather, it was a legitimisation crisis.

7 The first edition was published in 1968.

8 The original French edition is dated 1972.

9 In addition to spin-off, the literature also includes spill-over, externalities, diffusion, and technology transfer (Hartley, 2017, p. 64). It is worth noting that Dunne and Sköns (2011) argued that "as a result of a long-term rapid development in many civilian technologies, the relative positions of military and civilian technology have been reversed in several areas of sophisticated technology" (p. 4). While military technology was leading civilian technology until the 1980s, by the 1990s the civilian technology led military technology in many areas, particularly electronics (e.g. IT and mobile phones). That is, the authors argued that there is no spin-off effect from the military to the civilian sectors; on the contrary, the technology transfer is from the civilian to the military sector. Also, there has been separation between civil and military technologies; for example in the case of jet engines (Hartley, 2017, p. 56). However, it is crucial to note that the state subsidies continued to develop weapon systems (Mazzucato, 2013, pp. 73–79). In fact, what matters more is not whether there is still spin-off or not, but how worthwhile the spin-off is. In other words, the existence of spin-off does not tell its market value and does not tell if subsidies pay off, because other industries might also create spin-off effect (Hartley, 2017, p. 19). In other words, it might be possible to produce the same technology at lower cost without relying on the military spill-over (Smith, 2009, p. 167).

10 Cypher criticised Mandel's analysis of the effect of milex for not presenting or citing any empirical evidence, referring to it as "the most muddled chapter in the book" (Cypher, 1985, p. 279). Rowthorn also criticised his work by arguing that his analysis of the role

of military production in absorbing surplus value draws on two incompatible theories. On the one hand, he argues for the surplus-absorbing capacity of milex, in line with Baran and Sweezy; on the other hand, he also notes that milex is accompanied by an equivalent decline in workers' consumption, which cannot help to prevent a realisation crisis (Rowthorn, 1980, p. 98).

11 In the same manner, Reich (1972) argues that capitalists may prefer military over civilian commodities because milex is "highly profitable and amenable to boondoggling", easily "expandable almost without limit", does not conflict with private-sector interests, produces arms that are "rapidly consumed or become obsolete very quickly", and increases wages less than social expenditure (pp. 298–302).

12 In fact, this criticism was raised by Friedman (1974) and Stevenson (1974) as well.

13 I would like to thank Duncan Foley for this comment.

6 An econometric analysis of the nexus of military expenditure and the profit rate

Introduction

Marx argued that the driving force of capitalism is the persistent search for higher rates of profit, imposed by fierce competition among capitalists. However, he also noted that there are internal contradictions in capitalist production systems that prevent their unlimited expansion. Marx argued that mechanisation of production is the key process in the accumulation of capital. It leads to higher labour productivity as workers use more sophisticated tools and machinery while increasing the organic composition of capital. This causes one key contradiction of capitalism: mechanisation reduces the profitability of capital. However, Marx also noted some countertendencies for the tendency for the rate of profit to fall, including raising the intensity of exploitation, depressing wages below their value, cheapening the elements of constant capital, and engaging in foreign trade. For Marx, the heart of the crisis-prone nature of capitalism was not the inevitable fall in the rate of profit. Rather, in his later years, he began to see the tendency of the rate of profit to fall as an empirical question, as discussed in Chapter 4.

Chapter 5 discussed the effect of milex on the rate of profit, which does so through capital productivity and the organic composition of capital, thereby playing a contradictory role in the context of the tendency of the rate of profit to fall. Luxemburg argued that if taxes are used to pay for weapons production, this can increase the profit rate because the indirect tax on the working class reduces wages (Luxemburg, 1913). This assumes that indirect taxes reduce variable capital because surplus value remains constant, which implies that any increase in the rate of surplus value is larger than the increase in the organic composition of capital. In a similar vein, Baran and Sweezy (1966) argued that milex helps to absorb the surplus without raising wages or capital.

Mandel (1978), on the other hand, argued that milex has a contradictory effect on the rate of profit. On the one hand, it increases the rate of profit for three reasons. Firstly, because of the so-called spin-off effect – that the spread of new technologies and products from the military to civilian sector reinforces profit rates in competitive civilian markets. Secondly, because the military sector is negotiated between state and industry, it is isolated from competition, which allows capitalists to enjoy more than the general rate of profit. Thirdly, milex increases the rate of surplus value through rising taxation of wages. On the other hand, although milex cheapens constant capital via the spin-off effect, overall, the organic composition of capital in the arms sector is usually higher than the social average. Thus, milex increases the average organic composition of capital, which in turn accelerates the tendency for the rate of profit to fall.

The discussions in Chapter 4 on the law of the tendency for the rate of profit to fall and in Chapter 5 on the possible counteracting effect of milex through absorbing the surplus showed that there are several tendencies and counteracting factors operating on the rate of profit. This suggests that the effect of milex on the rate of profit is a more empirical than theoretical question. This chapter therefore presents a comprehensive empirical analysis of the effect of milex on the rate of profit.

The chapter examines the relationship in question in a panel model, using two different sets of the rate of profit. The first set is the rate of profit calculated on the Penn World Tables. This set covers 31 major countries for 1950–2014. The second set is mainly based on the profit rate in the Extended Penn World Table. This set covers 27 countries for 1963–2008.

Literature survey

There are only five country case studies (Georgiou, 1992; Kollias and Maniatis, 2003; Dunne et al., 2013; Ansari, 2018; Elveren and Özgür, 2018) and two panel studies (Elveren and Hsu, 2016, 2018) that investigate the effect of milex on the rate of profit. Chapter 6 reviews the time-series studies on the U.S., the U.K., the former West Germany, Turkey, and Greece.

Elveren and Hsu (2016) examined the relationship of 24 OECD countries during 1963–2008 by employing a panel ARDL model. This first panel study of the nexus of milex and the rate of profit revealed two major findings. First, while there is a positive linkage between milex and profit rates for the whole period, the impact of milex is negative in the post-1980 era. Second, there is weak evidence that, while there is positive linkage between milex and profit rates for arms-exporting countries, the linkage is negative for non-arms-exporting countries.

Following up, Elveren and Hsu (2016), Elveren and Hsu (2018) considered income inequality specifically, which is a crucial variable that has not received much attention in the context of the economic effect of milex (Ali, 2007; Töngür and Elveren, 2017, Taşıran and Elveren, 2017). Elveren and Hsu (2018) examined 32 major countries for 1963–2008. The new data set included major countries like Argentina, Germany, China, India, Brazil, South Korea, South Africa, and Mexico. They used an extensive data set for income inequality, the Estimated Household Income Inequality data set, provided by the University of Texas Inequality Project (UTIP). They also improved the dummy variables to better test the difference between arms-exporting and arms-importing countries. Employing a fixed effect, a dynamic fixed effect, and a Generalised Method of Moment model, they showed that milex has a positive effect on the rate of profit and that increasing income inequality boosts profit rates. Their findings also suggest that, while milex has a positive impact on the profit rate for both arms-exporting countries and net-arms exporters, the relationship is not that significant for arms-importing countries. The study also provides some new evidence on the relationship in question through a Granger causality analysis. It shows that bidirectional causality exists only for one third of the countries; however, there is a clear distinction between country groups in that profit rates Granger cause milex in arms-importing countries, whereas milex causes profit rates in arms-exporting countries. This is an important finding because it suggests that countries like Turkey or Greece buy more arms when their economy is growing (e.g. higher GDP/higher profit rates) whereas countries like the U.S. or the U.K. grow more and enjoy higher profit rates while producing and selling arms.

In a similar vein but within a broader setting, Taşıran and Elveren (2017) analysed the nexus of milex-inequality profits for the first time for 21 countries for the period of 1988–2008. The authors employed the non-parametric technique of Partial Least Squares Path Modelling to examine this threevariate setting to better understand the internal relationships of the dependent variables together with their respective explanatory set of variables. The method is particularly useful because the theoretical foundation of the problem is scarce, measurements are not well-defined, and the empirical distributions of the dependent variables are not clear. The findings of the general pooled analysis suggest that milex has a relatively small positive effect on profit rates. However, when unobserved heterogeneity is taken into account, the results differ substantially. Accordingly, first, milex has a larger negative effect on the rate of profit when overall profit rates are higher. Second, milex has a positive effect on profits when milex is smaller. Third, when inequality is low, higher milex leads to lower profits. Fourth, when inequality is high, higher milex leads to both higher profits.

Data

The biggest controversy within Marxist economics is determining and quantifying which variables to use, as Marxist variables are not directly quantifiable and operational. Generally, this is achieved by modifying data based on value theory by choosing those measures that best match with Marxist categories[1] (Dunne, 1991).

Marx defined the general rate of profit as the total surplus value produced by productive labour divided by the total stock of fixed capital. The proxies that Marxist researchers use for surplus value and capitalist value are, respectively, corporate surplus and fixed stock capital, while the gross profit rate (i.e. the ratio of surplus value to invested capital) provides the measure of the dependent variable, namely profit. Derived from the Extended Penn World Tables[2] v. 4.0 (EPWT), profit can be calculated from the following formula:

$$Profit = 100^{*}(1\text{-}wage\ share)^{*}productivity\ of\ capital$$

Here, *wage share* refers to employee compensation's share of Gross Domestic Product, based on the local currency's current prices, while *productivity of capital* – specifically output-capital ratio – is real Gross Domestic Product in 2005 purchasing power parity (Chain Index) divided by estimated capital stock.

The market valuation of outputs and aggregated capital measures from the market valuation of different capital goods provide the aggregated national output measures that constitute the EPWT data. However, such aggregation is problematic because it conceals how variations in capital measurements can be caused either by changes in price and composition in capital or by uniform changes in the quantity of capital.

The Perpetual Inventory Method (PIM) enables the capital stock in EPWT to be determined by using the real investment share of GDP in the Penn World Table v. 5.6 with straight-line depreciation (Foley and Marquetti, 1997).

Inevitably, issues with the Penn World Tables data set are reflected in the EPWT data (Foley and Marquetti, 1997). First, the investment data maybe of insufficiently high quality. Second, it is assumed that all categories have similarly short lives as assets because the investment data is left uncategorised according to type of gross fixed capital formation while represented as a short series. Consequently, there may be inconsistent underestimation of the size of capital stock if countries vary in how their specific gross fixed capital formation is composed.

The second main data set is the Penn World Tables. The rate of profit is calculated as suggested in Roberts (2015).

Profit rate = (Real GDP – (Real GDP* share of labour compensation in GDP))/(capital stock + (Real GDP* share of labour compensation in GDP))

Or, referring to the legend of PWT, profit rate = (rgdpo – (rgdp*labsh))/(ck + (rgdp*labsh))

The basic correlation between the two series for the overlapping period (e.g. 1963–2008) is 0.4239, ranging from a high value of 0.8968 for Norway and a low value of -0.5431 for Chile.

Because of inconsistent definitions and its strategic manipulation by governments, milex data is problematic. Several issues therefore need to be clarified. First, the distinction between milex (or defence spending) and arms spending should be noted because arms spending is only part of milex, which also includes payments to military personnel and all spending on military facilities. That is, milex refers to "spending on the military in general, including spending on personnel (i.e. the salaries and benefits of troops and civilian staff), operations and maintenance (i.e. spending on general supplies, services, and transport), equipment (e.g. arms, other military equipment, and non-military equipment), construction (e.g. of military bases), and research and development" (SIPRI, 2017). Thus, arms spending constitutes only 10–30 percent of defence spending (Hartley, 2017, p. 6).

Second, even assuming that the authorities are honest about the information they release, milex data are intrinsically problematic because there is no consistency across countries of what exactly is measured. Even for the same country, particularly developing countries, it is very likely that different sources present different values. One should therefore be careful in interpretation. For instance, it matters what is included in milex because of the significant differences depending on whether spending on intelligence services, paramilitary forces, and pension payments for retired army members are included. Moreover, nuclear or space research has both civilian and military aspects (Smith, 2009, p. 90). Differentials in inflation and exchange rates between countries must also be considered, usually by converting current currencies into U.S. dollars using purchasing power parity. However, a better alternative is perhaps to measure milex as a percentage of GDP or the central government budget – which is commonly called *the military burden*. Accordingly, this chapter measures milex as a percentage of GDP, taken from the Stockholm International Peace Research Institute (SIPRI), the standard data set for milex. Regarding the above concerns, the data provided by the SIPRI is virtually problem-free in comparison of countries.

Kollias and Maniatis (2003) note that, depending on the assumptions (full employment, structure of milex in terms of R&D, personnel expenditures, etc.) and the short-term/long-term distinction, milex may have positive or negative effects on the profit rate. The positive effects include increasing demand, avoiding the rise in organic composition of capital and the accompanying fall in the profit rate, increasing labour productivity, increasing the rate of surplus value, and bringing about international trade dominance. Negative impacts include crowding out of investment, reducing productivity through purchase of "unreproductive" goods, increasing the organic composition of capital by expanding a capital-intensive sector, and taxing capital income.

Our GDP data was taken from the Penn World Tables as output-side real GDP at chained PPPs in 2005 US$. We predict that higher GDP leads to higher capital accumulation: that is, higher GDP is associated with higher rates of profit.

Unemployment rate data was obtained from the World Bank.[3] An increase in the rate of unemployment reduces wage bargaining power and lowers the wage rate, thereby increasing the rate of surplus value and the rate of profit. However, rising unemployment puts downward pressure on effective demand, raising the organic composition of capital and possibly reducing the rate of profit at the same time.

Our EPWT data include 27 major countries for 1963–2008. In addition to the OECD countries covered in Elveren and Hsu (2016), namely Australia, Austria, Belgium, Canada, Chile, Denmark, Finland, France, Greece, Ireland, Israel, Italy, Japan, Luxembourg, Netherlands, New Zealand, Norway, Portugal, Spain, Sweden, Switzerland, the U.K., and the U.S., the extended data set used in our analysis also covers four other major countries, Brazil, Germany, South Africa, and South Korea, but excludes Turkey as inconsistent in calculation method. South Africa's data are taken from EPWT and included in the analysis because the goal is to cover as many countries as possible, in contrast to Elveren and Hsu (2016), who focused exclusively on OECD countries. Brazil's data are taken from Roberts (2015) and calculated based on EPWT, with a correlation

Table 6.1 Countries included in analyses

Elveren and Hsu (2016)			*EPWT*	*PWT*
Australia	Greece	Norway	Elveren and Hsu (2016)	EPWT
Austria	Ireland	Portugal	Turkey (excluded)	Argentina
Belgium	Israel	Spain	Brazil	India
Canada	Italy	Sweden	Germany	Mexico
Chile	Japan	Switzerland	South Africa	Turkey
Denmark	Luxembourg	Turkey	South Korea	
Finland	Netherlands	U.K.		
France	New Zealand	U.S.		

coefficient of 1 for the overlapping period. Germany's and South Korea's data are taken from Esteban Maito, with correlation coefficients of 0.894 and 0.867 for the overlapping periods, respectively.

The second data set used in our analysis is the Penn World Tables (PWT) data, which covers 31 countries for 1960–2014. In addition to the countries in EPWT, it also covers Argentina, India, Mexico, and Turkey. Table 6.1 shows the countries included.

As both T and N are large, we conducted a panel ARDL cointegration test for four different time periods, 1960–2014, 1963–2008, 1980–2008, and 1980–2014, with and without unemployment to determine the overall impact of milex.

Method

Standard panel models are unable to capture the dynamic relationship among our variables of interest. One widely used method for dynamic panel data analysis is GMM, particularly for the common cases of large N and small T data. However, this method has some shortcomings as it is mostly employed in the case of short time periods, capturing only short-term dynamics. Kiviet (1995) therefore warns that the homogeneity assumptions on the slope coefficients of lagged dependent variables can create significant biases in GMM estimations. Therefore, GMM estimations are likely to lead to inconsistent and misleading long-run coefficients if the slope coefficients are not identical (Pesaran and Smith, 1995).

It used to be argued that long-run relationships only exist in the context of cointegration among integrated variables (Johansen, 1995; Philipps and Hansen, 1990). However, Pesaran and Smith (1995), who introduced the mean group, and Pesaran et al. (1999), who introduced the pooled mean group, provided a new technique that has made it possible to derive consistent and efficient estimates of the parameters in a long-run relationship between both integrated and stationary variables in a panel data structure. These methods, the autoregressive distributed lag models, (the so-called 'ARDL approach'), allow the variables in question, *profit*, *milex*, *GDP*, and *unemployment*, to be I(0) and I(1).

There are three issues that need to be highlighted for the panel ARDL cointegration analysis that we use. First, the stationary condition is that the coefficient of the error-correction term is negative and not lower than -1, for stabilising adjustment in the error correction model. Our results meet this requirement. Second, although the regressors don't need to be strictly exogenous, residuals must be serially uncorrelated. The second requirement is resolved by including lags for the dependent and independent variables in error correction form (which handles endogeneity as well), with lag length determined by the Schwarz Information Criterion (SC). Third, both the number of years (T) and the number of countries (N) must be large to prevent bias in the average estimators and avoid heterogeneity. Finally, our model satisfies the third requirement by having 24 countries and time periods of 29 years (i.e. 1980–2008) and 46 years (i.e. 1963–2008).[4]

Based on Pesaran et al. (1999), using the autoregressive distributed lag ARDL (p,q), the dynamic heterogeneous panel regression equation with the error correction model is formed as follows:

$$\Delta(y_i)_t = \sum_{j=1}^{p-1} \gamma^i_j \Delta(y_i)_{t-j} + \sum_{j=0}^{q-1} \delta^i_j \Delta(X_i)_{t-j} + \varphi^i \left[(y_i)_{t-1} - \left\{ \beta^i_0 + \beta^i_1 (X_i)_{t-1} \right\} \right] + \epsilon_{it} \qquad (1)$$

Where y is the profit rate; X represents the explanatory variables, including milex, real GDP, global profit rate, and unemployment; p and q refer to the lags of the dependent and independent variables, respectively; γ and δ are the short-run coefficients for profit rates and its determinants, respectively; β is the long-run coefficient; ϕ is the coefficient of the speed of adjustment to the long-run equilibrium ϵ and is a time-varying disturbance term; and i and t refer to country and time, respectively.[5] The long-run regression coefficient in the square brackets in (1) is derived from equation (2) as follows:

$$(y_i)_t = \beta^i_0 + \beta^i_1 (X_i)_t + \mu_{i,t} \text{ where } \mu_{i,t} \sim I(0) \qquad (2)$$

Various multi-country methods can allow for parameter differences across countries, including the fully heterogeneous coefficient model, which allows for complete diversity in cross-country parameters, given a sufficient size of time-series data, a mean group estimator created by Pesaran and Smith (1995), in which the cross-country dimension is also large, and a fully homogeneous coefficient model, which requires that all slope and intercept coefficients be equivalent for all countries.

In between these extremes, there are many estimators, such as the following: the dynamic fixed effects (DFE) estimator, which equalises all slope coefficients across countries and the pooled mean group (PMG) estimator of Pesaran et al. (1999), which equalises long-run slope coefficients across countries and creates consistent estimates of the mean of short-run coefficients across countries.

Results and discussion

Panel data models are likely to present cross-sectional dependence in the errors, which may be caused by common shocks and unobserved components that form part of the error term. In addition to major panel unit root tests, I therefore also utilised CADF and CIPS unit root tests, as suggested by Pesaran (2007), which allow for cross-sectional dependence. All variables were used in their natural logarithmic forms. Tests showed that the variables were a mix of I(0) and I(1) and that no variable was I(2), allowing us to employ the ARDL approach. The results for 1963–2008 are provided in Table 6.2, while the very similar results for 1980–2008 are provided in Table A5 in the Appendix A.

Cross-sectional dependence was tested by Pesaran's CD test (Pesaran, 2004) and other major tests suggested by Frees (1995) and Friedman (1937). All tests rejected the null hypothesis of cross-sectional independence. I was therefore able to control for cross-sectional dependence by incorporating the global profit variable, which is the cross-sectional mean of the profit rate. These results are provided in Table 6.3.

Here I emphasise the results of the rate of profit taken from EPWT. The results based on PWT is provided in the Appendix. There are three sets of analysis. The basic analysis is for 1963–2008 without unemployment, as presented in Table 6.4. The second set includes unemployment, a crucial variable with direct linkages to the profit rate. Table 6.5 shows the results for 1980–2008, both with and without unemployment, to compare with the whole period.

Table 6.2 Panel unit root tests (1963–2008)

Variables	*Deterministic Terms*	*LLC*	*IPS*	*Breitung*	*CADF*	*CIPS*
Levels						
Profit (EPWT)	Intercept, trend	−2.501***	−0.292	0.131	2.201	−2.166
Profit (PENN)	Intercept, trend	0.341	1.697	0.475	−2.508	−2.742***
Milex	Intercept, trend	−1.158	−3.112***	−0.968	−2.581*	−2.805***
GDP	Intercept, trend	−0.488	−0.513	0.917	−1.792	−1.872
First Differences						
ΔProfit (EPWT)	Intercept	−21.666***	−20.657***	−11.279***	−3.145***	−4.975***
ΔProfit (PENN)	Intercept	−16.396***	−19.261***	−9.175***	−3.362***	−5.011***
ΔMilex	Intercept	−27.143***	−26.340***	−15.757***	−3.410***	−5.233***
ΔGDP	Intercept	−17.832***	−18.384***	−12.051***	−2.999***	−4.922***

Notes: The number of lags is determined according to SC. For CADF, the number of lags is 2; for CIPS, the maximum lag number is taken as 2 for unemployment and 3 for other variables.

Significance is denoted by *** at 1%, ** at 5%, and * at 10% level.

Table 6.3 Cross-sectional independence tests (1963–2008)

Profit (EPWT)	*Pesaran's Test*	*Frees' Test*	*Friedman's Test*
Test Statistic	34.221	5.942	362.953
Probability	0.0000	0.0000	0.0000
Profit (PENN)			
Test Statistic	19.011	6.459	182.214
Probability	0.0000	0.0000	0.0000

Table 6.4 The long- and short-run effects of milex on profit rates (1963–2008)

	Pooled Mean Group	*Mean Group*	*Dynamic Fixed Effect*
Long-Run Coefficients			
Milex	0.517***	−0.233	0.552***
	[0.519]	[0.565]	[0.159]
GDP	−0.973***	−4.150**	−1.008***
	[0.113]	[1.842]	[0.166]
Global profit	1.425***	−0.730	0.177
	[0.208]	[1.500]	[0.391]
Time trend	0.060***	0.147**	0.052***
	[0.006]	[0.068]	[0.008]
Short-Run Coefficients			
Error Correction Coefficient	−0.040***	−0.126***	−0.040***
	[0.011]	[0.021]	[0.006]
ΔProfit (−1)	0.378***	0.324***	0.372***
	[0.013]	[0.018]	[0.016]
ΔMilex	−0.070***	−0.070***	−0.043***
	[0.021]	[0.019]	[0.012]
ΔGDP	0.297***	0.476***	0.323***
	[0.053]	[0.059]	[0.029]
ΔGlobal profit	0.513***	0.363***	0.567***
	[0.075]	[0.073]	[0.042]
Intercept	0.307***	2.204***	0.544***
	[0.106]	[0.447]	[0.096]
No. Countries	27	27	27
No. Observations	1188	1188	1188

Standard errors in brackets. Significance denoted by *** at 1%, ** at 5%, and * at 10% level.

Finally, the third analysis considers the possible effect of a country's role in the arms trade (i.e. arms exporter or arms importer). These results are provided in Tables 6.6, 6.7, and 6.8 for both time periods, and with or without unemployment. All the analyses used several methods based on different assumptions, as explained in the previous section. This strategy allows one to check the signs of the variables for robustness.

Table 6.5 The long- and short-run effects of milex on profit rates (1980–2008)

Long Run	*Pooled Mean Group*		*Mean Group*		*Dynamic Fixed Effect*	
	1	*2*	*1*	*2*	*1*	*2*
Milex	−0.123***	0.009	0.085	0.084	0.154	0.290**
	[0.044]	[0.027]	[0.149]	[0.182]	[0.128]	[0.134]
GDP	−1.177***	−1.071***	−0.174	−1.282***	−0.614***	−0.850***
	[0.101]	[0.087]	[0.357]	[0.380]	[0.169]	[0.176]
Unemployment	0.393***		0.146**		0.448***	
	[0.035]		[0.070]		[0.084]	
Global profit	0.087	0.639***	0.862**	0.520	−1.287**	−0.901
	[0.209]	[0.134]	[0.357]	[0.433]	[0.593]	[0.577]
Time trend	0.036***	0.028***	0.009	0.046***	0.024***	0.039***
	[0.003]	[0.002]	[0.006]	[0.011]	[0.007]	[0.008]
Short Run						
Error Correction Coefficient	−0.114***	−0.122***	−0.366***	−0.285***	−0.069***	−0.071***
	[0.018]	[0.025]	[0.037]	[0.027]	[0.010]	[0.010]
ΔMilex	−0.089	−0.137*	−0.079*	−0.122**	−0.052***	−0.080***
	[0.056]	[0.077]	[0.048]	[0.050]	[0.019]	[0.019]
ΔGDP	0.334***	0.380***	0.350***	0.540***	0.397***	0.392***
	[0.068]	[0.071]	[0.074]	[0.777]	[0.038]	[0.038]
ΔUnemployment	−0.031**		−0.011		−0.018**	
	[0.012]		[0.012]		[0.007]	
ΔGlobal profit	0.590***	0.566***	0.427***	0.410***	0.752***	0.813***
	[0.088]	[0.095]	[0.142]	[0.103]	[0.073]	[0.075]
Intercept	1.870***	1.794***	1.499	3.335***	0.963***	1.127***
	[0.271]	[0.416]	[1.039]	[0.766]	[0.174]	[0.180]
No. Country	27	27	27	27	27	27
No. Obser.	756	783	756	783	756	783

Standard errors in brackets. Significance denoted by *** at 1%, ** at 5%,and * at 10% level.

Table 6.4, which reports the results of the DFE, PMG, and MG estimations for 1963–2008, shows both long-term relations and a short-term adjustment mechanism. The most important finding is that both the PMG and DFE estimations reveal a very significant positive effect of milex on profit rates in the long run.[6] Since the model includes a time trend, the GDP coefficient should be interpreted in terms of its deviation from trend. In all three estimations, the negative coefficient suggests that profits are counter-cyclical, which might be the case if workers can increase their share during a boom and capital-output ratio is constant. The positive and significant PMG coefficient of *global profit* suggests that, overall, there is a global pattern of profit rates. The time trend has a highly significant positive impact, not just in all three estimations, but also in almost all other specifications, which suggests there is no tendency for the profit rate to fall.

Regarding the short-run dynamics, the error correction coefficient is negative and less than −1, which suggests that the panel error correction model

Table 6.6 The long- and short-run effects of milex on profit rates for arms-exporting versus arms-importing countries (1963–2008)

Long run	*Pooled Mean Group*		*Mean Group*		*Dynamic Fixed Effect*	
	Exporter	*Importer*	*Exporter*	*Importer*	*Exporter*	*Importer*
Milex	0.552***	1.265***	0.884	−1.504*	0.527**	0.937**
	[0.064]	[0.349]	[0.742]	[0.811]	[0.259]	[0.395]
GDP	−1.109***	0.217	−0.560	−8.607**	−1.930***	−0.831***
	[0.157]	[0.182]	[0.827]	[3.722]	[0.688]	[0.224]
Global profit	1.457***	4.515***	−0.026	−1.705	−0.769	0.801
	[0.251]	[0.859]	[0.721]	[3.329]	[0.783]	[0.728]
Time trend	0.068***	0.023***	0.031	0.292**	0.081***	0.049***
	[0.008]	[0.008]	[0.025]	[0.143]	[0.028]	[0.012]
Short run						
Error Correction Coefficient	−0.047*	**−0.020**	−0.164***	−0.075***	−0.035***	−0.034***
	[0.025]	**[0.021]**	[0.032]	[0.023]	[0.012]	[0.009]
ΔProfit (−1)	0.397***	0.374***	0.337***	0.323***	0.400***	0.372***
	[0.017]	[0.017]	[0.018]	[0.033]	[0.023]	[0.026]
ΔMilex	−0.026*	−0.134**	−0.046**	−0.100***	−0.007	−0.060***
	[0.016]	[0.052]	[0.020]	[0.034]	[0.016]	[0.019]
ΔGDP	0.304***	0.244***	0.539***	0.399***	0.353***	0.289***
	[0.081]	[0.078]	[0.089]	[0.080]	[0.043]	[0.041]
ΔGlobal profit	0.494***	0.472***	0.218**	0.454***	0.511***	0.564***
	[0.108]	[0.094]	[0.099]	[0.070]	[0.051]	[0.067]
Intercept	0.421**	−0.337	2.715***	1.669***	1.001***	0.300*
	[0.200]	[0.226]	[0.683]	[0.603]	[0.171]	[0.155]
No. Countries	14	12	14	12	14	12
No. Observ.	616	528	616	528	616	528

Standard errors in brackets. Significance denoted by *** at 1%, ** at 5%, and * at 10% level.

holds for each estimator. As expected, GDP and the lagged value of the profit rate[7] have positive impacts on profit rates, whereas milex has a negative impact. This finding is consistent through all specifications. Overall, the results reported in Table 6.4 are highly consistent, suggesting that milex has a positive impact on the profit rate. However, the relationship in question requires further analysis as unemployment, a crucial variable, was omitted due to lack of data for the whole period.

Table 6.5 includes unemployment, with a shorter time period. The table reports the results for 1980–2008, both with and without the unemployment rate for comparison purposes. The results also show the highly significant negative effect (in five out of six model specifications) of GDP (i.e. profits are counter-cyclical) on the profit rates, as reported in Table 6.4. All three estimators show a positive long-run effect of unemployment on the profit rate, which strongly supports the concept of a reserve army of unemployed and is in line with counter-cyclical profits.

Table 6.7 The long- and short-run effects of milex on profit rates (with unemployment) for arms-exporting versus arms-importing countries (1980–2008)

Long run	*Pooled Mean Group*		*Mean Group*		*Dynamic Fixed Effect*	
	Exporter	*Importer*	*Exporter*	*Importer*	*Exporter*	*Importer*
Milex	−0.002	−0.573***	0.182	0.020	−0.010	−0.002
	[0.047]	[0.107]	[0.142]	[0.293]	[0.112]	[0.268]
GDP	−1.018***	−1.481***	−0.185	−0.089	−1.184***	−0.551*
	[0.092]	[0.246]	[0.236]	[0.415]	[0.247]	[0.295]
Unemployment	0.278***	0.594***	0.050	0.305**	0.156***	0.893***
	[0.029]	[0.081]	[0.040]	[0.135]	[0.047]	[0.247]
Global Profit	−0.153	0.646*	0.936***	0.947	−0.763	0.686
	[0.231]	[0.360]	[0.238]	[0.755]	[0.492]	[1.013]
Time trend	0.036***	0.032***	0.014*	−0.0008	0.039***	0.008
	[0.003]	[0.007]	[0.008]	[0.010]	[0.010]	[0.011]
Short run						
Error Correction Coefficient	−0.154***	−0.087***	−0.447***	−0.253***	−0.111***	−0.051***
	[0.033]	[0.014]	[0.039]	[0.056]	[0.019]	[0.012]
ΔMilex	−0.005	−0.199	−0.027	−0.154	0.015	−0.071***
	[0.030]	[0.130]	[0.039]	[0.095]	[0.026]	[0.027]
ΔGDP	0.386***	0.648***	0.341***	0.333***	0.331***	0.427***
	[0.084]	[0.237]	[0.120]	[0.093]	[0.060]	[0.051]
ΔUnemployment	−0.025	0.344*	−0.015	−0.010	−0.001	−0.031***
	[0.020]	[0.130]	[0.015]	[0.022]	[0.009]	[0.011]
ΔGlobal profit	0.677***	0.396***	0.299**	0.361**	0.706***	0.586***
	[0.118]	[0.126]	[0.142]	[0.163]	[0.091]	[0.109]
Intercept	2.369***	1.591***	1.146	1.268	2.214***	0.301
	[0.509]	[0.270]	[1.721]	[1.092]	[0.326]	[0.247]
No. Countries	14	12	14	12	14	12
No. Observations	392	336	392	336	392	336

Standard errors in brackets. Significance denoted by *** at 1%, ** at 5%, and * at 10% level.

The short-run dynamics among the variables is consistent across all model specifications and in line with the findings in Table 6.4, except for milex, which has a less significant impact.

Table 6.5 suggests that milex has had no significant positive impact on the rate of profit during the neo-liberal period. This is another crucial finding. Out of six model specifications, only one model shows a significant positive impact, four models suggest a positive but insignificant impact, and just one shows a very significant negative impact. This might be due to the changing structure of major economies in the neo-liberal era. With the rise of the financial sector and the rentier class, the increasing share of profits earned by firms has begun to be used for interest payments, dividends, and other unproductive expenditure, causing a smaller fraction of profits to be reinvested in the capital stock.

Finally, it is important to consider the distinction between each country's role in the arms trade because milex affects the rate of profit through several

Table 6.8 The long- and short-run effects of milex on profit rates for arms exporters versus arms importers (1980–2008)

Long run	*Pooled Mean Group*		*Mean Group*		*Dynamic Fixed Effect*	
	Exporter	*Importer*	*Exporter*	*Importer*	*Exporter*	*Importer*
Milex	−0.010	−0.208**	0.394*	−0.290	−0.008	0.632*
	[0.029]	[0.101]	[0.236]	[0.279]	[0.101]	[0.336]
GDP	−0.796***	−2.059***	−0.639**	−2.080***	−1.265***	−0.701**
	[0.095]	[0.289]	[0.254]	[0.758]	[0.218]	[0.314]
Global profit	0.556***	1.952***	0.430	0.713	−0.597	1.216
	[0.134]	[0.347]	[0.349]	[0.904]	[0.439]	[1.110]
Time trend	0.019***	0.065***	0.031***	0.064***	0.042***	0.031**
	[0.002]	[0.010]	[0.007]	[0.023]	[0.008]	[0.013]
Short run						
Error Correction Coefficient	−0.179***	−0.074**	−0.362***	−0.195***	−0.123***	−0.051***
	[0.045]	[0.029]	[0.038]	[0.024]	[0.019]	[0.013]
ΔMilex	−0.024	−0.209*	−0.099***	−0.151	−0.012	−0.113***
	[0.040]	[0.126]	[0.016]	[0.109]	[0.026]	[0.028]
ΔGDP	0.400***	0.380***	0.535***	0.537***	0.367***	0.407***
	[0.083]	[0.142]	[0.113]	[0.119]	[0.060]	[0.052]
ΔGlobal profit	0.570**	0.470***	0.344***	0.383**	0.698***	0.695***
	[0.123]	[0.128]	[0.119]	[0.158]	[0.092]	[0.116]
Intercept	2.126***	1.566**	2.828**	3.957***	2.541***	0.336
	[0.607]	[0.638]	[1.183]	[1.062]	[0.320]	[0.269]
No. Countries	14	12	14	12	14	12
No. Observations	406	348	406	348	406	348

Standard errors in brackets. Significance denoted by *** at 1%, ** at 5%, and * at 10% level.

negative and positive mechanisms, among which the negative consequences of arms production are more likely to be realised in arms-importing countries than arms-producing countries. While arms exports contribute to the balance of payments, provide jobs, and maintain industrial capacity, arms-producing countries externalise the wasteful effects of arms production by exporting.

It is therefore plausible to expect a difference between a country like Greece, which is mainly an arms importer, with the U.S. as the world's largest arms exporter. More specifically, we can expect milex to both benefit and disadvantage arms exporters. On the one hand, milex, because it requires R&D spending and provides employment, can increase the profit rate. For instance, such countries may be more dominant internationally, gain access to resources more cheaply, and impose unfavourable trade terms on others, while raising labour productivity domestically due to militarily inspired technological advances. On the other hand, milex can have negative effects on arms exporters if the organic composition of capital is raised when military technology is transferred to the civilian sector or if surplus value is not used productively for investment, et cetera. However, productivity in arms-importing countries will probably fall because resources must be diverted into buying "unreproductive" military items. Therefore, this exercise is both theoretically legitimate and empirically appropriate because estimation methods may not be able to represent this heterogeneity completely. Thus, in line with Elveren and Hsu (2016), I explore the relationship with regard to each country's role in the arms trade.

Accordingly, the analysis was extended to repeat each model specification in Tables 6.4 and 6.5 for fourteen arms-exporting countries versus twelve arms-importing countries to better understand the impact of milex on profitability.[8] Tables 6.6, 6.7, and 6.8 report the results. The error correction model holds in 17 out of 18 cases, while the short-run dynamics yield highly consistent results across all regressions except for milex. The most important overall finding from Tables 6.6, 6.7, and 6.8 is that, comparing within estimators, there is no significant evidence in 18 cases that, while milex has a positive effect on the rate of profits for arms exporters, its effect for non-exporters is negative. In other words, there is no clear evidence that milex has a differential effect on profit rates depending on a country's role in the arms trade since only 3 out of 17 model specifications show a significant negative impact of milex in the case of arms-importing countries.

GDP has a significant negative sign in 14 out of 18 cases, while unemployment has a significant positive sign in 5 out of 6 model specifications, strengthening the findings of Tables 6.4 and 6.5. The positive impact of unemployment on the rate of profit suggests that the effect is realised through changes in distribution in these economies from the working class to the capital-investing rentier class, rather than via a reduction in demand due to any decline in workers' wages. This is strong evidence that there is a reserve army of the unemployed in that higher unemployment rates lower workers' bargaining power, push down wages, change the organic composition of capital, and increase profit rates.

Regarding global profit, although the results are not as strong over the whole period, it remains safe to argue that (based on four significant positive signs out of twelve cases, with no significant negative impact), there is a global pattern of profit rates in the neo-liberal era as well. Except for one case (negative and significant), the time trend has a positive and significant sign in 23 specifications and a positive sign in 3 out of 27 model specifications in total. This can be interpreted as general counter evidence that there is a tendency for the profit rate to fall for the period in question in a panel context, in addition to comprehensive studies in the Marxist literature.

Overall, the findings suggest a highly significant positive relationship between milex and profit rates for 1963–2008, which supports and strengthens Elveren and Hsu (2016). However, there is no positive impact for the post-1980 period, contrary to the highly significant evidence provided in Elveren and Hsu (2016). Rather, the findings here suggest that milex has had an insignificant effect on profitability during the neo-liberal era. There is very weak evidence that, while milex has a positive effect on the rate of profit for arms-exporting countries, the effect is negative for arms importers. Although this is only weak evidence, it still supports the similar, and perhaps somewhat stronger, evidence in Elveren and

Hsu (2016) because the set of arms-exporting and arms-importing countries are different in this analysis. In general, the different findings from Elveren and Hsu (2016) suggest the necessity of further investigation to better understand the nexus of milex and profit. One easy way to do so is to conduct a robustness check with a different data set. To this end, I repeated the whole analysis with the profit rate taken from PWT for 1950–2014. All results are provided in the Appendix A.

Overall, my findings based on PWT support the positive impact of milex for the whole period. They are also very similar for the post-1980 period in that there is no significant negative impact; rather, the results are mixed and very weak. Overall, this indicates that milex had an insignificant impact during this period, while also providing very weak evidence for the differentiation between arms-exporting and arms-importing countries.

Conclusion

The findings above demonstrate the necessity to develop the analysis further in two main ways. First, panel data studies intrinsically provide limited information due to heterogeneity between countries, so such findings should be supported by further country-level analyses. This also allows longer time periods and other alternative dependent variables to be used. Second, there may be a non-linear relationship between milex and the rate of profit. That is, the effect of milex may change at different levels of the rate of profit. Regarding the former, Chapter 7 provides two basic analyses for 31 countries: the ARDL Bounds Test (Pesaran et al., 2001) and a Granger causality test, based on the procedure proposed by Toda and Yamamoto (1995). Regarding the latter issue (e.g. non-linearity), Chapter 7 extends the discussion on the U.S. by utilising a non-linear ARDL model and a Markov Switching model.

Notes

1 The key point in this transformation process is the fact that the price is a measure of value and that Ricardo finds that values are proportional to prices, which is empirically proven. (That is, the value price distortion is empirically very small.) (Ochoa, 1984; Shaikh, 1984; Petrovic, 1987 cited in Dunne, 1991).

2 The data was constructed by Duncan Foley and Adalmir Marquetti, based on the Penn World Tables and other sources. It is worth noting that profit rates in major countries in EPWT have highly similar patterns to those in major studies that compute profit rates in traditional Marxist thought. (See Roberts, 2012.)

3 Missing years are completed based on the IMF World Economic Outlook.

4 I used the 'xtpmg' command in Stata for non-stationary heterogeneous panel data models, provided by Blackburne and Frank (2007).

5 I adopted a general model to examine the relationship in question in line with Georgiou (1992), Dunne et al. (2013), and Elveren and Hsu (2016).

6 One can notice that while the short-run coefficients are very similar for all estimates, the long-run MG coefficients are very different. It may result from some outliers distorting the MG estimates.

7 The shorter time period of 1980–2008 does not have a lagged value for the dependent variable due to the lack of degrees of freedom. Pesaran et al. (1999) also note that, in cases of shorter time periods, the lagged dependent variable causes biased estimations, even when the number of N is large (p. 627).

8 The arms-exporting countries are Austria, Belgium, France, Germany, Israel, Netherlands, New Zealand, Portugal, South Africa, Spain, Sweden, Switzerland, the U.K., and the U.S., according to SIPRI (SIPRI, 2018). Because of its negligible milex, Luxembourg is excluded. The other countries are treated as arms importing.

References

Ali, H. E. (2007). Military expenditures and inequality: Empirical evidence from global data. *Defence and Peace Economics*, 18(6), pp. 519–535.

Ansari, S. (2018). US fiscal policy, manufacturing stagnation, and the shift to financialization in the era of globalization: An econometric analysis, 1973–2015. *Review of Political Economy*, 30(4), pp. 595–614. doi:10.1080/09538259.2018.1504388

Baran, P. and Sweezy, P. (1966). *Monopoly capital: An essay on the American economic and social order*. New York: Monthly Review Press.

Blackburne, E. F. and Frank, M.W. (2007). Estimation of nonstationary heterogeneous panels. *The Stata Journal*, 7(2), pp. 197–208.

Dunne, P. (1991). *Quantitative Marxism*. Cambridge: Polity Press.

Dunne, P., Pieroni, L. and D'Agostino, G. (2013). *Military spending and the falling rate of profit in the US*. Available at: www.sipri.org/research/armaments/milex/ICES2013/papers/archive/dunne-pieroni-agostino-milex-falling-rate-of-profit-in-usa

Elveren, A. Y. and Hsu, S. (2016). Military expenditures and profit rates: Evidence from OECD countries. *Metroeconomica*, 67(3), pp. 551–577.

Elveren, A.Y. and Hsu, S. (2018). The effect of military expenditure on profit rates: Evidence from major countries. *World Journal of Applied Economics*, 4(2), pp. 75–94.

Elveren, A.Y. and Özgür, G. (2018). *The effect of military expenditures on the profit rates in Turkey*. MPRA Paper 88848, University Library of Munich, Germany.

Foley, D. and Marquetti, A. (1997). *Economic growth from a classical perspective*. Available at: http://citeseerx.ist.psu.edu/viewdoc/download?doi=10.1.1.38.9954&rep=rep1&type=pdf

Frees, E. W. (1995). Assessing cross-sectional correlation in panel data. *Journal of Econometrics*, 69(2), pp. 393–414.

Friedman, M. (1937). The use of ranks to avoid the assumption of normality implicit in the analysis of variance. *Journal of the American Statistical Association*, 32(200), pp. 675–701.

Georgiou, G. (1992). Military expenditure and the rate of profit: Some empirical results. *International Review of Applied Economics*, 16(3), pp. 344–361.

Hartley, K. (2017). *The economics of arms*. Croydon: Agenda Publishing.

Johansen, S. (1995). *Likelihood-based inference in cointegrated vector autoregressive models*. Oxford and New York: Oxford University Press.

Kiviet, J. (1995). On bias, inconsistency, and efficiency of various estimators in dynamic panel data models. *Journal of Econometrics*, 68(1), pp. 53–78.

Kollias, C. and Maniatis, T. (2003). Military expenditure and the profit rate in Greece. *Defence and Peace Economics*, 14(2), pp. 117–127.

Luxemburg, R. (1951) [1913]: *The accumulation of capital*. London: Routledge and Kegan Paul.

Mandel, E. (1978). *Late capitalism*. New York: Verso.

Ochoa, E. M. (1984). *Labour values and prices of production: An interindustry study of the US economy, 1947–1972*. PhD Thesis, University of Michigan, Ann Arbor, MI.

Pesaran, H. (2004). *General diagnostic tests for cross section dependence in panels*. Cambridge Working Papers in Economics No. 0435. University of Cambridge, Faculty of Economics, Cambridge, UK.

Pesaran, H. (2007). A simple panel unit root test in the presence of cross-section dependence. *Journal of Applied Economics*, 22, pp. 265–312.

Pesaran, M. H., Shin, Y. and Smith, R. (1999). Pooled mean group estimation of dynamic heterogeneous panels. *Journal of the American Statistical Association*, 94, pp. 621–634.

Pesaran, M. H., Shin, Y. and Smith, R. J. (2001). Bounds testing approaches to the analysis of level relationships. *Journal of Applied Econometrics*, 16, pp. 289–326.

Pesaran, H. and Smith, R. (1995). Estimating long-run relationships from dynamic heterogeneous panels. *Journal of Econometrics*, 68(1), pp. 79–113.

Petrovic, P. (1987). The deviation of production prices from labour values: Some methodology and empirical evidence. *Cambridge Journal of Economics*, 11, pp. 197–210.

Philipps, P. and Hansen, B. (1990). Statistical inference in instrumental variables regression with I(1) processes. *The Review of Economic Studies*, 57(1), pp. 99–125.

Roberts, M. (2012). *A world of profit*. Available at: http://thenextrecession.files.wordpress.com/2012/09/a-world-rate-of-profit.pdf

Roberts, M. (2015). *Revisiting a world rate of profit*. Available at: https://thenextrecession.files.wordpress.com/2015/12/revisiting-a-world-rate-of-profit-june-2015.pdf

Shaikh, A. (1984). The transformation from Marx to Sraffa. In: E. Mandel and A. Freeman, eds., *Ricardo, Marx, Sraffa: The Langston memorial volume*. London: Verso.

SIPRI. (2018). Available at: www.sipri.org

Smith, R. (2009). *Military economics the interaction of power and money*. New York: Palgrave Macmillan.

Taşıran, A. C. and Elveren, A. Y. (2017). *Soft modelling of military expenditures, inequality and profits*. Allied Social Science Association Annual Meeting, Chicago, IL. Available at: www.aeaweb.org/conference/2017/preliminary/paper/DRSifQkh

Toda, H. Y. and Yamamoto, T. (1995). Statistical inference in vector autoregressions with possibly integrated processes. *Journal of Econometrics*, 66(1–2), pp. 225–250.

Töngür, Ü. and Elveren, A. Y. (2017). The nexus of economic growth, military expenditures, and income inequality. *Quality and Quantity*, 51(4), pp. 1821–1842.

7 Analysis of the nexus of military expenditure and profit

Country cases

Introduction

The chapter examines the effect of milex on the rate of profit, using the autoregressive distributed lag model (ARDL) Bounds Test, a non-linear ARDL, and the Toda-Yamamoto method for 31 countries for different time periods, ranging from 1950 to 2016. The main goal is to provide some complementary evidence to the relationship between milex and the profit rate, which was discussed in detail in Chapter 6.

It is worthwhile to support panel data analyses with time-series investigations, for two main reasons. First, panel studies cannot capture the full dynamics of the relationship in question for each country. Second, particularly in the case of strongly balanced data, the analysis prevents the longest time period available being used. Time-series studies, although they have their own handicaps, allow us to overcome these shortcomings.

The following section provides a brief literature survey of time-series analysis on the effect of milex on the rate of profit. Sections 7.3 and 7.4 present the data and method, respectively, whereas section 7.5 gives the results and discussion. Finally, the conclusion section summarises the findings.

Literature survey

In addition to the two panel studies (Elveren and Hsu, 2016, 2018) reviewed in the previous chapter, there are five time-series studies that deal with the effect of milex on the rate of profit.

Georgiou (1992) used an Ordinary Least Square (OLS) method to examine the effect of milex on profit rates in the U.K., the U.S., and the former West Germany for 1958–1987 with respect to Luxemburg's and Mandel's views. Georgiou investigates the effect of the share of milex in GDP on the rate of profit by controlling for the rate of growth of nominal GDP, unemployment rates, and a time trend. His profit rate is taken from Hill (1979) and updated with the OECD National Accounts, in which the rate of profit is gross operating surplus divided by the stock of fixed and working capital. The study finds that unemployment has a positive effect on the rate of profit in all three countries, whereas the effect of milex is only significant in the case of the U.S.

Kollias and Maniatis (2003) examined the case of Greece during 1962–1994. They calculated the rate of profit based on the methodology proposed in Shaikh and Tonak (1994), using the Greek National Accounts and Input-Output data. They employed an Autoregresive Distributed Lag (ARDL) model to investigate the relationship between milex and the rate of profit by controlling for unemployment rate, profit-wage ratio, and time trend. The basic difference from Georgiou's model is that they examine the effect of profit-wage ratio instead of the growth of nominal GDP. The profit-wage ratio behaves in the same way as the profit share. They find that, while milex has a positive effect on the profit rate in the short run, it has an inverse relationship in the long run in the case of Greece. They argue that, "given the small size of the domestic domestic military sector, and the negligible funds devoted to military R&D", milex's positive effect in the short run is due to the lagged impact on effective demand of military wages and salaries, which represents more than half the total defence budget (Kollias and Maniatis, 2003, pp. 123–124). On the other hand, they also argue that it is a drain of resources diverted to the purchase of "unreproductive" commodities, which slows down productivity growth, thereby reducing priobitability.

Dunne et al. (2013) examined the case of the U.S. for 1959–2010, adopting the model specification of Georgiou (1992) to examine the effect of unemployment, GDP, the time trend, and milex as a share of GDP. They used the updated rate of profit calculated by Bakir and Campbell (2006). Regarding GDP, they used both current and constant prices. They used OLS with some dynamic specification for comparison with Georgiou (1992). Regarding the OLS analysis, while milex has no significant effect on the rate of profit in the case of GDP with constant prices, the effect is significant and positive in the case of GDP with current prices, as Georgio (1992) found. The results are supported by the OLS with a dynamic specification. They argue that, while the evidence on the positive long-run relationship between the military burden and the profit rate is consistent with a Luxemburg-type story, the evidence of the positive effect of unemployment on the rate of profit is not that significant.

Recently, my co-author and I examined Turkey, which has one of the highest levels of milex (Elveren and Özgür, 2018) and is the sixth-largest arms importer. Its average ratio of milex to GDP during 1950–2008 rose as high as 3.58 percent.[1] As is the case in other countries, although there is a substantial literature on the effect of milex on economic growth (see Töngür and Elveren, 2016), there is no study of the relationship between milex and the profit rate in Turkey. To fill this gap, we investigated the possible relationship between milex and the profit rate in Turkey for 1950–2008, using both ARDL and a Markov-Switching autoregression model to determine a non-linear relationship between the variables in question. The effect of milex on profit rates was negative during turbulent years and positive in more tranquil years. Our findings also suggest that negative effects outweigh positive effects, but the probability of positive effects prevailing is larger. In other words, milex reduces the profit rate more during economic recessions but raises profitability at other times. These findings are evidence for the Marxist argument that milex helps overcome the fall in profit rates.

Finally, Ansari (2018) examined the role of government consumption expenditure and milex on the rate of profit in the case of the U.S. Using an ARDL model and covering the 1973–2015 period, he found a positive impact of milex on profitability for both the entire period and 1973–1993 specifically.

Data

This chapter uses the same data as in the analyses in Chapter 6. However, the time-series analysis allows for a few more alternative dependent variables to be added (e.g. profit rates) for some countries and to analyse a longer time period. Milex as a percentage of GDP is taken from the Stockholm International Peace Research Institute (SIPRI), the standard data set for milex. GDP data is taken from the Penn World Tables, namely output-side real GDP at chained PPPs in 2005 U.S. dollars. Data for unemployment rates are taken from the World Bank's World Development Indicators.

In addition to the Extended Penn World Tables and Penn World Tables, there are alternative calculations of profit rates, such as those by Esteban Maito for a few countries, by Michael Roberts for G-6 countries based on the Eurostat AMECO database, by Erdogan Bakir for the U.S., and by Benan Eres and Hakan Ongan for Turkey. The details of these calculations will be presented alongside discussion of the results.

Our PWT profit rate is calculated based on Roberts (2015), who uses net capital stock at constant prices (code: OKNDE), net national income at market prices (code: AUVNNE), nominal compensation of employees (code: AUWCDE), and GFCF price deflator (code: NLAPIGTE) according to the following formula:

$$\text{Profit rate} = (\text{AUVNNE-AUWCDE}) / \\ ((\text{OKNDE}^{\star}\text{NLAPIGTE})/100) + (\text{AUWCDE}))$$

The chapter analyses all the countries covered in Chapter 6 for different time periods, ranging from 1950 to 2016, namely Argentina, Australia, Austria, Belgium, Brazil, Canada, Chile, Denmark, Finland, France, Germany, Greece, Ireland, Israel, India, Italy, Japan, Luxembourg, Mexico, Netherlands, New Zealand, Norway, Portugal, South Africa, South Korea, Spain, Sweden, Switzerland, Turkey, the U.K., and the U.S.

Method

ARDL bounds testing approach

$$\pi_t = \beta_0 + \beta_1 T + \beta_2 M_t + \beta_3 G_t + \beta_4 U_t + \varepsilon_t \quad (1)$$

Where π = ln(profit), M = ln(milex), G = ln(GDP), U = ln(unemployment), and T is time. The β s are the long-run coefficients while ε_t is a white noise error term.

The first step of the bounds-testing approach is to estimate the following unrestricted error correction model using OLS (Pesaran et al., 2001):

$$\begin{aligned}\Delta\pi_t &= c + dT +_1 \varnothing\pi_{t-1} + \varnothing_2 M_{t-1} + \varnothing_3 G_{t-1} + \varnothing_4 U_{t-1} + \sum_{i=1}^{k} \varphi_{1,i}\Delta\pi_{t-1} \\ &+ \sum_{i=1}^{l} \varphi_{2,i}\Delta M_{t-1} + \sum_{i=1}^{m} \varphi_{3,i}\Delta G_{t-1} + \sum_{i=1}^{n} \varphi_{4,i}\Delta U_{t-1} + u_t\end{aligned} \quad (2)$$

Where $\varnothing$ are the long-run multipliers, c is a drift term, ϕ are the short-run coefficients, and u_t is a white noise error term.

The second step is to conduct an F-test on the joint hypothesis that the long-run multipliers of the lagged level variables are all equal to zero, against the alternative hypothesis that at least one long-run multiplier is non-zero. For each of the conventional significance levels, two sets of critical values are given for the lower and the upper bound. While the lower bound shows the critical values when all variables are assumed to be I(0), the upper bound assumes them to be I(1). If the F-statistic lies above the upper bound, the null hypothesis of no cointegration can be rejected. On the other hand, if it is below the lower bound, the null hypothesis is not rejected. If the F-statistic lies between the bounds, the result of the inference is inconclusive.

$$\begin{aligned}\pi_t &= \alpha_c + \alpha_d T + \sum_{i=1}^{k} \alpha_{1,i}\pi_{t-i} + \sum_{i=0}^{l} \alpha_{2,i} M_{t-i} \\ &+ \sum_{i=0}^{m} \alpha_{3,i} G_{t-i} + \sum_{i=0}^{n} \alpha_{4,i} U_{t-i} + w_t\end{aligned} \quad (3)$$

where w_t is an error term and k, l, m, and n are the lag lengths of the single variables.

$$\begin{aligned}\Delta\pi_t &= \theta_c + \theta_d \Delta T + \theta_{ect} ECT_{t-1} + \sum_{i=1}^{k} \theta_{1,i}\Delta\pi_{t-1} \\ &+ \sum_{i=1}^{l} \theta_{2,i}\Delta M_{t-i} + \sum_{i=1}^{m} \theta_{3,i}\Delta G_{t-i} + \sum_{i=1}^{n} \theta_{4,i}\Delta U_{t-i} + v_t\end{aligned} \quad (4)$$

where ECT_{t-1} is the resulting error correction term, and θ_{ect} is the coefficient that shows the percental annual correction of a deviation from the long-run equilibrium the year before.

Non-linear ARDL

Following from Equation (2), a non-linear ARDL model can be written as follows (Shin et al., 2013):

$$\begin{aligned}\Delta\pi_t &= c + dT + \varnothing_1\pi_{t-1} + \varnothing_2 M_{t-1}^{POS} + \varnothing_3 M_{t-1}^{NEG} \\ &+ \varnothing_4 G_{t-1} + \varnothing_5 U_{t-1} + \sum_{i=1}^{k} \varphi_{1,i}\Delta\pi_{t-1} + \sum_{i=1}^{l} \varphi_{2,i}\Delta M_{t-1}^{POS} \\ &+ \sum_{i=1}^{m} \varphi_{3,i}\Delta M_{t-1}^{NEG} + \sum_{i=1}^{n} \varphi_{4,i}\Delta G_{t-1} + \sum_{i=1}^{p} \varphi_{5,i}\Delta U_{t-1} + u_t\end{aligned} \tag{5}$$

Where $M^{POS} = \sum_{j=1}^{t} \max(\Delta M_j, 0)$ and $M^{NEG} = \sum_{j=1}^{t} \min(\Delta M_j, 0)$

Markov switching model

A Markov Switching Autoregression (MSAR) model allows us to investigate the variables that exhibit different patterns under different regimes. The model was introduced by Quandt (1972), and Goldfeld and Quandt (1973), and developed by Hamilton (1989). The model predicts regimes that cannot be observable. The random switches between the regimes are called Markov processes. The coefficients of variables and autocorrelation terms may change under these regimes. The MSAR model which captures all these properties is formed as:

$$y_t = \mu_t + x_t\alpha + z_t\beta_{s_t} + \sum_{i=1}^{p} \varphi_{i,s_t}(y_{t-i} - \mu_{s_{t-i}} - x_{t-i}\alpha + z_{t-i}\beta_{s_{t-i}}) + \varepsilon_{t,s} \tag{6}$$

Where y_t is dependent variable, μ_t is state invariant constant term, x_t is vector of exogenous variables with state invariant coefficients α, z_t, vector of exogenous variables with state-dependent coefficients β_{st}, $\phi_{i,st}$ is i[th] AR term in state s_t, and $\varepsilon_{t,s} \sim$ iid $N(0,\sigma_s^2)$ where σ_s^2 is state-dependent variance.

The number of regimes can be exogenously determined in the Markov switching models. In our particular model, the number of regimes is two. Thus, the probability transition matrix is as follows:

$$P = \begin{bmatrix} p_{11} & p_{12} \\ p_{21} & p_{22} \end{bmatrix} \tag{7}$$

where,

$$\sum_{i,j=1}^{2} p_{ij} = 1 \tag{8}$$

p_{11} is the probability of regime 1 to continue in the next period given that the process is already in regime 1. Similarly, p_{22} refers to the probability of regime 2 to continue in the next period. p_{12} and p_{21} reflect the probability of switching from one regime to another. By definition, the sum of $p_{11} + p_{12}$ or $p_{21} + p_{22}$ is equal to one as stated in equation (8).

Toda-Yamamoto method

As presented in Chapter 1, X is said to Granger-cause Y if Y can be better predicted using the lagged values of both X and Y than it can by using the lagged values of Y alone. Toda and Yamamoto (1995) introduced a method to address possible bias in the basic Granger causality approach due to model specification, lag selection, and the existence of the I(2) variable. In the Toda-Yamamoto procedure, the $(k + d_{max})^{th}$ order VAR models are estimated with the lagged d_{max} vector, which guarantees the asymptotic distribution of the Wald statistic. The lag length (k) and the maximum order of integration (d_{max}) for the variables in the system are determined in the following VAR setting:

$$profit = \mu + \sum_{i=1}^{k} \alpha_i profit_{t-i} + \sum_{j=k+1}^{d_{max}} \alpha_j profit_{t-j} + \sum_{i=1}^{k} \beta_i milex_{t-i} + \sum_{j=k+1}^{d_{max}} \beta_j milex_{t-j}$$
$$+ \sum_{i=1}^{k} \delta_i GDP_{t-i} + \sum_{j=k+1}^{d_{max}} \delta_j GDP_{t-j} + \sum_{i=1}^{k} \theta_i unemp_{t-i} + \sum_{j=k+1}^{d_{max}} \theta_j unemp_{t-j}$$

Results and discussion

Below are the results of two sets of analyses: for the U.S. and other countries. First, I discuss the results of the U.S. in detail, including the unit root test, and linear and non-linear ARDL procedure. Second, I will summarise the findings of other countries based on a linear ARDL analysis, providing the unit roots tests and the short-term results in the Appendix B.

Results for U.S.A.

Table 7.1 shows that the first difference of all variables is stationary. In other words, none of the variables is I(2), allowing us to proceed with the ARDL analysis. This finding is supported by Table 7.2, which shows possible breaks in the series.

As a part of the robustness check and to utilise the longest time range available, we conducted two sets of analysis as in the previous chapter: with and

Table 7.1 ADF unit root test results

Series	*Prob.*	*Lag*	*Obs*
D(GDP)	0.0000	0	65
D(MILEX)	0.0000	0	65
D(PROFIT1)	0.0000	0	65
D(PROFIT2)	0.0000	0	44
D(PROFIT3)	0.0000	0	63
D(PROFIT4)	0.0001	1	52
D(UNEMPLOYMENT)	0.0000	1	64

Table 7.2 Breakpoint unit root test results

Variables	*Breakpoint Unit Root Test*
First Differences	
ΔProfit1	−8.494***
ΔProfit2	−7.216***
ΔProfit3	−7.912***
ΔProfit4	−6.604***
ΔMilex	−9.283***
ΔGDP	−7.893***
ΔUnemployment	−8.045***

Note: *** refers to p<0.01

without unemployment. Table 7.3 presents the results of the ARDL Bounds Test, where the model specification includes unemployment. Profit1, Profit2, Profit3, and Profit4 are PWT, EPWT, Erdoğan Bakır's (2015), and Michael Roberts's (2015) (e.g. AMECO) calculations, respectively.

The table has four main parts: the short-run results, the long-run results, the major diagnostic tests, and the results of the Bounds Test. Functional form is tested by the Ramsey's Regression Specification Error Test. This shows if the second power of the fitted values from the original regression should be included. The null hypothesis is that the coefficients of the powers of the fitted values are all zero. Normality (i.e. if the residuals are normally distributed) is tested by the Jarque-Bera Test. Heteroscedasticity is tested by the Breusch-Pagan-Godfrey test, which is a Lagrange multiplier test of the null hypothesis of no heteroskedasticity. Finally, serial correlation (i.e. existence of the relationship between dependent variable and its lagged version), which is the most important issue for the robustness of the results, is tested by the Breusch-Godfrey LM test. The tests show that none of the models has serial correlation.

The bottom row of the table presents the Bounds Test F-Statistic and the lower bound, I(0), and upper bound, I(1), for the closest actual sample size, for 10, 5, and 1 percent significant levels. Since our sample sizes are relatively small, we preferred to use the results of actual sample size rather than asymptotic values. As noted above, if the F-statistic is below the lower bound, it can be concluded that there is no cointegration, whereas if the statistic is above the upper bound, the test suggests the existence of cointegration. If the statistic is between the lower and upper bound, it is inconclusive. The Bound Test results suggest that there is cointegration at 1 percent significance level for each model.

Regarding the short-run results, the table shows, as expected, that the lagged value of profit rate is highly significant and positive in all models. While GDP has a positive effect on the rate of profit, the lagged value of GDP has a negative effect. Similarly, except for Profit2, higher unemployment increases the profit

Table 7.3 Results of ARDL bounds test (with unemployment)

USA	*Profit1* *1951–2014* *ARDL* *(1, 0, 1, 1)*	*Profit2* *1964–2008* *ARDL* *(1, 0, 1, 0)*	*Profit3* *1951–2016* *ARDL* *(1, 0, 1, 1)*	*Profit4* *1961–2014* *ARDL* *(1, 0, 1, 1)*
Short-Run Coefficients				
Profit (−1)	0.823***	0.703***	0.727***	0.816***
	(0.062)	(0.079)	(0.079)	(0.075)
Milex	0.021	−0.002	0.113*	0.0007
	(0.014)	(0.021)	(0.067)	(0.019)
GDP	1.764***	0.665***	4.602***	1.895***
	(0.197)	(0.220)	(0.887)	(0.307)
GDP (−1)	−1.856***	−1.264***	−4.865***	−2.301***
	(0.201)	(0.167)	(0.910)	(0.292)
Unemployment	0.161***	−0.007	0.326***	0.099**
	(0.025)	(0.026)	(0.109)	(0.046)
Unemployment	−0.124***		−0.252**	−0.111***
(−1)	(0.024)		(0.109)	(0.039)
Trend	0.003**	0.017***	0.012**	0.014***
	(0.001)	(0.005)	(0.005)	(0.003)
Intercept	1.591**	9.890***	3.758	6.265***
	(0.736)	(2.944)	(2.944)	(1.876)
Long-Run Coefficients				
Milex	0.120	−0.008	0.417*	0.004
	(0.094)	(0.072)	(0.247)	(0.104)
GDP	−0.521	−2.021***	−0.965	−2.215***
	(0.339)	(0.692)	(0.809)	(0.636)
Unemployment	0.207*	−0.026	0.272	−0.065
	(0.114)	(0.082)	(0.205)	(0.144)
Trend	0.021*	0.058***	0.046*	0.080***
	(0.011)	(0.021)	(0.025)	(0.020)
R-squared	0.870	0.954	0.775	0.982
SER	0.016	0.021	0.076	0.020
Serial correlation	0.032	1.638	1.218	2.252
	[0.856]	[0.208]	[0.303]	[0.140]
Functional form	2.216	0.018	4.921	4.828
	[0.118]	[0.891]	[0.030]	[0.033]
Normality	2.439	41.740	20.187	6.920
	[0.295]	[0.0000]	[0.0000]	[0.031]
Heteroscedasticity	0.311	0.907	1.218	1.270
	[0.945]	[0.500]	[0.181]	[0.286]
Bounds Test	18.198***	8.587***	8.717***	16.727***
F-Statistic	10% 3.12 3.94	10% 3.22 4.05	10% 3.12 3.94	10% 3.13 3.95
Actual Sample Size	5% 3.62 4.53	5% 3.82 4.71	5% 3.62 4.53	5% 3.69 4.58
	1% 4.84 5.84	1% 5.15 6.28	1% 4.84 5.84	1% 4.99 6.01

Note: Standard errors in parentheses, probabilities in brackets. ***, **, and * refer to $p<0.01$, $p<0.05$, $p<0.1$, respectively.

rate in the short run. The table also shows that, except for the case of Profit3, there is no significant relationship between milex and the rate of profit.

Regarding the long-run results, the most important result is that milex has a positive sign in three out of four specifications, with only one significant at the 10 percent level. It is safe to consider this as strong evidence because different measures of the profit rates do not change the positive sign. This positive effect of milex on the rate of profit supports Luxemburg's view that milex is an important stimulant of capital accumulation. However, the findings on the effect of unemployment on the rate of profit are not strong, with only one out of four specifications having a significant (only at 10 percent) positive sign.[2]

Because the model specifications have a time trend, the GDP coefficient is interpreted in terms of its deviation from the trend. The negative coefficient suggests that profits are counter-cyclical, which might be the case if workers can increase their share in the boom and the capital-output ratio is constant. All models show the same findings, although only two of them are significant. Finally, all model specifications yield a significant positive effect of the time trend, suggesting no tendency for the profit rate to fall.

Table 7.4 shows the results for the case without unemployment, which are highly similar to the results of Table 7.3 with unemployment. This supports our findings in that results are not sensitive to the model specification.

Table 7.5 below shows the results for the post-1980 period. Compared to the results in Table 7.3, the key finding is that, although milex has a positive effect in the three models, the only significant coefficient has a negative sign. This suggests that milex more likely has had no positive impact on the rate of profit in the post-1980 period.

Finally, we repeated the same analyses (with and without unemployment) to investigate the non-linear relationship between milex and the rate of profit. It is important to see if milex has a different effect when it increases or decreases. Since the long-term relationship is important in this particular analysis, the tables only present the long-run results, along with the major diagnostic tests and the Bounds Test as before.

Table 7.6 shows that the results for the effect of GDP are the same. However, in the case of unemployment, the table presents a stronger positive effect on the rate of profit compared to the linear case. Here three rather than two of the four model specifications have a positive sign, and two rather than one are significant at the 10 percent level. This is some more supportive evidence for Luxemburg's view on the role of milex in general and the reserve army of unemployed specifically. Regarding the key variable, milex, Table 7.6 allows us to see how it affects the rate of profit when it decreases or increases. The results are highly mixed and not significant. Therefore, it is safe to focus on the case of Profit3, where only milex-negative is significant. Accordingly, the negative sign of milex-positive means that as milex increases, the rate of profit declines, and the positive sign of milex-negative means that as milex declines it reduces the

Table 7.4 Results of ARDL bounds test (without unemployment)

USA	*Profit1* *1952–2014* *ARDL (2, 1, 2)*	*Profit2* *1965–2008* *ARDL (2, 0, 2)*	*Profit3* *1951–2016* *ARDL (1, 1, 1)*	*Profit4* *1963–2014* *ARDL (3, 2, 3)*
Short-Run Coefficients				
Profit (−1)	1.006***	0.455***	0.612***	1.205***
	(0.122)	(0.159)	(0.072)	(0.155)
Profit (−2)	−0.187*	0.246*		−0.701***
	(0.094)	(0.130)		(0.231)
Profit (−3)				0.375**
				(0.143)
Milex	−0.043	−0.005	−0.052	−0.084
	(0.031)	(0.020)	(0.103)	(0.053)
Milex (−1)	0.054*		0.187**	0.159*
	(0.032)		(0.084)	(0.089)
Milex (−2)				−0.095*
				(0.053)
GDP	0.700***	0.614***	2.660***	1.228***
	(0.123)	(0.201)	(0.485)	(0.162)
GDP (−1)	−1.394***	−1.045***	−2.845***	−2.039***
	(0.175)	(0.273)	(0.465)	(0.281)
GDP (−2)	0.674***	−0.380		0.984**
	(0.161)	(0.276)		(0.409)
GDP (−3)				−0.509*
				(0.294)
Trend	0.0007	0.023***	0.010*	0.011***
	(0.001)	(0.006)	(0.005)	(0.003)
Intercept	0.688	13.017***	2.964	5.182***
	(0.876)	(3.284)	(2.980)	(1.782)
Long-Run Coefficients				
Milex	0.059	−0.016	0.349*	−0.171
	(0.095)	(0.069)	(0.094)	(0.184)
GDP	−0.107	−2.721***	−0.478	−2.798**
	(0.323)	(0.899)	(0.531)	(1.104)
Trend	0.004	0.080***	0.026*	0.096***
	(0.009)	(0.027)	(0.015)	(0.033)
R-squared	0.845	0.952	0.755	0.984
SER	0.018	0.020	0.078	0.019
Serial correlation	1.689	0.729	0.170	1.969
	[0.194]	[0.489]	[0.681]	[0.135]
Functional form	5.062	0.011	8.359	8.629
	[0.028]	[0.916]	[0.005]	[0.005]
Normality	0.128	50.171	1.719	9.378
	[0.937]	[0.0000]	[0.423]	[0.009]
Heteroscedasticity	0.989	0.699	0.822	0.235
	[0.454]	[0.671]	[0.557]	[0.993]
Bounds Test	1.827	7.051***	9.200***	3.396
F-Statistic	10% 3.53 4.20	10% 3.62 4.33	10% 3.53 4.20	10% 3.57 4.28
Actual Sample Size	5% 4.12 4.90	5% 4.33 5.07	5% 4.12 4.90	5% 4.22 5.03
	1% 5.54 6.45	1% 5.87 6.87	1% 5.54 6.45	1% 5.80 6.79

Note: Standard errors in parentheses, probabilities in brackets. ***, **, * refer to $p<0.01$, $p<0.05$, and $p<0.1$, respectively.

Table 7.5 Results of ARDL bounds test (post-1980)

USA	*Profit1 1980–2014 ARDL (1, 1, 1, 1)*	*Profit2 1980–2008 ARDL (1, 1, 1, 0)*	*Profit3 1980–2016 ARDL (1, 0, 0, 1)*	*Profit4 1980–2014 ARDL (1, 0, 1, 0)*
Short-Run Coefficients				
Profit (−1)	0.729***	0.641***	0.288*	0.549***
	(0.094)	(0.130)	(0.142)	(0.118)
Milex	−0.148**	−0.104	0.054	−0.062**
	(0.064)	(0.070)	(0.094)	(0.024)
Milex (−1)	0.161**	0.113		
	(0.059)	(0.068)		
GDP	1.759***	0.682*	0.218	1.675***
	(0.307)	(0.367)	(0.440)	(0.239)
GDP (−1)	−1.600***	−1.312***		−1.597***
	(0.399)	(0.242)		(0.174)
Unemployment	0.213***	−0.003	−0.350***	0.061
	(0.047)	(0.073)	(0.119)	(0.040)
Unemployment (−1)	−0.140**		0.456***	
	(0.057)		(0.092)	
Trend	−0.003	0.018	0.0002	0.003
	(0.006)	(0.012)	(0.012)	(0.005)
Intercept	−1.955	10.515	−2.532	−0.488
	(3.293)	(6.990)	(6.795)	(2.597)
Long-Run Coefficients				
Milex	0.049	0.023	0.076	−0.138**
	(0.094)	(0.073)	(0.129)	(0.061)
GDP	0.586	−1.758	0.306	0.172
	(0.812)	(1.119)	(0.643)	(0.381)
Unemployment	0.267	−0.008	0.149	0.137
	(0.176)	(0.202)	(0.168)	(0.114)
Trend	−0.013	0.051	0.0004	0.008
	(0.022)	(0.032)	(0.017)	(0.010)
R-squared	0.885	0.924	0.758	0.985
SER	0.016	0.018	0.070	0.019
Serial correlation	0.148	0.0007	0.0007	0.341
	[0.703]	[0.978]	[0.977]	[0.564]
Functional form	0.175	0.016	0.433	0.613
	[0.678]	[0.898]	[0.515]	[0.440]
Normality	0.956	6.736	1.815	3.782
	[0.619]	[0.034]	[0.403]	[0.150]
Heteroscedasticity	0.687	0.616	2.146	1.260
	[0.698]	[0.736]	[0.077]	[0.307]
Bounds Test	9.605***	8.825***	8.026***	12.375***
F-Statistic	10% 3.29 4.17	10% 3.37 4.27	10% 3.29 4.17	10% 3.29 4.17
Actual Sample Size	5% 3.93 4.91	5% 4.04 5.09	5% 3.93 4.91	5% 3.93 4.91
	1% 5.65 6.92	1% 5.66 6.98	1% 5.65 6.92	1% 5.65 6.92

Note: Standard errors in parentheses, probabilities in brackets. ***, **, * refer to $p<0.01$, $p<0.05$, and $p<0.1$, respectively.

Table 7.6 Long-term results of non-linear ARDL (with unemployment)

USA	*Profit1* *1951–2014* *ARDL* *(1, 0, 0, 1, 1)*	*Profit2* *1965–2008* *ARDL* *(2, 0, 1, 1, 2)*	*Profit3* *1950–2016* *ARDL* *(1, 1, 1, 1, 0)*	*Profit4* *1961–2014* *ARDL* *(1, 0, 0, 1, 1)*
Long-Run Coefficients				
Milex-Positive	0.173	−0.216	−1.004	0.378
	(0.228)	(0.267)	(0.629)	(0.403)
Milex-Negative	0.076	0.160	1.227**	−0.294
	(0.191)	(0.247)	(0.501)	(0.321)
GDP	−0.549	−2.262***	−0.136	−2.596***
	(0.363)	(0.824)	(0.636)	(0.870)
Unemployment	0.203*	0.041	0.283*	−0.097
	(0.115)	(0.118)	(0.164)	(0.142)
Trend	0.018	0.076**	0.078**	0.073***
	(0.013)	(0.030)	(0.030)	(0.020)
R-squared	0.870	0.958	0.808	0.982
SER	0.016	0.020	0.071	0.020
Serial correlation	0.030	0.326	1.144	1.934
	[0.861]	[0.723]	[0.705]	[0.171]
Functional form	3.639	1.100	2.727	5.309
	[0.061]	[0.302]	[0.104]	[0.026]
Normality	2.312	25.365	9.180	5.869
	[0.314]	[0.0000]	[0.010]	[0.053]
Heteroscedasticity	0.773	0.854	1.859	1.288
	[0.627]	[0.590]	[0.078]	[0.273]
Bounds Test	14.924***	6.783***	8.661***	14.238***
F-Statistics	10% 2.84 3.74	10% 2.95 3.86	10% 2.84 3.74	10% 2.86 3.78
Actual Sample Size	5% 3.30 4.28	5% 3.47 4.47	5% 3.3 4.28	5% 3.35 4.36
	1% 4.34 5.55	1% 4.62 5.86	1% 4.34 5.55	1% 4.45 5.61

Note: Standard errors in parentheses, probabilities in brackets. ***, **. * refer to $p<0.01$, $p<0.05$, $p<0.1$, respectively.

rate of profit as well. The results for the case without unemployment presented in Table 7.7 are very similar.

Additionally, we estimated an MSAR model as outlined above. The model includes *profit1* and *milex*. The estimation also includes the state-dependent first order autoregressive term, AR(1). The model specification is determined according to the Schwarz's Bayesian Information Criterion (SBIC). Table 7.8 shows the results of the MSAR model.

The results show that the model has a very high explanatory power, and milex is statistically significant at 1 percent. Milex and AR(1) are the state-dependent variables. AR(1) term is statistically significant and has a positive sign in both regimes. There is a negative relationship between milex and profit rates in regime 1, whereas the effect of milex on profit rates is positive in regime 2.

Table 7.7 Results of non-linear ARDL bounds test (without unemployment)

USA	*Profit1* *1952–2014* *ARDL* *(2, 0, 1, 2)*	*Profit2* *1965–2008* *ARDL* *(2, 0, 1, 2)*	*Profit3* *1952–2016* *ARDL* *(1, 1, 1, 1)*	*Profit4* *1963–2014* *ARDL* *(3, 0, 2, 3)*
Long-Run Coefficients				
Milex-Positive	−0.197	−0.190	−0.619	0.494
	(0.266)	(0.224)	(0.496)	(0.736)
Milex-Negative	0.241	0.163	0.941**	−0.647
	(0.224)	(0.185)	(0.399)	(0.717)
GDP	0.056	−2.415***	−0.202	−3.454*
	(0.319)	(0.809)	(0.543)	(1.873)
Trend	0.011	0.081***	0.061**	0.085**
	(0.012)	(0.027)	(0.023)	(0.036)
R-squared	0.848	0.955	0.791	0.985
SER	0.018	0.020	0.073	0.019
Serial correlation	0.752	0.169	0.103	2.023
	[0.476]	[0.844]	[0.749]	[0.128]
Functional form	4.391	0.001	5.732	8.457
	[0.041]	[0.978]	[0.020]	[0.006]
Normality	0.564	43.585	1.324	10.913
	[0.754]	[0.0000]	[0.515]	[0.004]
Heteroscedasticity	0.964	0.693	1.821	0.226
	[0.479]	[0.709]	[0.092]	[0.995]
Bounds Test	1.708	5.953**	8.742***	2.635
F-Statistics	10% 3.12 3.94	10% 3.22 4.05	10% 3.12 3.94	10% 3.17 4.00
Actual Sample Size	5% 3.62 4.53	5% 3.82 4.71	5% 3.62 4.53	5% 3.73 4.66
	1% 4.84 5.84	1% 5.15 6.28	1% 4.84 5.84	1% 5.05 6.18

Note: Standard errors in parentheses, probabilities in brackets. ***, **. * refer to p<0.01, p<0.05, p<0.1, respectively.

Table 7.8 Results of MSAR model

d(profit1)	*Regime 1*	*Regime 2*
	Coefficient	*Coefficient*
d(milex)	−0.103***	0.065***
	(0.029)	(0.022)
AR(1)	1.184***	0.731***
	(0.081)	(0.077)
Intercept	−1.696**	2.604***
	(0.837)	(0.812)
R-squared	0.954	0.7766

Note: Standard errors in parentheses, probabilities in brackets. ***, **. * refer to p<0.01, p<0.05, p<0.1, respectively.

Table 7.9 Transition probabilities and expected duration

	Trans. Probabilities	
Regime 1	P_{11}	0.255
	P_{12}	0.744
Regime 2	P_{21}	0.225
	P_{22}	0.774

The analysis allows us to see the probabilities of these regimes occurring. The transition probabilities of the regimes are given in Table 7.9 below. The probability of a process that started in regime 1 to stay in regime 1 is 0.255 and to switch to regime 2 is 0.744. These probabilities show that the expected duration of regime 1 is shorter than that of regime 2. Similarly, the probability of a regime 2 process remaining is 0.774 and switching to regime 1 is 0.225. That is, the findings in Table 7.9 suggest that milex has a positive impact on profit rates in most years and a negative impact occurs in few years.

Summary of the long-term results of all countries

Table 7.10 summarises the long-term results when the dependent variable is the profit rate based on the Penn World Table. The complete tables are provided in the Appendix B. Overall, milex and unemployment have a significant effect on the rate of profit in about one third of countries. While milex has a positive sign in 11 and a negative sign in 17 countries in Model 1 with unemployment, it has a positive sign in 18 and a negative sign in 12 countries in the case of the model specification without unemployment in Model 2. Regarding Model 1, milex has a significant sign in 9 out of 28 countries: 4 are positive while 5 are negative; regarding Model 2, milex has a significant sign in only 7 out of 30 countries: 2 are positive while 5 are negative. The results are much clearer in the case of unemployment in Model 1, with 22 positive signs versus only 6 negative signs. Although only 8 out of those positive signs were significant, this is still very strong evidence for the reserve army of the unemployed. Turning to the role of countries in the arms trade, the findings suggest that milex is more likely to have a negative impact in the case of arms-importing countries, although the evidence is not very strong.

Table 7.11 summarises the long-term results when the dependent variable is the profit rate taken from EPWT. The results are very similar in terms of the distribution of positive and negative signs for both unemployment and milex. However, it is worth noting that milex has a more strongly significant effect on the rate of profit in Model 2, as 11 countries out of 28 have significant signs, with 4 positive and 7 negative.

Overall, considering Table 7.10 and Table 7.11 together, it is safe to argue that a negative effect is more likely to be observed, regardless of which rate of profit is used or the role of each country in the arms trade. Milex has a positive

Table 7.10 Summary of long-term results (dependent variable: PWT)

Countries	*Model 1: With Unemployment*				*Model 2: Without Unemployment*		
	Milex	*GDP*	*Unemp*	*Trend*	*Milex*	*GDP*	*Trend*
Argentina	−0.256**	0.188	−0.131**	−0.018*	−0.508*	0.026	−0.111
Australia	1.093*	5.179**	0.291**	−0.173**	0.071	−0.754	0.033*
Austria	−1.176	1.907	0.280	−0.098	−0.619*	0.202	−0.027
Belgium	−0.404	−0.469	0.478	−0.010	0.596	0.037	0.009
Brazil	0.206**	0.359*	0.109**	−0.042***	−0.074	−0.351	−0.011
Canada	−0.757***	−1.006**	0.072	0.017	−0.427**	−0.666	0.013
Chile	−0.085	0.264***	0.080	−0.031***	0.029	0.130	−0.022***
Denmark	0.964	0.316	0.071	0.003	0.733	−0.615	0.022
Finland	−0.805**	−1.699	0.182	0.043	−0.406*	−1.470***	0.045***
France	−2.010***	−1.912***	0.601***	−0.007	4.404	−1.991	−0.028
Germany	−0.642*	−0.047	0.067	−0.018	−0.549***	−0.188	−0.007
Greece	NA	NA	NA	NA	0.250	−0.514	0.013
Indonesia	−2.127	0.553	2.102**	−0.247**	−0.056	2.614	−0.191
Ireland	NA	NA	NA	NA	0.004	0.258	−0.022
Israel	0.009	−0.171	−0.193***	0.009	−0.268	−1.188*	0.050
Japan	−0.099	0.037	0.372**	−0.016***	0.078	0.188**	−0.015***
Luxembourg	0.428	0.349	−0.071	0.002	0.054	0.705***	−0.024***
Mexico	−0.433	−0.335	0.037	0.003	0.036	0.184	−0.007
Netherlands	−1.812	−0.314	0.036	−0.031	0.034	−0.302	0.019
N. Zealand	2.132*	4.766**	0.092	−0.103**	0.742	0.568	−0.007
Norway	−0.954	0.013	0.390*	−0.019	−0.226	0.045	0.002
Portugal	0.042	0.290	−0.042	−0.026	0.163**	0.398**	−0.030***
S. Africa	−0.052	−3.899	0.832	0.064	0.879	−4.802	0.158
S. Korea	0.739*	0.648	0.354	−0.028	0.456*	0.189	−0.007
Spain	0.376	−0.283	−0.143	0.009	−0.007	−0.176	−0.006
Sweden	0.042	2.064***	0.068	−0.061**	0.364	−0.842	0.027
Switzerland	−0.099	−0.638	0.050	0.011	0.848	−1.932	0.069
Turkey	−0.109	−0.370**	−0.003	0.011	−0.049	−0.284	0.008
U.K.	−0.427	1.401**	0.327***	-0.063***	-4.892	−14.971	0.218
U.S.	0.120	−0.521	0.207*	0.021*	0.059	−0.107	0.004

effect on the rate of profit in Australia, Brazil, Israel, Italy, and New Zealand, whereas the opposite is true for Argentina, Austria, Canada, Finland, France, Germany, Ireland, and Norway. On the other hand, Portugal and South Korea show ambiguous effects, with both positive and negative effects for different profit rates.

In the case of the existence of I(2) variables, we followed the Toda-Yamamoto procedure to analyse the relationship between milex and the rate of profit. The results of those analyses are presented in the Appendix C. In the case of Greece, out of four model specifications (two different profit rates with and without unemployment), causality runs from profit to milex in one case and from milex to profit rate in the other. In India, the results suggest causality runs from profit to milex, whereas there is a strong causality from milex to the profit rate for Italy in one of the two models.

Table 7.11 Summary of long-term results (dependent variable: EPWT)

Countries	*Model 1: With Unemployment*				*Model 2: Without Unemployment*		
	Milex	*GDP*	*Unemp*	*Trend*	*Milex*	*GDP*	*Trend*
Australia	−0.959	−4.375	0.198	0.145	−0.452	−5.949**	0.204**
Austria	−0.998***	−0.863***	0.113**	0.008	−0.846***	−2.218***	0.062***
Belgium	−0.177	1.587***	0.091	0.035***	−0.004	−1.172***	0.031***
Brazil	−0.654	0.865	−0.725	−0.026	0.168	−0.756	0.039
Canada	0.388***	−1.809***	0.183**	0.041**	−0.200***	−0.752***	0.016**
Chile	0.381	−1.554***	−0.443	0.071**	0.264	−1.242**	0.042**
Denmark	1.138	−0.693	0.038	0.024	0.643	−1.247**	0.035***
Finland	−0.335	−1.510	0.166	0.050*	−0.444	−1.932***	0.071***
France	0.140	−0.910***	0.091*	0.025***	0.378	−0.849***	0.031***
Germany	−0.323	18.414	−0.465	−0.612	−6.693	134.101	−4.787
Ireland	NA	NA	NA	NA	−0.972**	−3.031	0.151
Israel	0.234*	−1.474***	0.141	0.074***	0.343***	−1.444***	0.079***
Italy	1.344**	1.309	0.153	−0.018	1.560*	1.580	−0.032
Japan	−0.488	−0.891***	0.025	0.029***	−0.497	−0.887***	0.030***
Luxembourg	0.561**	−0.356	−0.079	0.044***	−0.294*	−0.556*	0.030***
Mexico	−1.221	−1.273	0.470	0.013	−0.533	−0.535*	0.014*
Netherlands	0.019	−0.414***	0.014	0.021***	0.088	−0.503***	0.026***
New Zealand	0.645*	1.790***	0.095**	−0.045**	1.689***	0.813	0.007
Norway	−1.046***	−0.627	0.257*	0.012	−0.058	−0.371	0.033**
Portugal	−0.678	−2.709	−0.037	0.076	−0.587*	−1.482**	0.032
S. Africa	−0.038	−0.702*	0.019	0.034**	−0.071	−1.309***	0.045***
S. Korea	−1.054***	0.062	0.319**	−0.078***	−0.481***	0.122	−0.062***
Spain	0.377	−1.087***	−0.070**	0.045***	0.053	−1.188***	0.040***
Sweden	0.313	−1.524	0.188*	0.047	0.463	−2.426	0.083
Switzerland	−0.213	−0.991	−0.005	0.010	−0.192*	−0.639**	0.002
U.K.	0.500	−0.038	0.232	0.014	0.687**	−0.879	0.043**
U.S.	−0.008	−2.021***	−0.026	0.058***	−0.016	−2.721***	0.080***

Conclusion

The goal of this chapter was to provide additional evidence to support the findings from the panel analyses discussed in the previous chapter. Employing ARDL Bounds Testing, non-linear ARDL, and the Toda-Yamamoto Granger causality methods, the chapter provided a complementary analysis of the effect of milex on the rate of profit for 31 countries for different time periods ranging from 1950 to 2016.

The chapter presented a full analysis of the U.S. and summarised the long-term results from 30 other countries. Regarding the U.S., the basic ARDL analysis for the whole period provided evidence, though not very strong, that milex is an important stimulant of capital accumulation. Regarding the post-1980 period, on the other hand, the findings suggest that milex is more likely to have an insignificant or negative impact. This is in line with the findings presented in Chapter 6 and in other panel data studies (Elveren and Hsu, 2016,

2018). The findings of the non-linear analysis, however, are not significant. For both analyses, linear and non-linear, the results are similar with respect to different model specifications (i.e. with or without unemployment).

Regarding the other major countries, the overall results are very similar for different profit variables (i.e. EPWT and PWT). In more than one third of countries, milex has a significant effect on the rate of profit. Thus, milex is more likely to have a negative than positive effect on the rate of profit, and milex is more likely to have a negative impact in arms-importing countries. For all countries, including the U.S., there is a very strong supportive evidence for the reserve army of unemployed.

Notes

1 The authors note that the ratio is high due to the low-intensity conflict in southeastern Turkey, Greek militarisation, aggressive military modernisation programmes, the effect of terrorism and wars in the Middle East, and NATO membership (Elveren and Özgür, 2018, p. 1).

2 In fact, in the case of profit1 in Table 7.3, the bounds test shows that there is a long-run relationship, but the long-run coefficients are not significant at the 5 percent level. The joint rejection of the null of zero individual coefficients suggests that variables are correlated. The same situation occurs in other analyses in the case of profit1 in Tables 7.4–7.7.

References

Ansari, S. (2018). US fiscal policy, manufacturing stagnation, and the shift to financialization in the era of globalization: An econometric analysis, 1973–2015. *Review of Political Economy*, 30(4), pp. 595–614. doi:10.1080/09538259.2018.1504388

Bakir, E. (2015). Capital accumulation, profitability, and crisis: Neoliberalism in the United States. *Review of Radical Political Economics*, 47(3), pp. 389–411.

Bakir, E. and Campbell, A. (2006). The effect of neoliberalism on the fall in the rate of profit in business cycles. *Review of Radical Political Economics*, 38(3), pp. 365–373.

Dunne, P., Pieroni, L. and D'Agostino, G. (2013). *Military spending and the falling rate of profit in the US*. Available at: www.sipri.org/research/armaments/milex/ICES2013/papers/archive/dunne-pieroni-agostino-milex-falling-rate-of-profit-in-usa

Elveren, A. Y. and Hsu, S. (2016). Military expenditures and profit rates: Evidence from OECD countries. *Metroeconomica*, 67(3), pp. 551–577.

Elveren, A.Y. and Hsu, S. (2018). The effect of military expenditure on profit rates: Evidence from major countries. *World Journal of Applied Economics*, 4(2), pp. 75–94.

Elveren, A.Y. and Özgür, G. (2018). *The effect of military expenditures on the profit rates in Turkey*. MPRA Paper 88848, University Library of Munich, Germany.

Georgiou, G. (1992). Military expenditure and the rate of profit: Some empirical results. *International Review of Applied Economics*, 16(3), pp. 344–361.

Goldfeld, S. M. and Quandt, R. E. (1973). A Markov model for switching regressions. *Journal of Econometrics*, 1(1), pp. 3–15.

Hamilton, J. D. (1989). A new approach to the economic analysis of nonstationary time series and the business cycle. *Econometrica*, 57(2), pp. 357–384.

Hill, T. P. (1979). *Profits and rates of return*. Paris: OECD.

Kollias, C. and Maniatis, T. (2003). Military expenditure and the profit rate in Greece. *Defence and Peace Economics*, 14(2), pp. 117–127.

OECD. (2001). *Measuring capital – OECD manual measurement of capital stocks, consumption of fixed capital and capital services*. Paris: OECD.

Pesaran, M. H., Shin, Y. and Smith, R. J. (2001). Bounds testing approaches to the analysis of level relationships. *Journal of Applied Econometrics*, 16, pp. 289–326.

Quandt, R. E. (1972). A new approach to estimating switching regressions. *Journal of the American Statistical Association*, 67(338), pp. 306–310.

Roberts, M. (2015). Revisiting a world rate of profit. *Paper for the 2015 conference of the association of heterodox economists*, Southampton Solent University July 2015.

Shaikh, A. and Tonak, E. A. (1994). *The political economy of national accounts: An alternate approach to the measurement of the wealth of nations*. New York: Cambridge University Press.

Shin, Y., Yu, B. and Greenwood-Nimmo, M. (2013). *Modelling asymmetric cointegration and dynamic multipliers in a nonlinear ARDL framework*. Festschrift: Springer.

Toda, H.Y. and Yamamoto, T. (1995). Statistical inference in vector autoregressions with possibly integrated processes. *Journal of Econometrics*, 66(1–2), pp. 225–250.

Töngür, Ü. and Elveren, A.Y. (2016). The impact of military spending and income inequality on economic growth in Turkey. *Defence and Peace Economics*, 27(3), pp. 433–452.

8 Conclusion

The main goal of this book was to investigate theoretically and empirically the effect of milex on the rate of profit from a Marxist perspective. Although there is an ever-growing empirical literature on the effect of milex on economic growth in the defence and peace economics, very few works have examined the role of milex in the capitalist economy with special attention to its effect on profit rates.

There are three main strategic and economic motives for milex in capitalist systems (Smith and Smith, 1983). First, capitalist states must protect the international capitalist system from external threats, such as communism or radical Islamic terrorism. Second, military power is the main tool for the core countries to sustain their hegemony over peripheral capitalist countries and to regulate rivalries between themselves. Third, military power is used against internal threats to protect the social order. In terms of the direct economic role of milex, one group argues that milex helps to maintain full employment and boosts economic growth and profit rates due to its surplus-absorbing function. The other view claims that other government spending could generate similar growth and employment performance; therefore, the motive for high milex is simply political – so strategic reasons matter, not economic ones. This book focused on a specific question within this framework: How strong is the surplus-absorbing function of milex? In other words, does milex actually counteract the tendency of the rate of profit to fall?

Chapter 2: Economic models of the military expenditure-growth nexus

The chapter had two goals: to present the major economic models explaining the effect of milex on economic growth and to summarise the findings of the associated literature. Although the core task of the defence economics literature is to assess the effect of milex on the economy (of which the effect on economic growth is the most popular), this book focused on its effect on the rate of profit. In fact, there is a significant relationship between economic growth and the rate of profit, as the findings of this book revealed. Therefore, it is important to assess the various short- and long-run effects of milex on economic growth. In the short run, the main effect is substitution between milex and other government spending. In the long run, the effect on economic growth is more diverse, including labour, capital, technology, debt, politics, society, external relations, and conflicts. Based on this theoretical background, using time-series, cross-sectional, or panel data, empirical studies have investigated how milex affects economic growth, either positively by boosting aggregate demand or negatively by crowding out public and private investments. The first part of Chapter 2 briefly presented the different econometric models adopted in these studies, such as the Feder-Ram model (Feder, 1983; Biswas and Ram, 1986), the Deger-Smith model (Deger and Smith, 1983; Deger, 1986), the augmented Solow-Swan growth model (Mankiw et al., 1992), the endogenous growth model (Barro, 1990), the new macroeconomic model (Romer, 2000; Taylor, 2000), and the causality approach. The second part of the chapter summarised the findings of the ever-growing literature since the seminal work of Benoit (1973, 1978). While Benoit concluded that milex has a positive effect on economic growth, later studies have provided conflicting results due to different model specifications (e.g. how the functional form is determined and how milex is measured), simultaneity problems, choices of time period (for example Cold War versus post–Cold War), country (e.g. developed versus developing), and whether non-linearity has been taken into account. Overall, however, it's worth noting that recent studies using more advanced methods have been more likely to suggest a negative impact.

Chapter 3: Military Keynesianism and the military-industrial complex

Chapter 3 addressed the positive effect of milex on economic growth associated with Military Keynesianism, which is the policy of using milex as a countercyclical economic tool. The chapter also examined the Military-Industrial Complex (MIC) in detail as a coalition of vested interests within the military and its industrial suppliers. This symbiotic coalition promotes bureaucratic over national needs by increasing milex. While Military Keynesianism considers milex as simply a part of government spending, providing no clear theory, the MIC with a substantial institutional view successfully explains the dynamics of milex from a long-run perspective.

The great 'success' of the war economy during WWII in terms of boosting business and creating full employment led to a broad ideological consensus by the 1950s that milex can be used as a "means for governmental control of the economy" (Melman, 1974, p. 16). The core principle of Military Keynesianism is that this kind of economy is both sustainable and required to promote growth. There were two similar views within Marxist thought explaining the positive impact of milex on economic performance. Baran and Sweezy's (1966) view of underconsumption suggests that milex prevents the realisation crisis by absorbing the surplus in the economy without increasing its productivity capacity. This is the key difference between milex and other types of government spending. The other view, the permanent arms economy, promoted by Michael Kidron, argues that milex prevents the economy from overheating (Kidron, 1970). Both theories emphasise why milex performs better than civilian government expenditure. (Chapter 5 developed this discussion.) The liberal school, on the other hand, argues for the negative impact of milex. Seymour Melman, the prominent figure of this view, showed that milex has a negative effect because the military sector creates economic inefficiencies by crowding out productive civilian investment (Melman, 1970, 1974; Rosen, 1973; Kaldor, 1981; Dumas, 1986). However, their criticisms are based on a suggestive empirical relationship between milex and labour productivity, balance of payments, and inflation, rather than a sophisticated theory.

During the interwar period, the MIC expanded by providing jobs to subcontractors of giant corporations in the arms industry and by supporting non-military firms (Duncan and Coyne, 2013). As a massive and politically powerful network with state authority, it has gained immense political support. The symbiotic coalition between the arms industry and the military service has become the key determinant of level of milex. Chapter 3 analysed the MIC through the works of John Kenneth Galbraith (despite the lack of an analysis of militarism and milex themselves) because he offers a valuable general theory regarding the power of corporations that can be usefully applied to military ones and the MIC specifically. In addition, as a public intellectual in the U.S. who also held major positions in four administrations, Galbraith had a critical effect on U.S. economic policy at various times from World War II up to the 1980s (even if somewhat lesser by then). In taking this approach, Chapter 3 offered a novel way to examine the origin and development of the MIC.

Chapter 4: Marxist crisis theories

The goal of Chapter 2 and Chapter 3 was to provide a general mainstream discussion on the economic role of milex. However, the book's fundamental aim was to contribute to understanding the effect of milex on economic performance, particularly the rate of profit, in Marxist thought. Accordingly, it attempted to summarise the theoretical views in two chapters (i.e. Chapters 4 and 5) and provided comprehensive empirical evidence in the final two chapters (i.e. Chapters 6 and 7).

Chapter 4 briefly summarised Marxist crisis theories. These theories explain the long-term economic crisis caused by the internal contradictions of capitalism, leading to the potential for underconsumption or overproduction and the tendency for the profit rate to fall. The tendency of stagnation is a key internal contradiction of the capitalist system. It happens whenever wage increases fail to keep up with the rate of expansion of output due to the resulting inadequate aggregate demand – unless capitalist demand for consumption or investment is able to absorb it. Rather than the underconsumptionist theory, Engels argued for an overproduction theory: that capitalist crises are due to the 'anarchy of production' in that there is no centralised coordination of decision-making regarding investment and production; instead, a host of individual profit-seeking companies decide for themselves (Engels, 1878). The underconsumptionist theories originate in Rosa Luxemburg's *The Accumulation of Capital* (1913), in which she claimed that capitalist expansion relies on non-capitalist systems. Applying these ideas to theorise stagnation, Sweezy (1942) argued that it is caused by both overaccumulation and underconsumption, and that capitalism's survival depends on unproductive spending. In *Monopoly Capital* (1966), Baran and Sweezy saw milex as a key element in this.

Another crisis theory, the profit/wage squeeze approach, was proposed by Glyn and Sutcliffe (1972). They argued that the main cause of the fall of the rate of profits in the U.K. was the decline in profit share caused by increasing union militancy. However, this theory failed to explain the current crisis empirically as real wages have deteriorated since the 1980s.

Chapter 4 focused on the tendency for the rate of profit to fall, a significant part of Marx's theory. The chapter briefly summarised i) what role the tendency for the falling rate of profit played in Marx's thinking, ii) different views on how to measure the rate of profit, and iii) alternative accounts for the sources of change in the rate of profit in recent empirical work. Marx argued that the fall in the rate of profit is due to the inner mechanism of capitalist production. For the younger Marx, the law of the tendency for the rate of profit to fall was "the most important law of political economy". He wanted to prove that the tendency for the organic composition of capital to rise due to mechanisation leads to a fall in the rate of profit despite the continued rise in the mass of profit. This leads capitalism to lurch between progressively more severe cyclical reductions in the rate of profit, resulting in increasingly intense socio-economic destabilisation. This was virtually the universal view among political economists until the late 20th century. However, a current reading of the now much more extensive available writings of Marx shows that he began to see the tendency of the rate of profit to fall as an empirical question in his later years, rather than an iron law.

Chapter 5: The effect of military expenditure on profitability in Marxist theories

Although there is no Marxist theory of militarism, the essential role of milex in capitalism was examined by several Marxist thinkers, revealing direct linkages between milex and the profit rate. Chapter 5 provided a brief discussion of these major views. While Marx did not explicitly discuss the economic effect of military production, Engels claimed that milex has no direct or indirect positive effect on the economy; on the contrary, it increases financial difficulties as armies are 'devilishly expensive'.

Rosa Luxemburg, a close follower of Marx's writings, provided a comprehensive framework to examine the role of milex in a capitalist economy. For Luxemburg, milex is a key means for realising surplus value. She argued that capitalism needs to expand, and militarism (e.g. force and state power) is the key mechanism of 'primitive accumulation'. Milex helps to build a political, social, and economic hegemony in the colonies, easing the further expansion of capital accumulation. It also favours capitalists by intensifying the exploitation and suppression of the working class. Thus, Luxemburg's views on the military's effects on the economy included both the short-term problems of Keynesian effective demand and the long-term dynamics of capital accumulation (Sweezy, 1942; Rowthorn, 1980).

Underconsumptionist theory was one interpretation of Luxemburg's theory that milex helps to absorb the surplus of the capitalist production system without increasing productive capacity. This view was further developed by Paul Baran and Paul Sweezy in *Monopoly Capital* (1966). They argued that milex helps capitalists obtain higher profit rates and lower levels of competition, increases aggregate demand, and absorbs surplus. Milex is distinct from other forms of state spending in this context because it absorbs the surplus without harming the interests of any powerful faction of the ruling class, and without raising wages or capital. This view led Baran and Sweezy to conclude that the U.S. was able to increase its power and preserve monopolistic capitalism during the 1940s and 1950s due to the key role played by high milex. Similarly, Michael Kidron argued that militarism stabilises the capitalist system by counteracting the "permanent threat of overproduction" (Kidron, 1970). However, Baran and Sweezy's and Kidron's views have been challenged both empirically and theoretically. Chapter 5 reviewed these debates on the economic effects of milex, emphasising the contradictory mechanisms through which milex affects the economy in general and the rate of profit particularly.

Chapter 5 also was an attempt to adapt the circuit of capital model of Foley (1982) to show the effect of milex on profit rates. Dividing the government sector into military and non-military sectors, a basic extension of the model shows that a higher share of the military sector increases the rate of profit through the realisation lag.

Chapter 6: An econometric analysis of the nexus of military expenditure and the profit rate

Military Keynesianism, discussed in Chapter 3, deals with the short-run effects of milex on the level of GDP and the rate of utilisation. Chapter 5, on the other hand, addressed the longer-run effects of milex on the rate of economic growth. The chapter underscored that, since there are several tendencies and counteracting tendencies operating on the rate of profit, the topic is more empirical than theoretical. Against this background, Chapters 6 and 7 provided comprehensive evidence on the nexus of milex and the profit rate. While Chapter 6 provided evidence based on a panel approach to the countries in question, Chapter 7 examined them individually, with special attention to the U.S. Both chapters use various quantitative methods and model specifications to better understand the dynamics of this nexus.

Chapter 6 presented evidence based on two major data sets, the Penn World Tables and Extended Penn World Tables. While the former covers 31 major countries for 1950–2014, the latter includes 27 countries for 1963–2008. The chapter provides three sets of analysis: for 1950–2014 (or 1963–2008) without unemployment; for 1980–2008 (or 1980–2014), both with and without unemployment; and for both periods with respect to a country's role in the arms trade as an arms exporter or importer. The first set of analyses for the whole period suggested four main findings: that milex has a positive impact on milex, that profits are counter-cyclical, that the profit rate does not tend to fall, and that there is a global pattern of profit rates. The second set of analyses for the neo-liberal era provided strong support for the reserve army of unemployed. Crucially, however, while the effect of GDP, time trends, and global profit are in line with the whole period, the results also show that milex no longer has a positive impact on the rate of profit in the neo-liberal era. Finally, the last set of analyses considered potential variation in the effects of milex because it influences the rate of profit through different mechanisms (both positively and negatively). Specifically, arms importers are more prone to suffer harmful effects of milex than arms exporters. There is no strong evidence that milex has a negative impact in the case of arms-importing countries and a positive impact in the case of arms-exporting countries. These findings are supported by the whole analysis based on the other main data set.

Overall, the findings support and strengthen Elveren and Hsu (2016)'s findings that there is a highly significant positive relationship between milex and profit rates for 1963–2008. However, contrary to the highly significant evidence provided in Elveren and Hsu (2016), the findings in Chapter 6 did not suggest that milex had negative effects during the neo-liberal era. Rather, the chapter shows an insignificant effect on profitability. Finally, although the findings provided only weak evidence on the differing impact of milex regarding the roles of countries in the arms trade, they still support the similar and somewhat stronger evidence in Elveren and Hsu (2016) because the set of arms-exporting and arms-importing countries and time periods are different in this analysis. Panel model analyses should therefore be complemented with time-series analyses when possible because the latter do not suffer from the potential problems resulting from heterogeneity that cannot be addressed fully in panel models. In addition, time-series analyses allow us to take advantage of the longest available data set of the rate of profit. Considering these issues, this book provided analyses for each country separately in Chapter 7.

Chapter 7: Analysis of the nexus of military expenditure and profit: country cases

Chapter 7 employed several linear and non-linear time-series methods to investigate the relationship in question for 31 countries for different time periods, ranging from 1950 to 2016. Regarding the U.S., the analysis for the whole period provided evidence, though not very strong, suggesting that milex is an important stimulant of capital accumulation. In the post-1980 period, on the other hand, the findings suggested that milex is more likely to have an insignificant or negative impact. This is in line with the previous findings in Chapter 6 and in other panel data studies (Elveren and Hsu, 2016, 2018). While the findings of a non-linear analysis were not significant, a Markov switching model provided supporting evidence of the positive impact of milex on the rate of profit. For both analyses, linear and non-linear, the results were similar with respect to different model specifications (e.g. with and without unemployment).

Regarding the other major countries, overall, the results were very similar for different profit variables (e.g. EPWT and PWT). Milex had a significant effect on the rate of profit in over a third of the countries. It is safe to argue that the negative effect of milex on the rate of profit is more common than the positive effect and that milex is more likely to have a negative impact in arms-importing countries. For all countries, including the U.S., there is very strong supportive evidence for the reserve army of unemployed.

References

Baran, P. and Sweezy, P. (1966). *Monopoly capital: An essay on the American economic and social order*. New York and London: Monthly Review Press.

Barro, R. J. (1990). Government spending in a simple model of endogeneous growth. *Journal of Political Economy*, 98(S5), pp. S103–S26.

Benoit, E. (1973). *Defence and economic growth in developing countries*. Boston, MA: Lexington Books.

Benoit, E. (1978). Growth and defense in developing countries. *Economic Development and Cultural Change*, 26(2), pp. 271–280.

Biswas, B. and Ram, R. (1986). Military expenditures and economic growth in less developed countries: An augmented model and further evidence. *Economic Development and Cultural Change*, 34(2), pp. 361–372.

Deger, S. (1986). Economic development and defense expenditure. *Economic Development and Cultural Change*, 35(1), pp. 179–196.

Deger, S. and Smith, R. (1983). Military expenditure and growth in less developed countries. *The Journal of Conflict Resolution*, 27(2), pp. 335–353.

Dumas, L. J. (1986). *The overburdened economy*. Berkeley and Los Angeles: University of California Press.

Duncan, T. K. and Coyne, C. J. (2013). The origins of the permanent war economy. *The Independent Review*, 18(2), pp. 219–240.

Elveren, A. Y. and Hsu, S. (2016). Military expenditures and profit rates: Evidence from OECD countries. *Metroeconomica*, 67(3), pp. 551–577.

Elveren, A.Y. and Hsu, S. (2018). The effect of military expenditure on profit rates: Evidence from major countries. *World Journal of Applied Economics*, 4(2), pp. 75–94.

Engels, F. (1878). *Anti-duhring*. Available at: www.marxists.org/archive/marx/works/1877/anti-duhring/ch15.htm#061

Feder, G. (1983). On exports and economic growth. *Journal of Development Economics*, 12(1–2), pp. 59–73.

Foley, D. (1982). Realization and accumulation in a Marxian model of the circuit of capital. *Journal of Economic Theory*, 28, pp. 300–319.

Glyn, A. and Sutcliffe, B. (1972). *British capitalism, workers and the profits Squeeze*. Harmondsworth: Penguin.

Kaldor, M. (1981). *The baroque arsenal*. New York: Hill and Wang.

Kidron, M. (1970). *Western capitalism since the war revised edition*. Harmondsworth: Pelican Books.

Luxemburg, R. (1951) [1913]. *The accumulation of capital*. London: Routledge and Kegan Paul.

Mankiw, N. G., Romer, D. and Weil, D. N. (1992). A contribution to the empirics of economic growth. *The Quarterly Journal of Economics*, 107(2), pp. 407–437.

Melman, S. (1970). *Pentagon capitalism: The political economy of war*. New York: McGraw-Hill.

Melman, S. (1974) [1985]. *The permanent war economy: American capitalism in decline*. New York: Simon & Schuster.

Romer, P. M. (2000). Keynesian macroeconomics without the LM curve. *Journal of Economic Perspectives*, 14(2), pp. 149–170.

Rosen, S. (ed.) (1973). *Testing the theory of the military-industrial complex*. Lexington, MA: Lexington Books.

Rowthorn, R. (1980). *Capitalism conflict & inflation essays in political economy*. London: Lawrence and Wishart.

Smith, D. and Smith, R. (1983). *The economics of militarism*. London: Pluto Press.

Sweezy, P. (1942). *The theory of capitalist development principles of Marxian political economy*. New York: Oxford University Press.

Taylor, J. B. (2000). Teaching modern macroeconomics at the principles level. *American Economic Review*, 90(2), pp. 90–94.

Appendix A: Panel studies (dependent variable is PWT Profit)

Table A.1 Panel unit root tests (1960–2014)

Variables	*Deterministic Terms*	*LLC*	*IPS*	*Breitung*	*CADF*	*CIPS*
Levels						
Profit	Intercept, trend	−5.144	1.079	−0.612	−2.487	−2.364
Milex	Intercept, trend	−3.573***	−5.144***	−2.036**	−2.919***	−3.146***
GDP	Intercept, trend	−0.491	0.870	3.123	−1.878	−2.021
First Differences						
ΔProfit	Intercept	−25.802***	−26.900***	−20.482***	−3.715***	−5.504***
ΔMilex	Intercept	−31.710***	−31.726***	−18.504***	−4.007***	−5.519***
ΔGDP	Intercept	−24.412***	−24.692***	−20.165***	−3.319***	−5.358***

Notes: The number of lags is determined according to SC. For CADF the number of lags is 2, for CIPS the max lag number is taken as 2 for unemployment and 3 for other variables.
Significance is denoted by *** at 1%, ** at 5%, and * at 10% level.

Table A.2 Cross-sectional independence tests (1960–2014)

	Pesaran's Test	*Frees' Test*	*Friedman's Test*
Test Statistic	21.820	6.709	229.461
Probability	0.0000	0.0000	0.0000

Table A.3 Panel unit root tests (1980–2014)

Variables	*Deterministic Terms*	*LLC*	*IPS*	*Breitung*	*CADF*	*CIPS*
Levels						
Profit	Intercept, trend	−1.084	−0.813	0.273	−2.796***	−2.804***
Milex	Intercept, trend	−0.370	0.205	0.775	−2.528	−2.907***

Variables	*Deterministic Terms*	*LLC*	*IPS*	*Breitung*	*CADF*	*CIPS*
GDP	Intercept, trend	0.271	0.414	0.875	−1.759	−1.687
Unemployment	Intercept, trend	−2.863***	−2.431***	−3.266***	−2.393	−2.209
First Differences						
ΔProfit	Intercept	−17.011***	−18.688***	−13.462***	−3.134***	−4.460***
ΔMilex	Intercept	−21.280***	−23.025***	−12.943***	−3.309***	−5.181***
ΔGDP	Intercept	−16.865***	−18.010***	−11.372***	−2.500***	−4.295***
ΔUnemployment	Intercept	−13.312***	−14.124***	−8.005***	−3.255***	−4.495***

Notes: The number of lags is determined according to SC. For CADF the number of lags is 2, for CIPS the max lag number is taken as 2 for unemployment and 3 for other variables.

Significance is denoted by *** at 1%, ** at 5%, and * at 10% level.

Table A.4 Cross-sectional independence tests (1980–2014)

	Pesaran's Test	*Frees' Test*	*Friedman's Test*
Test Statistic	21.205	6.018	187.320
Probability	0.0000	0.0000	0.0000

Table A.5 Panel unit root tests (1980–2008)

Variables	*Deterministic Terms*	*LLC*	*IPS*	*Breitung*	*CADF*	*CIPS*
Levels						
Profit (EPWT)	Intercept, trend	2.895	4.699	5.666	−1.819	−1.617
Profit (PENN)	Intercept, trend	1.853	−2.072**	0.615	−2.526	−2.676**
Milex	Intercept, trend	−1.233	−1.588*	−2.226**	−2.428	−3.074***
GDP	Intercept, trend	−0.250	−1.059	5.551	−1.431	−1.471
Unemployment	Intercept, trend	−1.758**	−2.376***	−0.507	−2.277	−2.308
First Differences						
ΔProfit (EPWT)	Intercept	−9.749***	−11.128***	−5.374***	−2.155**	−3.647***
ΔProfit (PENN)	Intercept	−10.495***	−13.355***	−3.369***	−2.841***	−4.064***
ΔMilex	Intercept	−15.178***	−17.261***	−7.701***	−2.976***	−4.701***
ΔGDP	Intercept	−11.048***	−12.098***	−6.004***	−2.197***	−3.743***
ΔUnemployment	Intercept	−14.215***	−15.744***	−9.421***	−2.729***	−4.062***

Notes: The number of lags is determined according to SC. For CADF the number of lags is 2, for CIPS the max lag number is taken as 2 for unemployment and 3 for other variables.

Significance is denoted by *** at 1%, ** at 5%, and * at 10% level.

Table A.6 Cross-sectional independence tests (1980–2008)

Profit (EPWT)	*Pesaran's Test*	*Frees' Test*	*Friedman's Test*
Test Statistic	11.778	4.775	107.357
Probability	0.0000	0.0000	0.0000
Profit (PENN)			
Test Statistic	11.821	5.541	112.686
Probability	0.0000	0.0000	0.0000

Table A.7 Long- and short-run effects of milex on profit rates (1963–2008)

	Pooled Mean Group	*Mean Group*	*Dynamic Fixed Effect*
Long-Run Coefficients			
Milex	0.060*	0.273	0.428**
	[0.036]	[0.191]	[0.179]
GDP	−0.652***	−0.148	−0.509***
	[0.090]	[0.319]	[0.177]
Global profit	0.171	1.122***	−0.090
	[0.111]	[0.306]	[0.539]
time trend	0.021***	0.006	0.026***
	[0.003]	[0.008]	[0.008]
Short-Run Coefficients			
Error Correction Coefficient	−0.072***	−0.268***	−0.039***
	[0.015]	[0.027]	[0.006]
Δmilex	−0.001	0.001	−0.022
	[0.029]	[0.035]	[0.014]
ΔGDP	0.554***	0.568***	0.598***
	[0.062]	[0.061]	[0.030]
ΔGlobal profit	0.793***	0.464***	0.798***
	[0.068]	[0.101]	[0.053]
Intercept	0.685***	0.265	0.292***
	[0.169]	[0.592]	[0.087]
No. Countries	27	27	27
No. Observations	1215	1215	1215

Standard errors in brackets. Significance denoted by *** at 1%, ** at 5%, and * at 10% level.

Table A.8 Long- and short-run effects of milex on profit rates (1980–2008)

Long Run	*Pooled Mean Group*		*Mean Group*		*Dynamic Fixed Effect*	
	1	*2*	*1*	*2*	*1*	*2*
Milex	−0.185***	0.045	−1.754	−0.272	−0.001	0.132
	[0.057]	[0.046]	[1.645]	[0.423]	[0.108]	[0.111]
GDP	−0.388***	−0.312***	−0.513	−0.205	−0.256*	−0.372***
	[0.122]	[0.052]	[1.426]	[0.586]	[0.136]	[0.131]

Long Run	*Pooled Mean Group*		*Mean Group*		*Dynamic Fixed Effect*	
	1	*2*	*1*	*2*	*1*	*2*
unemployment	0.444***		0.058		0.264***	
	[0.069]		[0.107]		[0.058]	
Global profit	1.421***	1.462***	0.780	1.046***	2.206***	1.795***
	[0.324]	[0.110]	[0.357]	[0.433]	[0.475]	[0.457]
time trend	−0.009	0.006***	−0.039***	−0.005	−0.001	0.009*
	[0.005]	[0.001]	[0.014]	[0.015]	[0.006]	[0.005]
Short Run						
Error Correction Coefficient	−0.073***	−0.164***	−0.398***	−0.382***	−0.097***	−0.098***
	[0.013]	[0.026]	[0.049]	[0.043]	[0.013]	[0.013]
Δmilex	−0.007	−0.041	0.036	−0.021	−0.040*	−0.066***
	[0.024]	[0.077]	[0.036]	[0.039]	[0.023]	[0.022]
ΔGDP	0.632***	0.588***	0.492***	0.559***	0.711***	0.656***
	[0.087]	[0.082]	[0.074]	[0.078]	[0.045]	[0.043]
ΔUnemp	0.013		−0.001		0.017*	
	[0.014]		[0.012]		[0.009]	
ΔGlobal profit	0.620***	0.638***	0.234**	0.419***	0.572***	0.668***
	[0.108]	[0.091]	[0.111]	[0.115]	[0.085]	[0.080]
Intercept	0.245***	0.406***	−2.712**	0.340	−0.028	0.220
	[0.051]	[0.065]	[1.104]	[0.779]	[0.194]	[0.183]
No. Country	27	27	27	27	27	27
No. Obser.	756	783	756	783	756	783

Standard errors in brackets. Significance denoted by *** at 1%, ** at 5%, and * at 10% level.

Table A.9 Long- and short-run effects of milex on profit rates (1980–2014)

Short Run	*Pooled Mean Group*		*Mean Group*		*Dynamic Fixed Effect*	
	1	*2*	*1*	*2*	*1*	*2*
Milex	0.254***	0.124**	−1.850	0.777	0.066	0.075
	[0.075]	[0.052]	[1.879]	[1.467]	[0.092]	[0.079]
GDP	−0.108	−0.220***	0.029	−0.451	−0.054	−0.110
	[0.122]	[0.063]	[0.613]	[0.767]	[0.103]	[0.085]
unemployment	0.480***		0.209**		0.227***	
	[0.063]		[0.090]		[0.048]	
Global profit	1.381***	0.388***	−0.348	1.414	0.926***	0.820***
	[0.164]	[0.106]	[1.343]	[0.993]	[0.208]	[0.194]
time trend	0.005	−0.0007	−0.017*	0.009	0.0002	0.003
	[0.003]	[0.002]	[0.010]	[0.007]	[0.004]	[0.003]
Short Run						
Error Correction Coefficient	−0.088***	−0.089***	−0.377***	−0.361***	−0.106***	−0.112***
	[0.013]	[0.018]	[0.039]	[0.037]	[0.011]	[0.011]
Δmilex	−0.036	−0.042	−0.005	−0.028	−0.044**	−0.060***
	[0.026]	[0.034]	[0.040]	[0.038]	[0.021]	[0.020]

(Continued)

Table A.9 (Continued)

Short Run	*Pooled Mean Group*		*Mean Group*		*Dynamic Fixed Effect*	
	1	*2*	*1*	*2*	*1*	*2*
ΔGDP	0.572***	0.540***	0.451***	0.540***	0.591***	0.552***
	[0.067]	[0.063]	[0.072]	[0.057]	[0.038]	[0.036]
ΔUnemp	0.009		−0.009		0.010	
	[0.012]		[0.016]		[0.008]	
ΔGlobal profit	0.608***	0.651***	0.284**	0.333***	0.563***	0.666***
	[0.073]	[0.085]	[0.110]	[0.097]	[0.066]	[0.063]
Intercept	−0.094***	0.373***	−2.287*	0.647	0.020	0.169
	[0.012]	[0.086]	[1.215]	[0.592]	[0.144]	[0.125]
No. Country	30	31	30	31	30	31
No. Obser.	1020	1085	1020	1085	1020	1085

Standard errors in brackets. Significance denoted by *** at 1%, ** at 5%, and * at 10% level.

Table A.10 Long- and short-run effects of milex on profit rates (1960–2014)

	Pooled Mean Group	*Mean Group*	*Dynamic Fixed Effect*
Long-Run Coefficients			
Milex	0.353***	−1.130	0.146
	[0.069]	[2.863]	[0.095]
GDP	−0.026	−8.426	−0.287***
	[0.043]	[1.842]	[0.100]
Global profit	−0.059	−2.946	0.211
	[0.188]	[3.164]	[0.352]
time trend	0.007***	0.146	0.012***
	[0.002]	[0.169]	[0.004]
Short-Run Coefficients			
Error Correction Coefficient	−0.059***	−0.213***	−0.050***
	[0.010]	[0.024]	[0.095]
Δmilex	−0.022	0.001	−0.020*
	[0.017]	[0.021]	[0.011]
ΔGDP	0.524***	0.560***	0.544***
	[0.047]	[0.049]	[0.026]
ΔGlobal profit	0.764***	0.515***	0.758***
	[0.059]	[0.082]	[0.048]
Intercept	0.119***	0.456*	0.237***
	[0.024]	[0.263]	[0.071]
No. Countries	31	31	31
No. Observations	1674	1674	1674

Standard errors in brackets. Significance denoted by *** at 1%, ** at 5%, and * at 10% level.

Table A.11 Long- and short-run effects of milex on profit rates, arms-exporting vs arms-importing (1963–2008)

Long run	*Pooled Mean Group*		*Mean Group*		*Dynamic Fixed Effect*	
	Exporter	*Importer*	*Exporter*	*Importer*	*Exporter*	*Importer*
Milex	0.039	0.352***	0.424	0.129	0.261	0.560
	[0.033]	[0.087]	[0.332]	[0.195]	[0.195]	[0.354]
GDP	−0.534***	−0.544***	−0.030	−0.290	−0.818***	−0.518*
	[0.049]	[0.085]	[0.549]	[0.350]	[0.296]	[0.311]
Global profit	1.439***	1.517***	1.232***	0.981**	0.400	−0.978
	[0.155]	[0.113]	[0.473]	[0.431]	[0.595]	[1.096]
Time trend	0.019***	0.019***	0.004	0.008	0.032***	0.028*
	[0.002]	[0.002]	[0.012]	[0.011]	[0.011]	[0.015]
Short run						
Error correction coefficient	−0.086***	−0.083**	−0.246***	−0.272***	−0.038***	−0.035***
	[0.030]	[0.037]	[0.039]	[0.035]	[0.008]	[0.012]
Δmilex	−0.039	0.057	−0.042	0.061	−0.021	0.001
	[0.024]	[0.052]	[0.037]	[0.064]	[0.016]	[0.022]
ΔGDP	0.438***	0.652***	0.462***	0.672***	0.432***	0.688***
	[0.070]	[0.100]	[0.070]	[0.104]	[0.040]	[0.045]
ΔGlobal profit	0.631***	0.817***	0.429***	0.606***	0.758***	0.932***
	[0.117]	[0.098]	[0.129]	[0.135]	[0.057]	[0.089]
Intercept	0.419***	0.344	0.321	0.242	0.401***	0.336**
	[0.155]	[0.160]	[0.912]	[0.846]	[0.153]	[0.138]
No. Countries	14	12	14	12	14	12
No. Observations	630	540	630	540	630	540

Standard errors in brackets. Significance denoted by *** at 1%, ** at 5%, and * at 10% level.

Table A.12 Long- and short-run effects of milex on profit rates (with unemployment), arms-exporting vs arms-importing (1980–2008)

Long run	*Pooled Mean Group*		*Mean Group*		*Dynamic Fixed Effect*	
	Exporter	*Importer*	*Exporter*	*Importer*	*Exporter*	*Importer*
Milex	−0.004	−0.457***	−3.461	0.053	−0.012	−0.222
	[0.034]	[0.160]	[3.141]	[0.380]	[0.137]	[0.237]
GDP	0.148	−0.574***	−1.908	1.053	0.167	−0.705**
	[0.105]	[0.193]	[2.655]	[0.820]	[0.264]	[0.298]
Unemployment	0.086***	0.599***	0.017	0.104	0.269***	0.377***
	[0.015]	[0.127]	[0.166]	[0.153]	[0.069]	[0.143]
Global Profit	1.262***	0.248	0.846	0.737	2.003***	2.127**
	[0.127]	[0.515]	[0.826]	[0.575]	[0.518]	[0.949]
Time trend	−0.0002	−0.007	−0.046**	−0.035	−0.015	0.014
	[0.004]	[0.006]	[0.020]	[0.024]	[0.010]	[0.011]

(*Continued*)

Table A.12 (Continued)

Short run	*Pooled Mean Group*		*Mean Group*		*Dynamic Fixed Effect*	
Error correction coefficient	−0.197***	−0.061***	−0.413***	−0.365***	−0.094***	−0.076***
	[0.060]	[0.020]	[0.069]	[0.079]	[0.016]	[0.018]
Δmilex	−0.042*	0.020	0.016	0.082	−0.015	−0.023
	[0.030]	[0.039]	[0.050]	[0.051]	[0.027]	[0.035]
ΔGDP	0.420***	0.743***	0.378***	0.593***	0.398***	0.886***
	[0.123]	[0.139]	[0.100]	[0.110]	[0.057]	[0.065]
Δunemployment	−0.016	0.034	−0.011	0.014	−0.006	0.045***
	[0.014]	[0.024]	[0.014]	[0.021]	[0.010]	[0.014]
ΔGlobal profit	0.586***	0.838***	0.212*	0.332*	0.585***	0.767***
	[0.136]	[0.182]	[0.120]	[0.198]	[0.091]	[0.136]
Intercept	−0.528***	0.516***	−2.297*	−3.363*	−0.452	0.382
	[0.144]	[0.187]	[1.387]	[1.936]	[0.320]	[0.294]
No. Countries	14	12	14	12	14	12
No. Observations	392	336	392	336	392	336

Standard errors in brackets. Significance denoted by *** at 1%, ** at 5%, and * at 10% level.

Table A.13 Long- and short-run effects of milex on profit rates, arms-exporters vs arms-importers (1980–2008)

Long run	*Pooled Mean Group*		*Mean Group*		*Dynamic Fixed Effect*	
	Exporter	*Importer*	*Exporter*	*Importer*	*Exporter*	*Importer*
Milex	0.079	0.480***	−0.850	0.334	0.107	0.075
	[0.053]	[0.116]	[0.630]	[0.574]	[0.157]	[0.188]
GDP	−0.231***	−0.250**	−0.514	0.140	−0.293	−0.514**
	[0.069]	[0.101]	[0.697]	[1.065]	[0.244]	[0.222]
Global profit	0.745***	1.846***	1.258***	0.892*	1.746***	1.628**
	[0.178]	[0.155]	[0.366]	[0.525]	[0.553]	[0.769]
Time trend	0.006**	0.012***	0.010	−0.004	0.005	0.014
	[0.002]	[0.003]	[0.012]	[0.031]	[0.009]	[0.009]
Short run						
Error correction coefficient	−0.149***	−0.146**	−0.383***	−0.361***	−0.086***	−0.092***
	[0.038]	[0.054]	[0.060]	[0.067]	[0.016]	[0.018]
Δmilex	−0.107***	−0.007	−0.026	0.002	−0.034	−0.045
	[0.025]	[0.079]	[0.034]	[0.079]	[0.026]	[0.035]
ΔGDP	0.457***	0.695***	0.468***	0.630***	0.427***	0.784***
	[0.101]	[0.145]	[0.096]	[0.131]	[0.057]	[0.062]
ΔGlobal profit	0.736***	0.717***	0.402**	0.468**	0.661***	0.824***
	[0.114]	[0.167]	[0.157]	[0.189]	[0.087]	[0.129]
Intercept	0.481***	0.005	0.912	−0.384	0.136	0.403
	[0.124]	[0.014]	[1.006]	[1.321]	[0.290]	[0.290]
No. Countries	14	12	14	12	14	12
No. Observations	406	348	406	348	406	348

Standard errors in brackets. Significance denoted by *** at 1%, ** at 5%, and * at 10% level.

Table A.14 Long- and short-run effects of milex on profit rates, arms-exporting vs arms-importing (1960–2014)

Long run	*Pooled Mean Group*		*Mean Group*		*Dynamic Fixed Effect*	
	Exporter	*Importer*	*Exporter*	*Importer*	*Exporter*	*Importer*
Milex	0.004	0.457***	−2.387	−0.093	0.252	0.042
	[0.036]	[0.126]	[6.452]	[0.153]	[0.182]	[0.140]
GDP	−0.523***	−0.030	−18.333	−0.283	−0.451	−0.288**
	[0.086]	[0.055]	[20.877]	[0.188]	[0.275]	[0.134]
Global profit	0.115	−0.579	−7.862	1.090**	0.129	0.022
	[0.124]	[0.381]	[6.898]	[0.357]	[0.597]	[0.507]
Time trend	0.016***	0.007**	0.311	0.010	0.018*	0.011*
	[0.002]	[0.003]	[0.378]	[0.008]	[0.010]	[0.006]
Short run						
Error correction coefficient	−0.068***	−0.054***	−0.160***	−0.240***	−0.035***	−0.055***
	[0.024]	[0.013]	[0.039]	[0.022]	[0.007]	[0.009]
Δmilex	−0.036**	0.005	−0.018	0.020	−0.014	−0.017
	[0.014]	[0.028]	[0.027]	[0.035]	[0.015]	[0.017]
ΔGDP	0.478***	0.570***	0.497***	0.602***	0.450***	0.552***
	[0.057]	[0.076]	[0.057]	[0.081]	[0.040]	[0.035]
ΔGlobal profit	0.696***	0.856***	0.499***	0.574***	0.711***	0.838***
	[0.097]	[0.078]	[0.107]	[0.122]	[0.054]	[0.074]
Intercept	0.579**	0.174***	0.441	0.533	0.233*	0.297***
	[0.242]	[0.048]	[0.436]	[0.345]	[0.127]	[0.109]
No. Countries	14	16	14	16	14	16
No. Observations	756	864	756	864	756	864

Standard errors in brackets. Significance denoted by *** at 1%, ** at 5%, and * at 10% level.

Table A.15 long- and short-run effects of milex on profit rates (with unemployment), arms-exporting vs arms-importing (1980–2014)

Long run	*Pooled Mean Group*		*Mean Group*		*Dynamic Fixed Effect*	
	Exporter	*Importer*	*Exporter*	*Importer*	*Exporter*	*Importer*
Milex	0.302***	−0.300***	−4.044	0.035	0.220	−0.159
	[0.108]	[0.114]	[4.016]	[0.230]	[0.163]	[0.161]
GDP	0.438*	−0.295***	−0.623	0.624	0.344	−0.256
	[0.237]	[0.107]	[1.180]	[0.544]	[0.296]	[0.167]
Unemployment	0.708***	0.450***	0.200	0.225*	0.316***	0.243***
	[0.106]	[0.093]	[0.142]	[0.126]	[0.080]	[0.087]
Global Profit	1.745***	−0.372*	−1.617	0.767**	1.017***	0.750**
	[0.210]	[0.213]	[2.870]	[0.365]	[0.303]	[0.346]
Time trend	−0.010	−0.008**	−0.019**	−0.018	−0.011	0.005
	[0.007]	[0.003]	[0.009]	[0.018]	[0.009]	[0.006]

(*Continued*)

Table A.15 (Continued)

Short run	*Pooled Mean Group*		*Mean Group*		*Dynamic Fixed Effect*	
Error correction coefficient	−0.077***	−0.078***	−0.365***	−0.377***	−0.079***	−0.101***
	[0.018]	[0.020]	[0.070]	[0.046]	[0.014]	[0.017]
Δmilex	−0.012	0.024	0.041	0.033	−0.009	−0.059*
	[0.034]	[0.036]	[0.061]	[0.055]	[0.027]	[0.033]
ΔGDP	0.451***	0.673***	0.402***	0.472***	0.407***	0.623***
	[0.090]	[0.108]	[0.109]	[0.102]	[0.056]	[0.054]
Δunemployment	−0.014	0.034	−0.018	0.002	−0.001	0.020
	[0.018]	[0.025]	[0.022]	[0.026]	[0.010]	[0.013]
ΔGlobal profit	0.552***	0.747***	0.257***	0.355*	0.636***	0.764***
	[0.094]	[0.106]	[0.098]	[0.198]	[0.071]	[0.107]
Intercept	−0.732***	0.533***	−1.232	−3.333	−0.417	0.327
	[0.181]	[0.153]	[0.854]	[2.309]	[0.270]	[0.223]
No. Countries	14	15	14	15	14	15
No. Observations	476	510	476	510	476	510

Standard errors in brackets. Significance denoted by *** at 1%, ** at 5%, and * at 10% level.

Table A.16 Long- and short-run effects of milex on profit rates, arms-exporters vs arms-importers (1980–2014)

Long run	*Pooled Mean Group*		*Mean Group*		*Dynamic Fixed Effect*	
	Exporter	*Importer*	*Exporter*	*Importer*	*Exporter*	*Importer*
Milex	0.603**	0.064	1.579	0.083	0.323*	−0.062
	[0.294]	[0.060]	[3.293]	[0.237]	[0.186]	[0.118]
GDP	−0.244	−0.248***	−0.766	−0.206	−0.007	−0.185
	[0.397]	[0.686]	[1.665]	[0.408]	[0.284]	[0.120]
Global profit	−0.053	0.400***	2.155	0.808***	0.905***	0.694**
	[0.488]	[0.112]	[2.219]	[0.180]	[0.334]	[0.287]
Time trend	0.008	0.00003	0.008	−0.009	0.004	0.004
	[0.012]	[0.002]	[0.010]	[0.012]	[0.009]	[0.004]
Short-run						
Error correction coefficient	−0.036***	−0.119***	−0.332***	−0.374***	−0.074***	−0.117***
	[0.013]	[0.031]	[0.062]	[0.046]	[0.014]	[0.015]
Δmilex	−0.031	−0.044	−0.332	0.066	−0.026	−0.072**
	[0.026]	[0.064]	[0.052]	[0.054]	[0.026]	[0.029]
ΔGDP	0.491***	0.569***	0.504***	0.550***	0.426***	0.562***
	[0.065]	[0.107]	[0.074]	[0.089]	[0.055]	[0.049]
ΔGlobal profit	0.725***	0.635***	0.329***	0.367**	0.652***	0.742***
	[0.108]	[0.133]	[0.121]	[0.156]	[0.071]	[0.098]
Intercept	0.166***	0.561***	1.053	0.363	−0.031	0.345*
	[0.064]	[0.161]	[0.865]	[0.879]	[0.259]	[0.188]
No. Countries	14	16	14	16	14	16
No. Observations	490	560	490	560	490	560

Standard errors in brackets. Significance denoted by *** at 1%, ** at 5%, and * at 10% level.

Appendix B: Time-series analyses

Note that for each table in this part, standard errors are in parenthesis, probability is in brackets, and significance is denoted by *** at 1%, ** at 5%, and * at 10% level. Unless indicated otherwise, Profit1 and Profit2 refer to profit rates of PWT and EPWT, respectively.

Table B.1 Results of ARDL bounds test: Argentina (with unemployment)

	Profit1 *1968–2014* *ARDL (2, 0, 2, 0)*	*Profit2* *1968–2011* *ARDL (1, 0, 1, 0)*	*Profit3* *1970–2011* *ARDL (1, 2, 1, 2)*
Short-Run Coefficients			
Profit (−1)	1.031*** (0.154)	0.466*** (0.109)	0.767*** (0.165)
Profit (−2)	−0.255 (0.158)		
Milex	−0.057* (0.028)	0.356*** (0.124)	0.229 (0.140)
Milex (−1)			0.056 (0.153)
Milex (−2)			−0.210* (0.105)
GDP	0.243** (0.105)	2.592*** (0.456)	0.578** (0.217)
GDP (−1)	−0.448*** (0.164)	−1.768*** (0.429)	−0.534** (0.253)
GDP (−2)	0.246** (0.104)		
Unemployment	−0.029 (0.021)	−0.162** (0.062)	−0.024 (0.058)
Unemployment (−1)			−0.003 (0.079)
Unemployment (−2)			0.116* (0.061)

(*Continued*)

Table B.1 (Continued)

	Profit1 1968–2014 ARDL (2, 0, 2, 0)	*Profit2* 1968–2011 ARDL (1, 0, 1, 0)	*Profit3* 1970–2011 ARDL (1, 2, 1, 2)
Short-Run Coefficients			
Trend	−0.004	−0.033**	−0.004
	(0.002)	(0.012)	(0.007)
Intercept	0.356	−7.208***	0.200
	(0.504)	(2.520)	(1.238)
Long-Run Coefficients			
Milex	−0.256**	0.667***	0.323
	(0.115)	(0.206)	(0.446)
GDP	0.188	1.544***	0.188
	(0.196)	(0.380)	(0.536)
Unemployment	−0131**	−0.303**	0.378
	(0.056)	(0.134)	(0.390)
Trend	−0.018*	−0.062***	−0.020
	(0.009)	(0.018)	(0.023)
R-squared	0.948	0.759	0.732
SER	0.040	0.193	0.089
Serial correlation	0.116	0.887	1.284
	[0.890]	[0.352]	[0.292]
Functional form	12.468	0.059	0.914
	[0.001]	[0.808]	[0.346]
Normality	42.068	2.557	4.432
	[0.0000]	[0.278]	[0.109]
Heteroscedasticity	6.176	0.604	0.719
	[0.0000]	[0.725]	[0.700]
Bounds Test	1.773	6.558***	2.725
F-Statistics	10% 3.22 4.05	10% 3.22 4.05	10% 3.264 4.094
Actual sample size	5% 3.82 4.71	5% 3.82 4.71	5% 3.85 4.782
	1% 5.15 6.28	1% 5.15 6.28	1% 5.258 6.526

Note: Profit2 and Profit3 are taken from Estaban Maito. While Profit2 uses reproduction cost with current dollars, Profit3 is calculated based on historical costs with current dollars.

Table B.2 Results of ARDL bounds test: Argentina (without unemployment)

	Profit1 1960–2014 ARDL (1, 0, 1)	*Profit2* 1960–2011 ARDL (1, 0, 1)	*Profit3* 1960–2011 ARDL (1, 0, 1)
Short-Run Coefficients			
Profit (−1)	0.901***	0.494***	0.600***
	(0.052)	(0.110)	(0.132)
Milex	−0.050***	0.237**	−0.013
	(0.018)	(0.096)	(0.045)

	Profit1 *1960–2014* *ARDL (1, 0, 1)*	*Profit2* *1960–2011* *ARDL (1, 0, 1)*	*Profit3* *1960–2011* *ARDL (1, 0, 1)*
Short-Run Coefficients			
GDP	0.186**	2.286***	0.550**
	(0.089)	(0.464)	(0.208)
GDP (−1)	−0.197**	−1.694***	−0.306**
	(0.086)	(0.436)	(0.217)
Trend	−0.001	−0.033***	−0.015**
	(0.002)	(0.012)	(0.006)
Intercept	0.477	−4.639*	−1.180
	(0.452)	(2.420)	(0.984)
Long-Run Coefficients			
Milex	−0.508*	0.470**	−0.033
	(0.276)	(0.175)	(0.109)
GDP	0.026	1.171***	0.611**
	(0.306)	(0.387)	(0.228)
Trend	−0.111	−0.068***	−0.039
	(0.397)	(0.019)	(0.011)
R-squared	0.959	0.717	0.785
SER	0.039	0.203	0.091
Serial correlation	2.117	2.216	1.839
	[0.1522]	[0.1435]	[0.181]
Functional form	4.856	1.032	0.663
	[0.032]	[0.315]	[0.419]
Normality	38.154	0.299	8.155
	[0.0000]	[0.861]	[0.016]
Heteroscedasticity	7.625	1.997	0.812
	[0.0000]	[0.096]	[0.547]
Bounds Test	2.547	5.507**	2.753
F-Statistics	10% 3.55 4.23	10% 3.5734.288	10% 3.573 4.288
Actual sample size	5% 4.18 4.95	5% 4.225 5.03	5% 4.225 5.03
	1% 5.67 6.57	1% 5.805 6.79	1% 5.805 6.79

Note: Profit2 and Profit3 are taken from Estaban Maito. While Profit2 uses reproduction cost with current dollars, Profit3 is calculated based on historical costs with current dollars.

Table B.3 Results of ARDL bounds test: Australia (with unemployment)

	Profit1 *1977–2014* *ARDL (1, 0, 2, 0)*	*Profit2* *1977–2008* *ARDL (1, 0, 1, 0)*	*Profit3* *1979–2011* *ARDL (2, 0, 2, 2)*
Short-Run Coefficients			
Profit (−1)	0.773***	0.780***	0.488***
	(0.091)	(0.094)	(0.132)
Profit (−2)			−0.574***
			(0.124)

(*Continued*)

Table B.3 (Continued)

	Profit1 1977–2014 ARDL (1, 0, 2, 0)	*Profit2* 1977–2008 ARDL (1, 0, 1, 0)	*Profit3* 1979–2011 ARDL (2, 0, 2, 2)
Short-Run Coefficients			
Milex	0.247**	−0.210*	−1.046***
	(0.091)	(0.121)	(0.180)
GDP	1.482***	0.480	−1.605***
	(0.234)	(0.347)	(0.381)
GDP (−1)	−0.972***	−1.442***	0.653
	(0.302)	(0.387)	(0.396)
GDP (−2)	0.664**		−1.859***
	(0.244)		(0.380)
Unemployment	0.066*	0.043	−0.127**
	(0.032)	(0.044)	(0.054)
Unemployment (−1)			0.157**
			(0.070)
Unemployment (−2)			−0.231***
			(0.050)
Trend	−0.039***	0.032	0.107***
	(0.014)	(0.019)	(0.025)
Intercept	−13.516***	12.042*	36.386***
	(0.014)	(6.463)	(8.487)
Long-Run Coefficients			
Milex	1.093*	−0.959	−0.964***
	(0.571)	(0.638)	(0.105)
GDP	5.179**	−4.375	−2.589***
	(2.382)	(3.609)	(0.556)
Unemployment	0.291**	0.198	−0.186***
	(0.138)	(0.161)	(0.038)
Trend	−0.173**	0.145	0.099***
	(0.084)	(0.124)	(0.019)
R-squared	0.944	0.905	0.979
SER	0.025	0.026	0.025
Serial correlation	0.314	0.854	0.583
	[0.732]	[0.364]	[0.567]
Functional form	0.595	2.419	1.212
	[0.446]	[0.132]	[0.283]
Normality	0.517	0.643	1.737
	[0.772]	[0.725]	[0.419]
Heteroscedasticity	0.733	3.131	1.656
	[0.645]	[0.019]	[0.155]
Bounds Test	3.896	8.101***	9.293***
F-Statistics	10% 3.26 4.09	10% 3.37 4.27	10% 3.29 4.176
Actual sample size	5% 3.85 4.78	5% 4.04 5.09	5% 3.936 4.918
	1% 5.25 6.52	1% 5.66 6.98	1% 5.654 6.926
	(inconclusive)		

Note: Profit3 taken from E. Maito.

Table B.4 Results of ARDL bounds test: Australia (without unemployment)

	Profit1 1953–2014 ARDL (2, 0, 3)	*Profit2* 1966–2008 ARDL (3, 1. 3)	*Profit3* 1963–2011 ARDL (3, 3, 3)
Short-Run Coefficients			
Profit (−1)	1.056***	1.177***	1.091***
	(0.129)	(0.172)	(0.155)
Profit (−2)	−0.290**	−0.740***	−0.360**
	(0.116)	(0.239)	(0.166)
Profit (−3)		0.388**	0.202**
		(0.150)	(0.096)
Milex	0.016	−0.233*	−0.256
	(0.037)	(0.115)	(0.232)
Milex (−1)		0.154	0.732*
		(0.113)	(0.386)
Milex (−2)			−0.852**
			(0.366)
Milex (−3)			0.391*
			(0.218)
GDP	1.159***	0.292	0.097
	(0.176)	(0.239)	(0.415)
GDP (−1)	−1.709***	−1.772***	1.953***
	(.259)	(0.287)	(0.429)
GDP (−2)	0.729**	1.441***	−3.173***
	(0.279)	(0.413)	(0.540)
GDP (−3)	−0.355**	−1.001***	0.739
	(0.167)	(0.338)	(0.492)
Trend	0.007*	0.035***	0.015
	(0.003)	(0.008)	(0.012)
Intercept	2.460*	12.737***	4.491
	(1.240)	(3.086)	(3.653)
Long-Run Coefficients			
Milex	0.071	−0.452	0.213
	(0.154)	(0.444)	(1.456)
GDP	−0.754	−5.949**	−5.711
	(0.455)	(2.588)	(7.546)
Trend	0.033*	0.204**	0.226
	(0.016)	(0.086)	(0.289)
R-squared	0.918	0.929	0.968
SER	0.031	0.025	0.040
Serial correlation	0.989	1.508	1.422
	[0.405]	[0.233]	[0.253]
Functional form	8.71	1.347	0.018
	[0.992]	[0.254]	[0.893]
Normality	32.678	1.260	0.382
	[0.000]	[0.532]	[0.825]

(*Continued*)

Table B.4 (Continued)

	Profit1 *1953–2014* *ARDL (2, 0, 3)*	*Profit2* *1966–2008* *ARDL (3, 1. 3)*	*Profit3* *1963–2011* *ARDL (3, 3, 3)*
Long-Run Coefficients			
Heteroscedasticity	1.696 [0.121]	0.713 [0.705]	0.532 [0.878]
Bounds Test	4.069	4.579**	3.207
F-Statistics	10% 3.54 4.23	10% 3.62 4.33	10% 3.573 4.288
Actual sample size	5% 4.18 4.93	5% 4.33 5.07	5% 4.225 5.03
	1% 5.62 6.50 (Inconclusive)	1% 5.87 6.87	1% 5.805 6.79

Note: Profit3 taken from E. Maito.

Table B.5 Results of ARDL bounds test: Austria (with unemployment)

	Profit1 *1967–2014* *ARDL (2, 0, 2, 0)*	*Profit2* *1970–2008* *ARDL (1, 2, 1, 3)*
Short-Run Coefficients		
Profit (−1)	1.486*** (0.129)	0.352*** (0.096)
Profit (−2)	−0.561*** (0.134)	
Milex	−0.088 (0.071)	−0.390*** (0.079)
Milex (−1)		−0.127 (0.095)
Milex (−2)		−0.128* (0.069)
GDP	0.884*** (0.205)	0.502*** (0.172)
GDP (−1)	−1.588*** (0.262)	−1.062*** (0.195)
GDP (−2)	0.848*** (0.215)	
Unemployment	0.021 (0.0186)	−0.031 (0.022)
Unemployment (−1)		0.002 (0.026)
Unemployment (−2)		0.030 (0.026)
Unemployment (−3)		0.072*** (0.025)

	Profit1 *1967–2014* *ARDL (2, 0, 2, 0)*		*Profit2* *1970–2008* *ARDL (1, 2, 1, 3)*	
Short-Run Coefficients				
Trend	−0.007**		0.005	
	(0.003)		(0.003)	
Intercept	−1.288		8.708***	
	(1.142)		(1.532)	
Long-Run Coefficients				
Milex	−1.176		−0.998***	
	(0.792)		(0.101)	
GDP	1.907		−0.863***	
	(1.712)		(0.165)	
Unemployment	0.280		0.113**	
	(0.322)		(0.042)	
Trend	−0.098		0.008	
	(0.059)		(0.005)	
R-squared	0.988		0.963	
SER	0.024		0.017	
Serial correlation	1.758		1.395	
	[0.186]		[0.268]	
Functional form	9.320		0.343	
	[0.004]		[0.563]	
Normality	0.094		0.603	
	[0.953]		[0.739]	
Heteroscedasticity	1.800		0.880	
	[0.106]		[0.569]	
Bounds Test	1.765		15.459***	
F-Statistics	10% 3.17	4.00	10% 3.26	4.09
Actual sample size	5% 3.73	4.66	5% 3.85	4.78
	1% 5.05	6.18	1% 5.25	6.52

Table B.6 Results of ARDL bounds test: Austria (without unemployment)

	Profit1 *1957–2014* *ARDL (4, 0, 2)*	*Profit2* *1964–2008* *ARDL (1,0, 1)*
Short-Run Coefficients		
Profit (−1)	1.441***	0.818***
	(0.129)	(0.096)
Profit (−2)	−0.534***	
	(0.168)	
Profit (−3)	0.355**	
	(0.158)	

(*Continued*)

Table B.6 (Continued)

	Profit1 *1957–2014* *ARDL (4, 0, 2)*	*Profit2* *1964–2008* *ARDL (1,0, 1)*
Short-Run Coefficients		
Profit (−4)	−0.360***	
	(0.094)	
Milex	−0.060	−0.153**
	(0.038)	(0.068)
GDP	0.663***	0.429**
	(0.147)	(0.205)
GDP (−1)	−1.413***	−0.832***
	(0.213)	(0.197)
GDP (−2)	0.769***	
	(0.168)	
Trend	−0.002	0.011***
	(0.002)	(0.003)
Intercept	0.106	5.032***
	(0.586)	(1.344)
Long-Run Coefficients		
Milex	−0.619*	−0.846***
	(0.323)	(0.301)
GDP	0.202	−2.218***
	(0.553)	(0.666)
Trend	−0.027	0.062***
	(0.018)	(0.020)
R-squared	0.993	0.960
SER	0.020	0.023
Serial correlation	1.565	0.224
	[0.200]	[0.638]
Functional form	7.104	4.231
	[0.010]	[0.046]
Normality	2.106	1.763
	[0.348]	[0.414]
Heteroscedasticity	1.293	0.949
	[0.265]	[0.460]
Bounds Test	3.198	10.073***
F-Statistics	10% 3.54 4.23	10% 3.62 4.33
Actual sample size	5% 4.18 4.93	5% 4.33 5.07
	1% 5.62 6.50	1% 5.87 6.87

Table B.7 Results of ARDL bounds test: Belgium (with unemployment)

	Profit1 *1969–2014* *ARDL (2, 1, 2, 0)*	*Profit2* *1969–2008* *ARDL (1, 1, 1, 0)*
Short-Run Coefficients		
Profit (−1)	1.357***	0.741***
	(0.141)	(0.081)
Profit (−2)	−0.441***	
	(0.144)	
Milex	−0.260***	−0.248***
	(0.094)	(0.089)
Milex (−1)	0.226**	0.202**
	(0.085)	(0.087)
Milex (−2)		−0.128*
		(0.069)
GDP	0.789***	0.131
	(0.131)	(0.128)
GDP (−1)	−1.352***	−0.541***
	(0.199)	(0.134)
GDP (−2)	0.523***	
	(0.177)	
Unemployment	0.040*	0.023
	(0.020)	(0.023)
Trend	−0.001	0.009***
	(0.002)	(0.002)
Intercept	0.625	5.503***
	(1.223)	(1.115)
Long-Run Coefficients		
Milex	−0.404	−0.177
	(0.502)	(0.198)
GDP	−0.469	1.587***
	(1.128)	(0.556)
Unemployment	0.478	0.091
	(0.295)	(0.110)
Trend	−0.010	0.035***
	(0.030)	(0.011)
R-squared	0.963	0.918
SER	0.025	0.025
Serial correlation	0.525	0.384
	[0.595]	[0.539]
Functional form	2.188	1.069
	[0.148]	[0.309]
Normality	1.262	0.414
	[0.532]	[0.812]
Heteroscedasticity	0.654	4.793
	[0.743]	[0.001]
Bounds Test	2.398	7.998***
F-Statistics	10% 3.22 4.05	10% 3.264 4.094
Actual sample size	5% 3.82 4.71	5% 3.85 4.782
	1% 5.15 6.28	1% 5.258 6.526

Table B.8 Results of ARDL bounds test: Belgium (without unemployment)

	Profit1 *1954–2014* *ARDL (2, 1, 2)*	*Profit2* *1964–2008* *ARDL (1, 1, 1)*
Short-Run Coefficients		
Profit (−1)	1.424***	0.689***
	(0.119)	(0.064)
Profit (−2)	−0.477***	
	(0.127)	
Milex	−0.108*	−0.226***
	(0.064)	(0.082)
Milex (−1)	0.140**	0.225***
	(0.061)	(0.075)
GDP	0.751***	0.177
	(0.106)	(0.117)
GDP (−1)	−1.391***	−0.541***
	(0.176)	(0.126)
GDP (−2)	0.641***	
	(0.141)	
Trend	0.0004	0.009***
	(0.002)	(0.001)
Intercept	0.038	5.087***
	(0.590)	(0.935)
Long-Run Coefficients		
Milex	0.596	−0.004
	(0.685)	(0.089)
GDP	0.037	−1.172***
	(1.017)	(0.236)
Trend	0.009	0.031***
	(0.038)	(0.008)
R-squared	0.955	0.937
SER	0.024	0.024
Serial correlation	0.335	0.419
	[0.716]	[0.521]
Functional form	0.972	0.105
	[0.328]	[0.747]
Normality	1.128	0.281
	[0.568]	[0.866]
Heteroscedasticity	1.409	6.918
	[0.214]	[0.000]
Bounds Test	1.869	11.516***
F-Statistics	10% 3.54 4.23	10% 3.62 4.33
Actual sample size	5% 4.18 4.93	5% 4.33 5.07
	1% 5.62 6.50	1% 5.87 6.87

Table B.9 Results of ARDL bounds test: Brazil (with unemployment)

	Profit1 *1976–2014* *ARDL (4, 2, 4, 2)*	*Profit2* *1975–2008* *ARDL (1, 0, 0, 1)*	*Profit3* *1977–2010* *ARDL (3, 3, 0, 3)*
Short-Run Coefficients			
Profit (−1)	1.004***	1.039***	0.556***
	(0.171)	(0.053)	(0.190)
Profit (−2)	−0.349		−0.226
	(0.209)		(0.261)
Profit (−3)	0.416**		0.443**
	(0.188)		(0.195)
Profit (−4)	−0.468***		
	(0.149)		
Milex	0.019	0.025*	−0.290
	(0.029)	(0.024)	(0.186)
Milex (−1)	−0.031		0.188
	(0.042)		(0.238)
Milex (−2)	0.093**		0.157
	(0.035)		(0.278)
Milex (−3)			0.283
			(0.235)
GDP	0.423***	−0.033	0.561
	(0.126)	(0.047)	(0.450)
GDP (−1)	−0.481**	−1.442***	
	(0.185)	(0.387)	
GDP (−2)	0.410*		
	(0.199)		
GDP (−3)	−0.547***		
	(0.178)		
GDP (−4)	0.338***		
	(0.113)		
Unemployment	−0.040	−0.012	−0.015
	(0.029)	(0.025)	(0.168)
Unemployment (−1)	0.058*	0.040	−0.094
	().032)	(0.028)	(0.195)
Unemployment (−2)	0.025		0.034
	(0.028)		(0.199)
Unemployment (−3)			0.300*
			(0.170)
Trend	−0.016***	0.001	−0.030
	(0.005)	(0.002)	(0.024)
Intercept	−0.272	0.212	−6.347
	(0.952)	(0.565)	(5.251)
Long-Run Coefficients			
Milex	0.206**	−0.654	1.489
	(0.084)	(0.861)	(1.203)
GDP	0.359*	0.865	2.478
	(0.206)	(1.491)	(1.660)

(*Continued*)

Table B.9 (Continued)

	Profit1 *1976–2014* *ARDL (4, 2, 4, 2)*	*Profit2* *1975–2008* *ARDL (1, 0, 0, 1)*	*Profit3* *1977–2010* *ARDL (3, 3, 0, 3)*
Long-Run Coefficients			
Unemployment	0.109**	−0.725	0.995
	(0.047)	(1.037)	(0.720)
Trend	−0.042***	−0.026	−0.136
	(0.009)	(0.063)	(0.090)
R-squared	0.996	0.948	0.909
SER	0.020	0.022	0.116
Serial correlation	0.022	2.769	1.162
	[0.978]	[0.109]	[0.361]
Functional form	5.698	0.005	1.338
	[0.028]	[0.939]	[0.265]
Normality	0.274	18.222	4.986
	[0.871]	[0.000]	[0.082]
Heteroscedasticity	0.255	1.357	0.425
	[0.995]	[0.270]	[0.936]
Bounds Test	3.859	1.492	2.697
F-Statistics	10% 3.29 4.17	10% 3.37 4.27	10% 3.37 4.27
Actual sample size	5% 3.93 4.91	5% 4.04 5.09	5% 4.04 5.09
	1% 5.65 6.92	1% 5.66 6.98	1% 5.66 6.98
	Inconclusive		

Note: Profit3 taken from E. Maito.

Table B.10 Results of ARDL bounds test: Brazil (without unemployment)

	Profit1 *1953–2014* *ARDL (1, 0, 1)*	*Profit2* *1964–2008* *ARDL (1, 0, 1)*	*Profit3* *1958–2010* *ARDL (1, 1, 0)*
Short-Run Coefficients			
Profit (−1)	0.937***	0.909***	0.881***
	(0.036)	(0.059)	(0.061)
Milex	−0.004	0.015	−0.111
	(0.021)	(0.024)	(0.129)
Milex (−1)			0.314**
			(0.122)
GDP	0.306***	0.128	0.097
	(0.085)	(0.099)	(0.144)
GDP (−1)	−0.327***	−0.196*	
	(0.086)	(0.101)	
Trend	−0.0007	0.003	−0.003
	(0.005)	(0.002)	(0.007)
Intercept	0.468	1.121*	−0.949
	(0.472)	(0.664)	(1.735)

	Profit1 *1953–2014* *ARDL (1, 0, 1)*	*Profit2* *1964–2008* *ARDL (1, 0, 1)*	*Profit3* *1958–2010* *ARDL (1, 1, 0)*
Long-Run Coefficients			
Milex	−0.074	0.168	1.711
	(0.350)	(0.297)	(1.156)
GDP	−0.351	−0.756	0.823
	(0.864)	(0.591)	(1.272)
Trend	−0.011	0.039	−0.030
	(0.038)	(0.032)	(0.060)
R-squared	0.989	0.935	0.907
SER	0.031	0.033	0.123
Serial correlation	0.003	0.689	0.003
	[0.949]	[0.411]	[0.954]
Functional form	0.221	2.316	1.338
	[0.639]	[0.136]	[0.265]
Normality	18.732	9.131	0.010
	[0.000]	[0.010]	[0.917]
Heteroscedasticity	2.891	1.566	4.053
	[0.022]	[0.192]	[0.003]
Bounds Test	5.971**	1.879	2.528
F-Statistics	10% 3.54 4.23	10% 3.62 4.33	10% 3.55 4.23
Actual sample size	5% 4.18 4.93	5% 4.33 5.07	5% 4.18 4.95
	1% 5.62 6.50	1% 5.87 6.87	1% 5.67 6.57

Note: Profit3 taken from E. Maito.

Table B.11 Results of ARDL bounds test: Canada (with unemployment)

	Profit1 *1967–2014* *ARDL (2, 3, 3, 0)*	*Profit2* *1970–2008* *ARDL (2, 1, 1, 3)*	*Profit3* *1967–2014* *ARDL (1, 2, 1, 0)*
Short-Run Coefficients			
Profit (−1)	0.903***	0.932***	0.965***
	(0.152)	(0.121)	(0.071)
Profit (−2)	−0.448***	−0.290**	
	(0.139)	(0.117)	
Milex	0.114	0.012	−0.191**
	(0.174)	(0.081)	(0.090)
Milex (−1)	−0.070	−0.151*	0.328**
	(0.248)	(0.082)	(0.124)
Milex (−2)	−0.153		−0.211***
	(0.243)		(0.077)
Milex (−3)	−0.304		
	(0.180)		
GDP	1.086***	0.368**	1.288***
	(0.298)	(0.160)	(0.161)

(*Continued*)

Table B.11 (Continued)

	Profit1 1967–2014 ARDL (2, 3, 3, 0)	*Profit2* 1970–2008 ARDL (2, 1, 1, 3)	*Profit3* 1967–2014 ARDL (1, 2, 1, 0)
Short-Run Coefficients			
GDP (−1)	−1.425***	−1.017***	−1.607***
	(0.449)	(0.160)	(0.182)
GDP (−2)	0.490		
	(0.459)		
GDP (−3)	−0.700*		
	(0.373)		
Unemployment	0.039	0.002	0.075***
	(0.037)	(0.030)	(0.022)
Unemployment (−1)		0.011	
		(0.040)	
Unemployment (−2)		−0.065	
		(0.046)	
Unemployment (−3)		0.116***	
		(0.035)	
Trend	0.009	0.014***	0.008**
	(0.007)	(0.003)	(0.003)
Intercept	8.350**	9.396***	3.911**
	(3.539)	(1.502)	(1.517)
Long-Run Coefficients			
Milex	−0.757***	0.388***	−2.129
	(0.139)	(0.095)	(4.402)
GDP	−1.006**	−1.809***	−9.198
	(0.458)	(0.510)	(20.975)
Unemployment	0.072	0.183**	2.185
	(0.068)	(0.069)	(4.923)
Trend	0.017	0.041**	0.243
	(0.013)	(0.015)	(0.547)
R-squared	0.886	0.969	0.963
SER	0.046	0.016	0.027
Serial correlation	1.073	1.450	0.523
	[0.374]	[0.253]	[0.597]
Functional form	1.797	1.386	1.004
	[0.188]	[0.249]	[0.322]
Normality	23.596	0.598	2.204
	[0.000]	[0.741]	[0.332]
Heteroscedasticity	1.219	0.827	2.334
	[0.309]	[0.614]	[0.037]
Bounds Test	5.078**	13.273***	5.214**
F-Statistics	10% 3.17 4.004	10% 2.97 3.74	10% 2.97 3.74
Actual sample size	5% 3.73 4.666	5% 3.38 4.23	5% 3.38 4.23
	1% 5.05 6.182	1% 4.3 5.23	1% 4.3 5.23

Note: Profit3 is taken from Roberts (2015), calculated based on AMECO.

Table B.12 Results of ARDL bounds test: Canada (without unemployment)

	Profit1 *1952–2014* *ARDL (2, 0, 1)*	*Profit2* *1965–2008* *ARDL (2, 0, 1)*	*Profit3* *1961–2014* *ARDL (1, 0, 1)*
Short-Run Coefficients			
Profit (−1)	1.011***	0.985***	0.773***
	(0.113)	(0.108)	(0.056)
Profit (−2)	−0.235**	−0.400***	
	(0.109)	(0.104)	
Milex	−0.095	−0.083**	−0.019
	(0.046)	(0.030)	(0.035)
GDP	0.802***	0.499***	1.471***
	(0.228)	(0.157)	(0.162)
GDP (−1)	−0.951***	−0.811***	−1.515***
	(0.207)	(0.146)	(0.148)
Trend	0.002	0.006**	0.003
	(0.002)	(0.002)	(0.002)
Intercept	2.423*	5.459***	0.948
	(1.395)	(1.197)	(0.966)
Long-Run Coefficients			
Milex	−0.427**	−0.200***	−0.087
	(0.205)	(0.059)	(0.150)
GDP	−0.666	−0.752***	−0.193
	(0.478)	(0.201)	(0.333)
Trend	0.013	0.016**	0.014
	(0.013)	(0.006)	(0.010)
R-squared	0.816	0.956	0.952
SER	0.046	0.020	0.031
Serial correlation	1.531	1.112	1.950
	[0.225]	[0.339]	[0.153]
Functional form	2.223	9.934	0.944
	[0.141]	[0.003]	[0.336]
Normality	125.393	0.066	1.718
	[0.000]	[0.967]	[0.423]
Heteroscedasticity	1.953	1.180	1.885
	[0.088]	[0.337]	[0.114]
Bounds Test	3.499	9.834***	5.506**
F-Statistics	10% 3.53 4.20	10% 3.62 4.33	10% 3.55 4.23
Actual sample size	5% 4.12 4.90	5% 4.33 5.07	5% 4.18 4.95
	1% 5.54 6.45	1% 5.87 6.87	1% 5.67 6.57

Note: Profit3 is taken from Roberts (2015), calculated based on AMECO.

Table B.13 Results of ARDL bounds test: Chile (with unemployment)

	Profit1 *1973–2014* *ARDL (2, 1, 1, 0)*	*Profit2* *1975–2008* *ARDL (2, 1, 1, 2)*
Short-Run Coefficients		
Profit (−1)	0.797***	0.936***
	(0.076)	(0.094)
Profit (−2)	−0.159*	−0.129
	(0.078)	(0.095)
Milex	−0.137**	−0.084
	(0.057)	(0.090)
Milex (−1)	0.106	0.158*
	(0.046**)	(0.086)
GDP	0.781***	0.719***
	(0.073)	(0.104)
GDP (−1)	−0.686***	−1.019***
	(0.077)	(0.095)
Unemployment	0.029	0.078*
	(0.023)	(0.044)
Unemployment (−1)		−0.038
		(0.050)
Unemployment (−2)		−0.125**
		(0.053)
Trend	−0.011***	0.013**
	(0.003)	(0.005)
Intercept	0.420	3.665
	(0.323)	(0.747)
Long-Run Coefficients		
Milex	−0.085	0.381
	(0.086)	(0.464)
GDP	0.264***	−1.554***
	(0.090)	(0.445)
Unemployment	0.080	−0.443
	(0.067)	(0.337)
Trend	−0.031***	0.071**
	(0.005)	(0.029)
R-squared	0.988	0.984
SER	0.022	0.028
Serial correlation	0.956	1.775
	[0.395]	[0.199]
Functional form	0.878	0.872
	[0.355]	[0.362]
Normality	1.698	0.818
	[0.427]	[0.664]
Heteroscedasticity	1.453	1.108
	[0.212]	[0.404]
Bounds Test	10.273***	13.388***
F-Statistics	10% 2.97 3.74	10% 2.97 3.74
Actual sample size	5% 3.38 4.23	5% 3.38 4.23
	1% 4.3 5.23	1% 4.3 5.23

Table B.14 Results of ARDL bounds test: Chile (without unemployment)

	Profit1 *1953–2014* *ARDL (2, 0, 1)*	*Profit2* *1967–2008* *ARDL (3, 3, 3)*
Short-Run Coefficients		
Profit (−1)	0.862***	1.110***
	(0.058)	(0.134)
Profit (−2)	−0.104*	−0.855***
	(0.056)	(0.167)
Profit (−3)		0.534***
		(0.107)
Milex	0.007	−0.058
	(0.008)	(0.051)
Milex (−1)		−0.064
		(0.080)
Milex (−2)		0.308***
		(0.083)
Milex (−3)		−0.130*
		(0.072)
GDP	0.768***	0.583***
	(0.051)	(0.134)
GDP (−1)	−0.737***	−1.254***
	(0.050)	(0.214)
GDP (−2)		1.128***
		(0.254)
GDP (−3)		−0.718***
		(0.176)
Trend	−0.005***	0.009*
	(0.001)	(0.004)
Intercept	0.560**	3.345**
	(0.244)	(1.346)
Long-Run Coefficients		
Milex	0.029	0.264
	(0.033)	(0.156)
GDP	0.130	−1.242**
	(0.113)	(0.543)
Trend	−0.022***	0.042**
	(0.004)	(0.019)
R-squared	0.994	0.981
SER	0.022	0.037
Serial correlation	0.939	2.018
	[0.397]	[0.142]
Functional form	1.064	0.986
	[0.306]	[0.331]
Normality	37.076	0.963
	[0.000]	[0.617]
Heteroscedasticity	0.860	1.991
	[0.529]	[0.073]
Bounds Test	12.244***	8.703***
F-Statistics	10% 3.38 4.02	10%3.38 4.02
Actual sample size	5% 3.88 4.61	5% 3.88 4.61
	1% 4.99 5.85	1% 4.99 5.85

Table B.15 Results of ARDL bounds test: Denmark (with unemployment)

	Profit1 *1971–2014* *ARDL (3, 0, 2, 0)*	*Profit2* *1972–2008* *ARDL (1, 1, 0, 1)*
Short-Run Coefficients		
Profit (−1)	1.244***	0.853***
	(0.150)	(0.071)
Profit (−2)	−0.132	
	(0.181)	
Profit (−3)	−0.207*	
	(0.114)	
Milex	0.091	−0.452***
	(0.117)	(0.110)
Milex (−1)		0.619***
		(0.099)
GDP	1.060***	−0.101
	(0.258)	(0.190)
GDP (−1)	−1.686***	
	(0.278)	
GDP (−2)	0.656***	
	(0.240)	
Unemployment	0.006	−0.022
	(0.016)	(0.030)
Unemployment (−1)		−0.038
		(0.050)
Unemployment (−2)		0.027
		(0.021)
Trend	0.0003	0.003
	(0.003)	(0.003)
Intercept	−0.242	1.428
	(1.990)	(2.354)
Long-Run Coefficients		
Milex	0.964	1.138
	(1.692)	(1.190)
GDP	0.316	−0.693
	(1.865)	(1.130)
Unemployment	0.071	0.038
	(0.218)	(0.133)
Trend	0.003	0.024
	(0.034)	(0.018)
R-squared	0.929	0.941
SER	0.030	0.023
Serial correlation	0.516	0.297
	[0.674]	[0.589]
Functional form	0.338	1.880
	[0.564]	[0.181]
Normality	7.707	0.437
	[0.021]	[0.803]
Heteroscedasticity	2.147	1.306
	[0.0523]	[0.282]
Bounds Test	1.495	7.494***
F-Statistics	10% 2.97 3.74	10% 2.97 3.74
Actual sample size	5% 3.38 4.23	5% 3.38 4.23
	1% 4.3 5.23	1% 4.3 5.23

Table B.16 Results of ARDL bounds test: Denmark (without unemployment)

	Profit1 *1953–2014* *ARDL (3, 0, 2)*	*Profit2* *1964–2008* *ARDL (1, 1, 1)*
Short-Run Coefficients		
Profit (−1)	1.162***	0.737***
	(0.120)	(0.052)
Profit (−2)	−0.085	
	(0.149)	
Profit (−3)	−0.190**	
	(0.092)	
Milex	0.083	−0.273**
	(0.061)	(0.103)
Milex (−1)		0.442***
		(0.110)
GDP	0.874***	0.119
	(0.143)	(0.206)
GDP (−1)	−1.369***	−0.447**
	(0.202)	(0.199)
GDP (−2)	0.424**	
	(0.169)	
Trend	0.002	0.009***
	(0.001)	(0.002)
Intercept	0.911	4.272**
	(0.594)	(2.110)
Long-Run Coefficients		
Milex	0.733	0.643
	(0.703)	(0.499)
GDP	−0.615	−1.247**
	(0.423)	(0.529)
Trend	0.022	0.035***
	(0.017)	(0.008)
R-squared	0.978	0.972
SER	0.026	0.023
Serial correlation	0.726	2.317
	[0.541]	[0.136]
Functional form	0.114	2.867
	[0.736]	[0.098]
Normality	31.830	2.356
	[0.000]	[0.307]
Heteroscedasticity	1.744	2.509
	[0.109]	[0.038]
Bounds Test	3.078	14.828***
F-Statistics	10% 3.38 4.02	10% 3.38 4.02
Actual sample size	5% 3.88 4.61	5% 3.88 4.61
	1% 4.99 5.85	1% 4.99 5.85

Table B.17 Results of ARDL bounds test: Finland (with unemployment)

	Profit1 *1968–2014* *ARDL (4, 0, 3, 1)*	*Profit2* *1968–2008* *ARDL (1, 1, 0, 1)*
Short-Run Coefficients		
Profit (−1)	1.342***	0.829***
	(0.128)	(0.060)
Profit (−2)	−0.700***	
	(0.194)	
Profit (−3)	0.506***	
	(0.144)	
Profit (−4)	−0.290***	
	(0.087)	
Milex	−0.114*	−0.057
	(0.117)	(0.064)
GDP	0.721***	0.741***
	(0.181)	(0.191)
GDP (−1)	−1.772***	−0.998***
	(0.248)	(0.162)
GDP (−2)	1.148***	
	(0.324)	
GDP (−3)	−0.339	
	(0.233)	
Unemployment	−0.042*	−0.036
	(0.023)	(0.023)
Unemployment	0.068***	0.065
(−1)	(0.023)	(0.023)
Trend	0.006	0.008*
	(0.100)	(0.005)
Intercept	2.849**	3.166*
	(1.268)	(1.568)
Long-Run Coefficients		
Milex	−0.805**	−0.335
	(0.380)	(0.329)
GDP	−1.699	−1.510
	(1.130)	(0.935)
Unemployment	0.182	0.166
	(0.139)	(0.145)
Trend	0.043	0.050*
	(0.031)	(0.029)
R-squared	0.970	0.972
SER	0.032	0.033
Serial correlation	1.953	0.597
	[0.127]	[0.445]
Functional form	3.112	0.347
	[0.087]	[0.559]
Normality	1.142	3.023
	[0.564]	[0.220]
Heteroscedasticity	2.046	1.261
	[0.050]	[0.299]
Bounds Test	5.558**	9.769***
F-Statistics	10% 3.22 4.05	10% 3.264 4.094
Actual sample size	5% 3.82 4.71	5% 3.85 4.782
	1% 5.15 6.28	1% 5.258 6.526

Table B.18 Results of ARDL bounds test: Finland (with unemployment)

	Profit1 *1958–2014* *ARDL (6, 0, 4)*	*Profit2* *1964–2008* *ARDL (1, 0, 1)*
Short-Run Coefficients		
Profit (−1)	1.404***	0.798***
	(0.143)	(0.039)
Profit (−2)	−0.974***	
	(0.240)	
Profit (−3)	0.881***	
	(0.236)	
Profit (−4)	−0.473***	
	(0.173)	
Profit (−5)	0.185	
	(0.146)	
Profit (−6)	−0.214	
	(0.094)	
Milex	−0.077*	−0.089
	(0.045)	(0.058)
GDP	0.794***	0.825***
	(0.147)	(0.162)
GDP (−1)	−1.841***	−1.215***
	(0.237)	(0.146)
GDP (−2)	1.391***	
	(0.358)	
GDP (−3)	−0.978**	
	(0.367)	
GDP (−4)	0.353	
	(0.214)	
Trend	0.008***	0.014***
	(0.002)	(0.003)
Intercept	3.341***	4.628***
	(0.988)	(1.128)
Long-Run Coefficients		
Milex	−0.406*	−0.444
	(0.226)	(0.268)
GDP	−1.470***	−1.932***
	(0.408)	(0.579)
Trend	0.045***	0.071***
	(0.013)	(0.018)
R-squared	0.968	0.965
SER	0.032	0.034
Serial correlation	0.439	2.635
	[0.847]	[0.112]
Functional form	1.262	0.644
	[0.267]	[0.427]
Normality	0.927	3.589
	[0.629]	[0.166]
Heteroscedasticity	1.165	0.733
	[0.335]	[0.602]
Bounds Test	4.714*	11.658***
F-Statistics	10% 3.55 4.23	10% 3.62 4.33
Actual sample size	5% 4.18 4.95	5% 4.33 5.07
	1% 5.67 6.57	1% 5.87 6.87

Table B.19 Results of ARDL bounds test: France (with unemployment)

	Profit1 *1971–2014* *ARDL (1, 0, 1, 3)*	*Profit2* *1968–2008* *ARDL (1, 3, 1, 0)*	*Profit3* *1971–2014* *ARDL (1, 1, 1, 3)*
Short-Run Coefficients			
Profit (−1)	0.729***	0.707***	0.717***
	(0.049)	(0.064)	(0.067)
Milex	−0.543***	−0.192	−0.689***
	(0.168)	(0.157)	(0.201)
Milex (−1)		0.311	0.386*
		(0.184)	(0.211)
Milex (−2)		−0.328**	
		(0.158)	
Milex (−3)		0.250**	
		(0.115)	
GDP	0.040	0.173	0.239
	(0.255)	(0.155)	(0.207)
GDP (−1)	−0.557**	−0.439**	−0.720***
	(0.204)	(0.161)	(0.212)
Unemployment	0.021	0.026**	0.010
	(0.062)	(0.012)	(0.052)
Unemployment	−0.013		−0.056
(−1)	(0.081)		(0.073)
Unemployment	−0.108		−0.004
(−2)	(0.078)		(0.065)
Unemployment	0.266***		0.102**
(−3)	(0.058)		(0.045)
Trend	0.002	0.007***	0.005**
	(0.003)	(0.002)	(0.002)
Intercept	8.312***	4.363***	7.486***
	(2.000)	(1.518)	(2.026)
Long-Run Coefficients			
Milex	−2.010***	0.140	−1.074**
	(0.462)	(0.322)	(0.405)
GDP	−1.912***	−0.910***	−1.705***
	(0.467)	(0.302)	(0.398)
Unemployment	0.601***	0.091*	0.184***
	(0.080)	(0.051)	(0.065)
Trend	−0.007	0.025***	0.018*
	(0.011)	(0.005)	(0.009)
R-squared	0.978	0.962	0.946
SER	0.029	0.017	0.023
Serial correlation	0.214	0.940	0.473
	[0.885]	[0.434]	[0.627]
Functional form	8.195	0.745	0.010
	[0.007]	[0.394]	[0.919]
Normality	1.389	0.711	2.876
	[0.499]	[0.700]	[0.237]
Heteroscedasticity	1.632	1.796	0.833
	[0.145]	[0.109]	[0.600]
Bounds Test	15.179***	12.289***	11.308***
F-Statistics	10%3.22 4.05	10% 3.26 4.09	10% 3.22 4.05
Actual sample size	5% 3.82 4.71	5% 3.85 4.78	5% 3.82 4.71
	1% 5.15 6.28	1% 5.25 6.52	1% 5.15 6.28

Note: Profit3 is taken from Roberts (2015), calculated based on AMECO.

Table B.20 Results of ARDL bounds test: France (without unemployment)

	Profit1 *1951–2014* *ARDL (1, 0, 0)*	*Profit2* *1964–2008* *ARDL (1,0, 1)*	*Profit3* *1962–2014* *ARDL (2, 1, 2)*
Short-Run Coefficients			
Profit (−1)	0.993***	0.698***	1.267***
	(0.046)	(0.064)	(0.067)
Profit (−2)			−0.361***
			(0.104)
Milex	0.028	0.114*	−0.456***
	(0.125)	(0.065)	(0.159)
Milex (−1)			0.447***
			(0.156)
GDP	−0.013	0.364**	0.398*
	(0.097)	(0.151)	(0.220)
GDP (−1)		−0.620***	−1.221***
		(0.140)	(0.294)
GDP (−2)			0.727***
			(0.196)
Trend	0.0001	0.009***	0.002
	(0.002)	(0.001)	(0.001)
Intercept	0.172	4.147***	1.484
	(1.410)	(1.464)	(1.687)
Long-Run Coefficients			
Milex	4.404	0.378	−0.094
	(39.477)	(0.262)	(1.277)
GDP	−1.991	−0.849***	−1.011
	(23.923)	(0.188)	(0.748)
Trend	−0.028	0.031***	0.0123
	(0.287)	(0.003)	(0.016)
R-squared	0.964	0.966	0.965
SER	0.057	0.018	0.027
Serial correlation	0.003	1.698	0.268
	[0.952]	[0.200]	[0.766]
Functional form	0.438	1.817	1.384
	[0.510]	[0.185]	[0.245]
Normality	74.909	2.074	1.698
	[0.000]	[0.354]	[0.427]
Heteroscedasticity	2.166	0.722	0.973
	[0.083]	[0.610]	[0.469]
Bounds Test	2.847	15.244***	1.653
F-Statistics	10% 3.53 4.20	10% 3.62 4.33	10% 3.55 4.23
Actual sample size	5% 4.12 4.90	5% 4.33 5.07	5% 4.18 4.95
	1% 5.54 6.45	1% 5.87 6.87	1% 5.67 6.57

Note: Profit3 is taken from Roberts (2015), calculated based on AMECO.

Table B.21 Results of ARDL bounds test: Germany (with unemployment)

	Profit1 *1971–2014* *ARDL* *(2, 0, 2, 0)*	*Profit2* *1964–2008* *ARDL* *(1, 0, 2, 2)*	*Profit3* *1963–2011* *ARDL* *(1, 1, 2, 1)*	*Profit4* *1962–2014* *ARDL* *(1, 3, 1, 0)*
Short-Run Coefficients				
Profit (−1)	1.290***	1.017***	0.907***	0.860***
	(0.122)	(0.055)	(0.064)	(0.077)
Profit (−2)	−0.389***			
	(0.118)			
Milex	−0.063*	0.005	−0.333***	−0.121
	(0.035)	(0.042)	(0.098)	(0.110)
Milex (−1)			0.176*	−0.005
			(0.103)	(0.139)
Milex (−2)				0.315**
				(0.137)
Milex (−3)				−0.340***
				(0.095)
GDP	0.654***	0.058	0.790***	0.403
	(0.131)	(0.163)	(0.225)	(0.256)
GDP (−1)	−1.373***	−0.687**	−1.978***	−0.885***
	(0.189)	(0.253)	(0.292)	(0.249)
GDP (−2)	0.714***	0.299	0.720***	
	(0.157)	(0.190)	(0.214)	
Unemployment	0.006	−0.0001	0.073***	0.020
	(0.007)	(0.015)	(0.023)	(0.017)
Unemployment (−1)		0.071***	−0.045*	
		(0.021)	(0.022)	
Unemployment (−2)		−0.062***		
		(0.014)		
Trend	−0.001	0.010***	0.008**	0.009**
	(0.001)	(0.002)	(0.003)	(0.003)
Intercept	0.392	4.252**	6.687***	6.967***
	(1.207)	(1.560)	(2.452)	(2.169)
Long-Run Coefficients				
Milex	−0.642*	−0.323	−1.695*	−1.090
	(0.368)	(1.923)	(0.856)	(0.688)
GDP	−0.047	18.414	−5.023*	−3.454*
	(0.857)	(61.645)	(2.696)	(1.826)
Unemployment	0.067	−0.465	0.298	0.149
	(0.080)	(1.174)	(0.319)	(0.194)
Trend	−0.018	−0.612	0.092*	0.068*
	(0.022)	(2.006)	(0.051)	(0.034)
R-squared	0.952	0.985	0.962	0.923
SER	0.021	0.017	0.031	0.039
Serial correlation	0.076	0.779	0.194	1.331
	[0.926]	[0.466]	[0.824]	[0.275]

	Profit1 *1971–2014* *ARDL* *(2, 0, 2, 0)*	*Profit2* *1964–2008* *ARDL* *(1, 0, 2, 2)*	*Profit3* *1963–2011* *ARDL* *(1, 1, 2, 1)*	*Profit4* *1962–2014* *ARDL* *(1, 3, 1, 0)*
Long-Run Coefficients				
Functional form	0.189	0.038	1.467	0.0007
	[0.665]	[0.846]	[0.233]	[0.978]
Normality	7.190	0.511	0.930	0.447
	[0.027]	[0.774]	[0.628]	[0.799]
Heteroscedasticity	0.843	0.562	1.281	1.211
	[0.570]	[0.817]	[0.277]	[0.313]
Bounds Test	1.872	13.826***	5.075**	5.786**
F-Statistics	10% 3.13 3.95	10% 3.22 4.05	10% 3.17 4.00	10% 3.13 3.95
Actual sample size	5% 3.69 4.58	5% 3.82 4.71	5% 3.73 4.66	5% 3.69 4.58
	1% 4.99 6.01	1% 5.15 6.28	1% 5.05 6.18	1% 4.99 6.01

Note: Profit3 is taken from E. Maito, and Profit4 is from Roberts (2015), calculated based on AMECO.

Table B.22 Results of ARDL bounds test: Germany (without unemployment)

	Profit1 *1953–2014* *ARDL (2, 0, 2)*	*Profit2* *1964–2008* *ARDL (1, 0, 2)*	*Profit3* *1963–2011* *ARDL (1, 0, 2)*	*Profit4* *1962–2014* *ARDL (2, 0, 2)*
Short-Run Coefficients				
Profit (−1)	1.317***	1.002***	0.860***	1.018***
	(0.102)	(0.055)	(0.039)	(0.142)
Profit (−2)	−0.435***			−0.172
	(0.094)			(0.124)
Milex	−0.064***	0.014	−0.089**	−0.070
	(0.021)	(0.052)	(0.040)	(0.065)
GDP	0.578***	0.194	0.843***	0.533**
	(0.106)	(0.169)	(0.182)	(0.257)
GDP (−1)	−1.315***	−1.290***	−1.851***	−1.471***
	(0.158)	(0.245)	(0.269)	(0.345)
GDP (−2)	0.714***	0.813***	0.816***	0.588**
	(0.114)	(0.192)	(0.186)	(0.276)
Trend	−0.001	0.010***	0.003*	0.008*
	(0.001)	(0.002)	(0.002)	(0.004)
Intercept	0.661	3.682**	3.046***	5.088*
	(0.448)	(1.802)	(0.896)	(2.555)
Long-Run Coefficients				
Milex	−0.549***	−6.693	−1.639***	−0.459
	(0.186)	(154.706)	(0.236)	(0.382)
GDP	−0.188	134.101	−1.375***	−2.272**
	(0.258)	(3516.457)	(0.430)	(0.952)

(*Continued*)

Table B.22 (Continued)

	Profit1 *1953–2014* *ARDL (2, 0, 2)*	*Profit2* *1964–2008* *ARDL (1, 0, 2)*	*Profit3* *1963–2011* *ARDL (1, 0, 2)*	*Profit4* *1962–2014* *ARDL (2, 0, 2)*
Long-Run Coefficients				
Trend	−0.007	−4.787	0.028	0.057**
	(0.010)	(124.594)	(0.017)	(0.024)
R-squared	0.955	0.975	0.979	0.909
SER	0.020	0.022	0.034	0.041
Serial correlation	0.031	0.0004	1.608	0.294
	[0.969]	[0.999]	[0.210]	[0.746]
Functional form	0.250	0.689	1.222	0.487
	[0.618]	[0.411]	[0.274]	[0.488]
Normality	11.036	0.636	0.094	12.603
	[0.004]	[0.727]	[0.953]	[0.001]
Heteroscedasticity	1.285	0.979	2.882	1.423
	[0.274]	[0.452]	[0.016]	[0.219]
Bounds Test	3.278	8.778***	5.147**	2.242
F-Statistics	10% 3.54 4.23	10% 3.62 4.33	10% 3.54 4.23	10% 3.55 4.23
Actual sample size	5% 4.18 4.93	5% 4.33 5.07	5% 4.18 4.93	5% 4.18 4.95
	1% 5.62 6.50	1% 5.87 6.87	1% 5.62 6.50	1% 5.67 6.57

Note: Profit3 is taken from E. Maito, and Profit4 is from Roberts (2015), calculated based on AMECO.

Table B.23 Results of ARDL bounds test: Greece (without unemployment)

	Profit1 *1953–2014* *ARDL (2, 0, 1)*
Short-Run Coefficients	
Profit (−1)	1.120***
	(0.101)
Profit (−2)	−0.263**
	(0.100)
Milex	0.035
	(0.045)
GDP	0.624***
	(0.115)
GDP(−1)	−0.698***
	(0.122)
Trend	0.001
	(0.002)
Intercept	1.059***
	(0.290)

	Profit1 *1953–2014* *ARDL (2, 0, 1)*
Long-Run Coefficients	
Milex	0.250
	(0.390)
GDP	−0.514
	(0.419)
Trend	0.013
	(0.021)
R-squared	0.983
SER	0.034
Serial correlation	0.660
	[0.520]
Functional form	0.005
	[0.942]
Normality	4.497
	[0.105]
Heteroscedasticity	1.323
	[0.262]
Bounds Test	7.190***
F-Statistics	10% 3.54 4.23
Actual sample size	5% 4.18 4.93
	1% 5.62 6.50

Table B.24 Results of ARDL bounds test: Indonesia

	Profit1 *1984–2014* *ARDL (1, 0, 4, 2)*	*Profit1 (without unemp)* *1974–2014* *ARDL (2, 0, 3)*
Short-Run Coefficients		
Profit (−1)	1.089***	1.469***
	(0.122)	(0.137)
Profit (−2)		−0.513***
		(0.147)
Milex	0.190***	−0.002
	(0.048)	(0.042)
GDP	0.587***	0.583***
	(0.110)	(0.111)
GDP(−1)	−0.585***	−0.767***
	(0.177)	(0.194)
GDP(−2)	−0.462**	−0.038
	(0.172)	(0.204)
GDP(−3)	−0.184	0.339***
	(0.174)	(0.119)

(*Continued*)

Table B.24 (Continued)

	Profit1 *1984–2014* *ARDL (1, 0, 4, 2)*	*Profit1 (without unemp)* *1974–2014* *ARDL (2, 0, 3)*
Short-Run Coefficients		
GDP(−4)	0.595***	
	(0.137)	
Unemployment	−0.091*	
	(0.045)	
Unemployment (−1)	0.029	
	(0.045)	
Unemployment (−2)	−0.126***	
	(0.037)	
Trend	0.022**	−0.008*
	(0.009)	(0.004)
Intercept	−0.399	−1.050**
	(0.727)	(0.483)
Long-Run Coefficients		
Milex	−2.127	−0.056
	(1.252)	(0.941)
GDP	0.553	2.614
	(0.761)	(1.952)
Unemployment	2.102**	
	(0.998)	
Trend	−0.247**	−0.191
	(0.090)	(0.118)
R-squared	0.996	0.993
SER	0.031	0.035
Serial correlation	2.296	1.499
	[0.106]	[0.235]
Functional form	21.447	16.581
	[0.0002]	[0.0003]
Normality	3.835	24.997
	[0.146]	[0.0000]
Heteroscedasticity	1.123	1.123
	[0.396]	[0.396]
Bounds Test	12.567***	2.762
F-Statistics	10% 3.37 4.27	10% 3.66 4.37
Actual sample size	5% 4.04 5.09	5% 4.36 5.13
	1% 5.66 6.98	1% 5.98 6.97

Table B.25 Results of ARDL bounds test: Ireland (without unemployment)

	Profit1 *1958–2014* *ARDL (2, 0, 2)*	*Profit2* *1964–2008* *ARDL (1, 1, 1)*
Short-Run Coefficients		
Profit (−1)	1.464***	0.915***
	(0.116)	(0.050)
Profit (−2)	−0.620***	
	(0.114)	
Milex	0.0007	−0.395***
	(0.033)	(0.100)
Milex (−1)		0.313***
		(0.100)
GDP	0.754***	0.443**
	(0.166)	(0.173)
GDP (−1)	−1.070***	−0.698***
	(0.242)	(0.172)
GDP (−2)	0.355**	
	(0.172)	
Trend	−0.003	0.012***
	(0.003)	(0.003)
Intercept	0.108	2.594***
	(0.575)	(0.670)
Long-Run Coefficients		
Milex	0.004	−0.972**
	(0.216)	(0.452)
GDP	0.258	−3.031
	(0.398)	(1.868)
Trend	−0.022	0.151
	(0.017)	(0.100)
R-squared	0.969	0.977
SER	0.036	0.034
Serial correlation	0.078	0.005
	[0.924]	[0.942]
Functional form	6.241	0.002
	[0.016]	[0.962]
Normality	54.629	3.961
	[0.000]	[0.137]
Heteroscedasticity	3.302	1.562
	[0.005]	[0.184]
Bounds Test	2.353	8.806***
F-Statistics	10% 3.55 4.23	10% 3.62 4.33
Actual sample size	5% 4.18 4.95	5% 4.33 5.07
	1% 5.67 6.57	1% 5.87 6.87

Table B.26 Results of ARDL bounds test: Israel (with unemployment)

	Profit1 *1968–2014* *ARDL (1, 3, 2, 1)*	*Profit2* *1967–2008* *ARDL (1, 3, 2, 0)*
Short-Run Coefficients		
Profit (−1)	0.782***	0.777***
	(0.066)	(0.089)
Milex	0.079**	0.110**
	(0.033)	(0.047)
Milex (−1)	0.025	0.039
	(0.036)	(0.050)
Milex (−2)	−0.046	−0.069
	(0.031)	(0.049)
Milex (−3)	−0.056*	−0.028
	(0.029)	(0.036)
GDP	0.578***	0.539***
	(0.132)	(0.175)
GDP (−1)	−0.870***	−1.263***
	(0.202)	(0.272)
GDP (−2)	0.254**	0.395*
	(0.119)	(0.228)
Unemployment	0.023	0.031
	(0.022)	(0.019)
Unemployment (−1)	−0.065***	
	(0.021)	
Trend	0.002	0.016***
	(0.001)	(0.004)
Intercept	0.946*	3.659***
	(0.504)	(0.837)
Long-Run Coefficients		
Milex	0.009	0.234*
	(0.098)	(0.122)
GDP	−0.171	−1.474***
	(0.185)	(0.521)
Unemployment	−0.193***	0.141
	(0.054)	(0.104)
Trend	0.009	0.074***
	(0.008)	(0.024)
R-squared	0.988	0.939
SER	0.020	0.031
Serial correlation	1.189	0.855
	[0.329]	[0.475]
Functional form	0.288	5.336
	[0.594]	[0.027]
Normality	1.189	2.430
	[0.551]	[0.296]
Heteroscedasticity	0.818	1.123
	[0.622]	[0.376]
Bounds Test	7.885***	4.815**
F-Statistics	10% 3.22 4.05	10% 3.26 4.09
Actual sample size	5% 3.82 4.71	5% 3.85 4.78
	1% 5.15 6.28	1% 5.25 6.52

Table B.27 Results of ARDL bounds test: Israel (without unemployment)

	Profit1 *1960–2014* *ARDL (1, 0, 1)*	*Profit2* *1964–2008* *ARDL (1, 0, 1)*
Short-Run Coefficients		
Profit (−1)	0.928***	0.690***
	(0.038)	(0.069)
Milex	−0.019*	0.106***
	(0.011)	(0.021)
GDP	0.337***	0.353*
	(0.103)	(0.184)
GDP (−1)	−0.422***	−0.800***
	(0.103)	(0.194)
Trend	0.003	0.024***
	(0.001)	(0.003)
Intercept	1.037**	4.899***
	(0.424)	(0.738)
Long-Run Coefficients		
Milex	−0.268	0.343***
	(0.225)	(0.079)
GDP	−1.188*	−1.444***
	(0.658)	(0.377)
Trend	0.050	0.079***
	(0.034)	(0.020)
R-squared	0.986	0.887
SER	0.025	0.038
Serial correlation	1.189	0.097
	[0.329]	[0.756]
Functional form	0.118	0.449
	[0.732]	[0.506]
Normality	8.562	2.588
	[0.013]	[0.274]
Heteroscedasticity	3.158	2.027
	[0.015]	[0.096]
Bounds Test	7.196***	12.630***
F-Statistics	10% 3.55 4.23	10% 3.62 4.33
Actual sample size	5% 4.18 4.95	5% 4.33 5.07
	1% 5.67 6.57	1% 5.87 6.87

Table B.28 Results of ARDL bounds test: Italy (with unemployment)

	Profit2 *1964–2008* *ARDL (1, 0, 1, 0)*	*Profit3* *1968–2014* *ARDL (2, 0, 2, 0)*
Short-Run Coefficients		
Profit (−1)	0.815***	1.305***
	(0.088)	(0.126)
Profit (−2)		−0.382***
		(0.117)
Milex	0.248**	0.167*
	(0.117)	(0.089)
GDP	0.904***	0.770***
	(0.229)	(0.187)
GDP (−1)	−0.662***	−1.497***
	(0.208)	(0.248)
GDP (−2)		0.818***
		(0.184)
Unemployment	0.028	0.029
	(0.047)	(0.028)
Trend	−0.003	−0.0006
	(0.004)	(0.001)
Intercept	−2.901**	−1.265*
	(1.331)	(0.713)
Long-Run Coefficients		
Milex	1.344**	2.195
	(0.621)	(1.479)
GDP	1.309	1.208
	(0.843)	(1.011)
Unemployment	0.153	0.392
	(0.253)	(0.497)
Trend	−0.018	−0.008
	(0.025)	(0.026)
R-squared	0.875	0.950
SER	0.037	0.031
Serial correlation	1.666	0.774
	[0.205]	[0.468]
Functional form	6.557	0.001
	[0.015]	[0.964]
Normality	8.124	2.045
	[0.017]	[0.359]
Heteroscedasticity	1.224	5.718
	[0.318]	[0.0001]
Bounds Test	3.042	2.128
F-Statistics	10% 3.26 4.09	10% 3.22 4.05
Actual sample size	5% 3.85 4.78	5% 3.82 4.71
	1% 5.25 6.52	1% 5.15 6.28

Note: Profit3 is taken from Roberts (2015), calculated based on AMECO.

Table B.29 Results of ARDL bounds test: Italy (without unemployment)

	Profit2 *1968–2008* *ARDL (1, 0, 2)*	*Profit3* *1962–2014* *ARDL (2, 0, 2)*
Short-Run Coefficients		
Profit (−1)	0.869***	1.324***
	(0.082)	(0.118)
Profit (−2)		−0.414***
		(0.110)
Milex	0.204**	0.147*
	(0.099)	(0.078)
GDP	0.883***	0.680***
	(0.203)	(0.174)
GDP (−1)	−1.154***	−1.449***
	(0.289)	(0.238)
GDP (−2)	0.477**	0.833***
	(0.190)	(0.179)
Trend	−0.004**	−0.0005
	(0.002)	(0.001)
Intercept	−2.445**	−0.749
	(0.904)	(0.585)
Long-Run Coefficients		
Milex	1.560*	1.646*
	(0.864)	(0.876)
GDP	1.580	0.712
	(1.045)	(0.612)
Trend	−0.032	−0.006
	(0.029)	(0.017)
R-squared	0.877	0.945
SER	0.035	0.031
Serial correlation	2.049	0.043
	[0.143]	[0.957]
Functional form	4.256	5.780
	[0.046]	[0.999]
Normality	39.521	1.670
	[0.000]	[0.433]
Heteroscedasticity	1.380	4.912
	[0.247]	[0.0004]
Bounds Test	2.808	2.348
F-Statistics	10% 3.62 4.33	10% 3.55 4.23
Actual sample size	5% 4.33 5.07	5% 4.18 4.95
	1% 5.87 6.87	1% 5.67 6.57

Note: Profit3 is taken from Roberts (2015), calculated based on AMECO.

Table B.30 Results of ARDL bounds test: Japan (with unemployment)

	Profit1 *1964–2014* *ARDL* *(1, 2, 1, 1)*	*Profit2* *1966–2007* *ARDL* *(3, 1, 1, 0)*	*Profit3* *1964–2010* *ARDL* *(1, 1, 0, 1)*	*Profit4* *1963–2014* *ARDL* *(2, 0, 2, 0)*
Short-Run Coefficients				
Profit (−1)	0.705***	0.738***	0.841***	1.017***
	(0.081)	(0.110)	(0.073)	(0.124)
Profit (−2)		0.302*		−0.310***
		(0.157)		(0.097)
Profit (−3)		−0.295***		
		(0.094)		
Milex	0.308	−1.033***	−1.815***	−0.418***
	(0.258)	(0.197)	(0.296)	(0.140)
Milex (−1)	0.217	0.909***	1.947***	
	(0.318)	(0.181)	(0.264)	
Milex (−2)	−0.555***			
	(0.191)			
GDP	0.866***	0.201	−0.061	1.191***
	(0.218)	(0.131)	(0.043)	(0.154)
GDP (−1)	−0.855***	−0.428***		−1.884***
	(0.215)	(0.143)		(0.287)
GDP (−2)				0.595**
				(0.220)
Unemployment	0.003	0.006	−0.106	0.025
	(0.045)	(0.026)	(0.068)	(0.030)
Unemployment (−1)	0.106**		0.208***	
	(0.044)		(0.063)	
Trend	−0.004***	0.007***	−0.006***	0.002**
	(0.001)	(0.002)	(0.002)	(0.001)
Intercept	0.588*	3.826***	1.495**	1.907***
	(0.319)	(0.764)	(0.722)	(0.398)
Long-Run Coefficients				
Milex	−0.099	−0.488	0.830	−1.430***
	(0.482)	(0.386)	(1.453)	(0.368)
GDP	0.037	−0.891***	−0.389	−0.333***
	(0.090)	(0.113)	(0.269)	(0.098)
Unemployment	0.372**	0.025	0.643	0.087
	(0.145)	(0.108)	(0.556)	(0.109)
Trend	−0.016***	0.029***	−0.040**	0.009**
	(0.003)	(0.005)	(0.019)	(0.003)
R-squared	0.967	0.995	0.993	0.978
SER	0.028	0.018	0.044	0.029
Serial correlation	0.742	0.894	2.117	0.586
	[0.482]	[0.455]	[0.153]	[0.561]
Functional form	0.001	2.108	1.726	2.236
	[0.972]	[0.156]	[0.196]	[0.142]
Normality	3.204	0.394	1.089	1.548
	[0.201]	[0.820]	[0.580]	[0.461]

	Profit1 *1964–2014* *ARDL* *(1, 2, 1, 1)*	*Profit2* *1966–2007* *ARDL* *(3, 1, 1, 0)*	*Profit3* *1964–2010* *ARDL* *(1, 1, 0, 1)*	*Profit4* *1963–2014* *ARDL* *(2, 0, 2, 0)*
Long-Run Coefficients				
Heteroscedasticity	1.708	1.197	3.239	0.824
	[0.118]	[0.330]	[0.008]	[0.585]
Bounds Test	5.816**	14.186***	5.933**	5.953**
F-Statistics	10% 3.17 4.00	10% 3.26 4.09	10% 3.22 4.05	10% 3.17 4.00
Actual sample size	5% 3.73 4.66	5% 3.85 4.78	5% 3.82 4.71	5% 3.73 4.66
	1% 5.05 6.18	1% 5.25 6.52	1% 5.15 6.28	1% 5.05 6.18

Note: Profit3 is taken from E. Maito, and Profit4 is from Roberts (2015), calculated based on AMECO.

Table B.31 Results of ARDL bounds test: Japan (without unemployment)

	Profit1 *1964–2014* *ARDL (2, 0, 2)*	*Profit2* *1966–2007* *ARDL (3, 1, 1)*	*Profit3* *1958–2010* *ARDL (3, 1, 2)*	*Profit4* *1962–2014* *ARDL (2, 2, 2)*
Short-Run Coefficients				
Profit (−1)	1.118***	0.733***	0.939***	1.129***
	(0.110)	(0.107)	(0.136)	(0.124)
Profit (−2)	−0.351***	0.299*	0.009	−0.395***
	(0.104)	(0.154)	(0.174)	(0.100)
Profit (−3)		−0.295***	−0.197*	
		(0.092)	(0.117)	
Milex	0.018	−1.034***	−0.667**	−0.689***
	(0.025)	(0.194)	(0.283)	(0.231)
Milex (−1)		0.903***	0.484*	0.715**
		(0.177)	(0.272)	(0.338)
Milex (−2)				−0.395**
				(0.195)
GDP	0.708***	0.193	1.297***	0.894***
	(0.145)	(0.134)	(0.309)	(0.225)
GDP (−1)	−1.313***	−0.427***	−2.299***	−1.458***
	(0.230)	(0.141)	(0.525)	(0.379)
GDP (−2)			0.975***	0.483*
			(0.360)	(0.249)
Trend	−0.003***	0.007***	−0.006**	0.002**
	(0.001)	(0.001)	(0.002)	(0.001)
Intercept	0.054	3.935***	1.253	1.639***
	(0.218)	(0.609)	(0.906)	(0.411)

(*Continued*)

Table B.31 (Continued)

	Profit1 *1964–2014* *ARDL (2, 0, 2)*	*Profit2* *1966–2007* *ARDL (3, 1, 1)*	*Profit3* *1958–2010* *ARDL (3, 1, 2)*	*Profit4* *1962–2014* *ARDL (2, 2, 2)*
Long-Run Coefficients				
Milex	0.078	−0.497	−0.738**	−1.387***
	(0.104)	(0.365)	(0.362)	(0.421)
GDP	0.188**	−0.887***	−0.102	−0.302***
	(0.071)	(0.106)	(0.179)	(0.095)
Trend	−0.015***	0.030***	−0.024**	0.009**
	(0.003)	(0.004)	(0.009)	(0.003)
R-squared	0.966	0.995	0.992	0.978
SER	0.027	0.017	0.049	0.029
Serial correlation	0.191	0.826	0.852	1.780
	[0.826]	[0.489]	[0.473]	[0.181]
Functional form	0.007	2.087	0.491	2.175
	[0.932]	[0.158]	[0.487]	[0.147]
Normality	72.731	0.368	0.207	1.685
	[0.000]	[0.831]	[0.901]	[0.430]
Heteroscedasticity	1.206	1.314	2.696	0.651
	[0.314]	[0.270]	[0.014]	[0.746]
Bounds Test	3.247	18.238***	2.032	4.563**
F-Statistics	10% 3.53 4.20	10% 3.66 4.37	10% 3.55 4.23	10% 3.55 4.23
Actual sample size	5% 4.12 4.90	5% 4.36 5.13	5% 4.18 4.95	5% 4.18 4.95
	1% 5.54 6.45	1% 5.98 6.97	1% 5.67 6.57	1% 5.67 6.57

Note: Profit3 is taken from E. Maito, and Profit4 is from Roberts (2015), calculated based on AMECO.

Table B.32 Results of ARDL bounds test: Luxembourg (with unemployment)

	Profit1 *1973–2014* *ARDL (3, 1, 1, 0)*	*Profit2* *1975–2008* *ARDL (1, 3, 1, 2)*
Short-Run Coefficients		
Profit (−1)	0.767***	0.446***
	(0.161)	(0.087)
Profit (−2)	−0.395**	
	(0.160)	
Profit (−3)	0.294*	
	(0.147)	
Milex	−0.001	−0.040
	(0.126)	(0.093)
Milex (−1)	0.144	0.135
	(0.127)	(0.112)

	Profit1 *1973–2014* *ARDL (3, 1, 1, 0)*	*Profit2* *1975–2008* *ARDL (1, 3, 1, 2)*
Short-Run Coefficients		
Milex (−2)		0.068
		(0.107)
Milex (−3)		0.147
		(0.109)
GDP	0.830***	0.491***
	(0.224)	(0.161)
GDP (−1)	−0.714***	−0.688***
	(0.213)	(0.171)
Unemployment	−0.023	−0.068
	(0.054)	(0.041)
Unemployment (−1)		−0.053
		(0.045)
Unemployment (−2)		0.078**
		(0.035)
Trend	0.0009	0.024**
	(0.008)	(0.008)
Intercept	−0.453	2.805**
	(1.065)	(1.119)
Long-Run Coefficients		
Milex	0.428	0.561**
	(0.431)	(0.206)
GDP	0.349	−0.356
	(0.437)	(0.246)
Unemployment	−0.071	−0.079
	(0.148)	(0.081)
Trend	0.002	0.044***
	(0.026)	(0.014)
R-squared	0.753	0.969
SER	0.072	0.045
Serial correlation	0.814	1.300
	[0.496]	[0.303]
Functional form	1.076	0.794
	[0.307]	[0.382]
Normality	10.286	0.156
	[0.005]	[0.924]
Heteroscedasticity	0.891	2.153
	[0.543]	[0.060]
Bounds Test	1.645	13.623***
F-Statistics	10% 3.26 4.09	10% 3.29 4.17
Actual sample size	5% 3.85 4.78	5% 3.93 4.91
	1% 5.25 6.52	1% 5.65 6.92

Table B.33 Results of ARDL bounds test: Luxembourg (without unemployment)

	Profit1 *1954–2014* *ARDL (4, 0, 4)*	*Profit2* *1965–2008* *ARDL (2, 0, 1)*
Short-Run Coefficients		
Profit (−1)	0.983***	0.849***
	(0.131)	(0.107)
Profit (−2)	−0.614***	−0.240**
	(0.172)	(0.106)
Profit (−3)	0.621***	
	(0.173)	
Profit (−4)	−0.412***	
	(0.130)	
Milex	0.023	−0.115*
	(0.033)	(0.066)
GDP	0.947***	0.845***
	(0.134)	(0.168)
GDP (−1)	−1.006***	−1.062***
	(0.208)	(0.154)
GDP (−2)	0.302	
	(0.240)	
GDP (−3)	−0.280	
	(0.241)	
GDP (−4)	0.335*	
	(0.170)	
Trend	−0.010**	0.012***
	(0.004)	(0.003)
Intercept	−1.533**	2.845***
	(0.742)	(0.821)
Long-Run Coefficients		
Milex	0.054	−0.294*
	(0.083)	(0.167)
GDP	0.705***	−0.556*
	(0.173)	(0.279)
Trend	−0.024***	0.030***
	(0.006)	(0.010)
R-squared	0.798	0.933
SER	0.057	0.058
Serial correlation	0.364	0.543
	[0.832]	[0.585]
Functional form	0.194	6.048
	[0.661]	[0.018]
Normality	25.962	3.404
	[0.000]	[0.182]
Heteroscedasticity	1.441	2.461
	[0.185]	[0.042]
Bounds Test	3.402	8.011***
F-Statistics	10% 3.54 4.23	10% 3.62 4.33
Actual sample size	5% 4.18 4.93	5% 4.33 5.07
	1% 5.62 6.50	1% 5.87 6.87

Table B.34 Results of ARDL bounds test: Mexico (with unemployment)

	Profit1 1980–2014 ARDL (1, 0, 1, 0)	*Profit2* 1981–2008 ARDL (1, 0, 1, 1)	*Profit3* 1982–2012 ARDL (1, 0, 1, 2)
Short-Run Coefficients			
Profit (−1)	0.783***	0.843***	0.436***
	(0.124)	(0.102)	(0.092)
Profit (−2)			
Profit (−3)			
Milex	−0.093	−0.190***	−0.033
	(0.066)	(0.048)	(0.047)
Milex (−1)			
Milex (−2)			
GDP	0.535**	0.236	1.365
	(0.210)	(0.156)	(0.156)
GDP (−1)	−0.608***	−0.434**	
	(0.218)	(0.159)	
Unemployment	0.008	0.028	−0.104**
	(0.025)	(0.021)	(0.037)
Unemployment (−1)		0.045**	0.101***
		(0.017)	(0.025)
Unemployment (−2)			−0.088***
			(0.018)
Trend	0.0006	0.002	−0.002
	(0.002)	(0.001)	(0.002)
Intercept	1.524	3.048***	0.886
	(1.030)	(1.059)	(0.984)
Long-Run Coefficients			
Milex	−0.433	−1.221	−0.059
	(0.262)	(0.963)	(0.084)
GDP	−0.335	−1.273	0.149
	(0.559)	(0.815)	(0.145)
Unemployment	0.037	0.470	−0.162***
	(0.123)	(0.366)	(0.049)
Trend	0.003	0.013	−0.004
	(0.014)	(0.011)	(0.004)
R-squared	0.835	0.885	0.931
SER	0.040	0.023	0.027
Serial correlation	0.435	0.311	2.020
	[0.515]	[0.583]	[0.158]
Functional form	1.390	0.023	3.191
	[0.248]	[0.879]	[0.088]
Normality	3.454	0.047	15.153
	[0.177]	[0.976]	[0.000]
Heteroscedasticity	3.634	1.379	1.595
	[0.008]	[0.267]	[0.183]
Bounds Test	1.681	10.460***	14.030***
F-Statistics	10% 3.29 4.17	10% 3.37 4.27	10% 3.37 4.27
Actual sample size	5% 3.93 4.91	5% 4.04 5.09	5% 4.04 5.09
	1% 5.65 6.92	1% 5.66 6.98	1% 5.66 6.98

Note: Profit3 is taken from E. Maito.

Table B.35 Results of ARDL bounds test: Mexico (without unemployment)

	Profit1 *1951–2014* *ARDL (1, 1, 1)*	*Profit2* *1972–2008* *ARDL (2, 0, 2)*	*Profit3* *1951–2012* *ARDL (1, 0, 1)*
Short-Run Coefficients			
Profit (−1)	0.812***	1.232***	0.508***
	(0.075)	(0.143)	(0.078)
Profit (−2)		−0.465***	
		(0.144)	
Milex	−0.103*	−0.124**	−0.107*
	(0.051)	(0.051)	(0.060)
Milex (−1)	0.110**		
	(0.054)		
GDP	0.627***	−0.091	0.954***
	(0.108)	(0.137)	(0.163)
GDP (−1)	−0.592***	−0.430**	−1.095***
	(0.102)	(0.194)	(0.152)
Trend	0.001	0.003*	0.005***
	(0.001)	(0.001)	(0.001)
Intercept	0.116	2.412**	3.258***
	(0.392)	(1.024)	(0.722)
Long-Run Coefficients			
Milex	0.036	−0.533	−0.219*
	(0.273)	(0.435)	(0.118)
GDP	0.184	−0.535*	−0.286***
	(0.170)	(0.286)	(0.088)
Trend	−0.007	0.014*	0.010***
	(0.006)	(0.007)	(0.003)
R-squared	0.854	0.839	0.745
SER	0.032	0.027	0.048
Serial correlation	2.472	0.724	1.193
	[0.121]	[0.493]	[0.279]
Functional form	0.388	0.696	1.421
	[0.535]	[0.411]	[0.238]
Normality	6.547	0.475	2.364
	[0.037]	[0.788]	[0.306]
Heteroscedasticity	3.858	2.207	2.101
	[0.002]	[0.063]	[0.078]
Bounds Test	2.502	5.029*	11.166***
F-Statistics	10% 3.53 4.20	10% 3.69 4.42	10% 3.54 4.23
Actual sample size	5% 4.12 4.90	5% 4.43 5.24	5% 4.18 4.93
	1% 5.54 6.45	1% 6.32 7.40	1% 5.62 6.50

Note: Profit3 is taken from E. Maito.

Table B.36 Results of ARDL bounds test: Netherlands (with unemployment)

	Profit1 1967–2014 ARDL (2, 0, 2, 0)	*Profit2* 1970–2008 ARDL (2, 3, 1, 3)	*Profit3* 1967–2011 ARDL (2, 0, 1, 0)
Short-Run Coefficients			
Profit (−1)	1.376***	0.172	0.566***
	(0.142)	(0.164)	(0.127)
Profit (−2)	−0.454***	−0.379***	−0.197
	(0.156)	(0.126)	(0.134)
Milex	−0.141	−0.435***	−0.047
	(0.098)	(0.108)	(0.158)
Milex (−1)		−0.046	
		(0.113)	
Milex (−2)		0.252**	
		(0.099)	
Milex (−3)		0.252**	
		(0.117)	
GDP	0.735***	−0.194	0.736**
	(0.194)	(0.135)	(0.327)
GDP (−1)	−1.184***	−0.305**	−1.192***
	(0.267)	(0.144)	(0.276)
Unemployment	0.028**	−0.016	0.0007
	(0.013)	(0.019)	(0.019)
Unemployment (−1)		0.004	
		(0.024)	
Unemployment (−2)		0.004	
		(0.022)	
Unemployment (−3)		0.025	
		(0.016)	
Trend	−0.002	0.025***	0.014***
	(0.002)	(0.004)	(0.005)
Intercept	0.639	9.596***	6.948***
	(1.076)	(1.856)	(2.310)
Long-Run Coefficients			
Milex	−1.812	0.019	−0.074
	(1.679)	(0.065)	(0.247)
GDP	−0.314	−0.414***	−0.721***
	(1.093)	(0.079)	(0.218)
Unemployment	0.036	0.014	0.001
	(0.332)	(0.011)	(0.031)
Trend	−0.031	0.021***	0.022***
	(0.046)	(0.002)	(0.007)
R-squared	0.972	0.986	0.689
SER	0.034	0.017	0.054
Serial correlation	0.499	0.240	0.562
	[0.611]	[0.866]	[0.575]

(*Continued*)

Table B.36 (Continued)

	Profit1 *1967–2014* *ARDL (2, 0, 2, 0)*	*Profit2* *1970–2008* *ARDL (2, 3, 1, 3)*	*Profit3* *1967–2011* *ARDL (2, 0, 1, 0)*
Long-Run Coefficients			
Functional form	8.485	2.491	0.596
	[0.006]	[0.127]	[0.444]
Normality	0.014	6.038	0.759
	[0.992]	[0.048]	[0.683]
Heteroscedasticity	1.306	0.727	0.958
	[0.268]	[0.721]	[0.475]
Bounds Test	1.988	10.445***	6.724***
F-Statistics	10% 3.17 4.00	10% 3.26 4.09	10% 3.22 4.05
Actual sample size	5% 3.73 4.66	5% 3.85 4.78	5% 3.82 4.71
	1% 5.05 6.18	1% 5.25 6.52	1% 5.15 6.28

Note: Profit3 is taken from E. Maito.

Table B.37 Results of ARDL bounds test: Netherlands (without unemployment)

	Profit1 *1956–2014* *ARDL (2, 0, 2)*	*Profit2* *1970–2008* *ARDL (2, 2, 1)*	*Profit3* *1956–2011* *ARDL (1, 0, 1)*
Short-Run Coefficients			
Profit (−1)	1.466***	0.498***	0.616***
	(0.115)	(0.150)	(0.076)
Profit (−2)	−0.561***	−0.252*	
	(0.114)	(0.125)	
Milex	0.003	−0.328***	0.039
	(0.058)	(0.110)	(0.091)
Milex (−1)		0.160	
		(0.099)	
Milex (−2)		0.234**	
		(0.109)	
GDP	0.703***	−0.133	0.750***
	(0.152)	(0.143)	(0.261)
GDP (−1)	−1.195***	−0.245	−1.152***
	(0.205)	(0.153)	(0.233)
GDP (−2)	0.463***		
	(0.160)		
Trend	0.001	0.019***	0.014***
	(0.002)	(0.003)	(0.003)
Intercept	0.484	6.676***	5.555***
	(0.788)	(1.647)	(1.741)

	Profit1 1956–2014 ARDL (2, 0, 2)	*Profit2 1970–2008 ARDL (2, 2, 1)*	*Profit3 1956–2011 ARDL (1, 0, 1)*
Long-Run Coefficients			
Milex	0.034	0.088	0.104
	(0.629)	(0.082)	(0.245)
GDP	−0.302	−0.503***	−1.048***
	(0.608)	(0.111)	(0.245)
Trend	0.019	0.026***	0.036***
	(0.019)	(0.002)	(0.008)
R-squared	0.969	0.978	0.876
SER	0.033	0.020	0.053
Serial correlation	0.326	1.462	1.662
	[0.723]	[0.248]	[0.203]
Functional form	8.647	0.006	5.555
	[0.004]	[0.127]	[0.022]
Normality	1.187	0.164	0.390
	[0.326]	[0.920]	[0.822]
Heteroscedasticity	1.306	2.513	1.325
	[0.268]	[0.032]	[0.268]
Bounds Test	1.626	11.954***	8.937***
F-Statistics	10% 3.54 4.23	10% 3.66 4.37	10% 3.55 4.23
Actual sample size	5% 4.18 4.93	5% 4.36 5.13	5% 4.18 4.95
	1% 5.62 6.50	1% 5.98 6.97	1% 5.67 6.57

Note: Profit3 is taken from E. Maito.

Table B.38 Results of ARDL bounds test: New Zealand (with unemployment)

	Profit1 1969–2014 ARDL (1, 2, 2, 0)	*Profit2 1971–2008 ARDL (1,2, 2, 2)*
Short-Run Coefficients		
Profit (−1)	0.872***	0.705***
	(0.057)	(0.076)
Profit (−2)		
Profit (−3)		
Milex	0.022	−0.050
	(0.076)	(0.073)
Milex (−1)	0.013	−0.0003
	(0.080)	(0.073)

(*Continued*)

Table B.38 (Continued)

	Profit1 *1969–2014* *ARDL (1, 2, 2, 0)*	*Profit2* *1971–2008* *ARDL (1,2, 2, 2)*
Short-Run Coefficients		
Milex (−2)	0.236***	0.240***
	(0.070)	(0.070)
GDP	0.974***	0.781***
	(0.185)	(0.204)
GDP (−1)	−0.968***	−0.804***
	(0.214)	(0.237)
GDP (−2)	0.601***	0.550***
	(0.186)	(0.184)
Unemployment	0.011	−0.0004
	(0.008)	(0.011)
Unemployment (−1)		−0.045***
		(0.015)
Unemployment (−2)		0.074***
		(0.013)
Trend	−0.013**	−0.013**
	(0.005)	(0.005)
Intercept	−6.151***	−4.456**
	(2.219)	(2.153)
Long-Run Coefficients		
Milex	2.132*	0.645*
	(1.123)	(0.319)
GDP	4.766**	1.790***
	(2.167)	(0.632)
Unemployment	0.092	0.095**
	(0.073)	(0.040)
Trend	−0.103**	−0.045**
	(0.048)	(0.017)
R-squared	0.934	0.965
SER	0.027	0.024
Serial correlation	0.263	0.812
	[0.770]	[0.455]
Functional form	1.285	3.553
	[0.264]	[0.071]
Normality	19.293	0.152
	[0.000]	[0.926]
Heteroscedasticity	1.299	1.788
	[0.271]	[0.108]
Bounds Test	4.870**	9.400***
F-Statistics	10% 3.22 4.05	10% 3.26 4.09
Actual sample size	5% 3.82 4.71	5% 3.85 4.78
	1% 5.15 6.28	1% 5.25 6.52

Table B.39 Results of ARDL bounds test: New Zealand (without unemployment)

	Profit1 *1958–2014* *ARDL (2, 2, 2)*	*Profit2* *1966–2008* *ARDL (3, 3, 2)*
Short-Run Coefficients		
Profit (−1)	1.113***	0.674***
	(0.135)	(0.121)
Profit (−2)	−0.198	−0.360***
	(0.139)	(0.126)
Profit (−3)		0.502***
		(0.094)
Milex	−0.045	−0.029
	(0.061)	(0.064)
Milex (−1)	0.002	0.008
	(0.073)	(0.067)
Milex (−2)	0.105*	0.106
	(0.060)	(0.067)
Milex (−3)		0.225***
		(0.058)
GDP	0.787***	0.573***
	(0.145)	(0.154)
GDP (−1)	−1.108***	−0.748***
	(0.208)	(0.184)
GDP (−2)	0.369**	0.324*
	(0.171)	(0.180)
Trend	−0.0006	0.001
	(0.002)	(0.004)
Intercept	−0.350	−1.277
	(1.034)	(2.125)
Long-Run Coefficients		
Milex	0.742	1.689***
	(0.749)	(0.565)
GDP	0.568	0.813
	(1.116)	(1.014)
Trend	−0.007	0.007
	(0.030)	(0.026)
R-squared	0.917	0.962
SER	0.029	0.023
Serial correlation	0.221	1.166
	[0.802]	[0.340]
Functional form	0.003	0.326
	[0.953]	[0.571]
Normality	24.049	15.536
	[0.000]	[0.0004]
Heteroscedasticity	0.765	0.918
	[0.648]	[0.534]
Bounds Test	2.101	14.461***
F-Statistics	10% 3.55 4.23	10% 3.62 4.33
Actual sample size	5% 4.18 4.95	5% 4.33 5.07
	1% 5.67 6.57	1% 5.87 6.87

Table B.40 Results of ARDL bounds test: Norway (with unemployment)

	Profit1 *1969–2014* *ARDL (1, 0, 1, 2)*	*Profit2* *1970–2007* *ARDL (2, 0, 1, 0)*
Short-Run Coefficients		
Profit (−1)	0.870***	1.006***
	(0.066)	(0.141)
Profit (−2)		−0.288**
		(0.133)
Milex	−0.123	−0.295**
	(0.132)	(0.132)
GDP	1.318***	0.041
	(0.150)	(0.161)
GDP (−1)	−1.317***	−0.218**
	(0.141)	(0.103)
Unemployment	0.132***	0.072***
	(0.030)	(0.023)
Unemployment (−1)	−0.014	
	(0.035)	
Unemployment (−2)	−0.066**	
	(0.030)	
Trend	−0.002	0.003
	(0.006)	(0.005)
Intercept	0.397	3.064*
	(1.440)	(1.662)
Long-Run Coefficients		
Milex	−0.954	−1.046***
	(0.940)	(0.361)
GDP	0.013	−0.627
	(1.048)	(0.378)
Unemployment	0.390*	0.257*
	(0.230)	(0.130)
Trend	−0.019	0.012
	(0.043)	(0.018)
R-squared	0.976	0.980
SER	0.046	0.036
Serial correlation	0.822	0.624
	[0.447]	[0.543]
Functional form	0.505	0.226
	[0.481]	[0.637]
Normality	3.461	2.618
	[0.177]	[0.270]
Heteroscedasticity	0.984	0.608
	[0.463]	[0.743]
Bounds Test	1.737	5.935**
F-Statistics	10% 3.22 4.05	10% 3.26 4.09
Actual sample size	5% 3.82 4.71	5% 3.85 4.78
	1% 5.15 6.28	1% 5.25 6.52

Table B.41 Results of ARDL bounds test: Norway (without unemployment)

	Profit1 *1952–2014* *ARDL (2, 0, 2)*	*Profit2* *1970–2007* *ARDL (2, 1, 0)*
Short-Run Coefficients		
Profit (−1)	1.221***	1.165***
	(0.129)	(0.152)
Profit (−2)	−0.331**	−0.415***
	(0.125)	(0.132)
Milex	−0.025	−0.331**
	(0.073)	(0.144)
Milex (−1)		0.317**
		(0.119)
GDP	1.286***	−0.092
	(0.119)	(0.161)
GDP (−1)	−1.754***	
	(0.221)	
GDP (−2)	0.473**	
	(0.211)	
Trend	0.0002	0.008
	(0.003)	(0.005)
Intercept	0.188	1.587
	(0.967)	(2.124)
Long-Run Coefficients		
Milex	−0.226	−0.058
	(0.648)	(0.727)
GDP	0.045	−0.371
	(0.828)	(0.546)
Trend	0.002	0.033**
	(0.029)	(0.013)
R-squared	0.964	0.975
SER	0.047	0.040
Serial correlation	0.781	0.534
	[0.462]	[0.591]
Functional form	0.012	0.798
	[0.918]	[0.378]
Normality	8.608	0.325
	[0.013]	[0.849]
Heteroscedasticity	0.768	0.196
	[0.615]	[0.975]
Bounds Test	2.043	3.333
F-Statistics	10% 3.53 4.20	10% 3.66 4.37
Actual sample size	5% 4.12 4.90	5% 4.36 5.13
	1% 5.54 6.45	1% 5.98 6.97

Table B.42 Results of ARDL bounds test: Portugal (with unemployment)

	Profit1 *1972–2014* *ARDL (2, 0, 2, 0)*	*Profit2* *1972–2007* *ARDL (1, 2, 1, 0)*
Short-Run Coefficients		
Profit (−1)	1.349***	0.831***
	(0.148)	(0.070)
Profit (−2)	−0.523***	
	(0.154)	
Milex	0.007	−0.007
	(0.030)	(0.096)
Milex (−1)		−0.328***
		(0.115)
Milex (−2)		0.221**
		(0.101)
GDP	0.609***	0.826***
	(0.125)	(0.246)
GDP (−1)	−1.054***	−1.283***
	(0.198)	(0.246)
GDP (−2)	0.496***	
	(0.155)	
Unemployment	−0.007	−0.006
	(0.011)	(0.023)
Trend	−0.004	0.012*
	(0.003)	(0.006)
Intercept	−0.040	5.503***
	(1.440)	(1.710)
Long-Run Coefficients		
Milex	0.042	−0.678
	(0.167)	(0.544)
GDP	0.290	−2.709
	(0.483)	(1.683)
Unemployment	−0.042	−0.037
	(0.060)	(0.143)
Trend	−0.026	0.076
	(0.017)	(0.058)
R-squared	0.994	0.940
SER	0.021	0.042
Serial correlation	0.901	0.791
	[0.416]	[0.464]
Functional form	5.575	2.607
	[0.024]	[0.118]
Normality	1.047	0.146
	[0.592]	[0.929]
Heteroscedasticity	3.586	1.211
	[0.004]	[0.328]
Bounds Test	1.283	7.260***
F-Statistics	10% 3.22 4.05	10% 3.29 4.17
Actual sample size	5% 3.82 4.71	5% 3.93 4.91
	1% 5.15 6.28	1% 5.65 6.92

Table B.43 Results of ARDL bounds test: Portugal (without unemployment)

	Profit1 *1953–2014* *ARDL (2, 0, 2)*	*Profit2* *1966–2008* *ARDL (1, 0, 1)*
Short-Run Coefficients		
Profit (−1)	1.383***	0.778***
	(0.113)	(0.060)
Profit (−2)	−0.559***	
	(0.119)	
Milex	0.028*	−0.130***
	(0.015)	(0.045)
GDP	0.632***	1.067***
	(0.076)	(0.197)
GDP (−1)	−1.063***	−1.396***
	(0.140)	(0.192)
GDP (−2)	0.501***	
	(0.115)	
Trend	−0.005**	0.007*
	(0.002)	(0.004)
Intercept	−0.265	4.406***
	(0.332)	(1.070)
Long-Run Coefficients		
Milex	0.163**	−0.587*
	(0.064)	(0.299)
GDP	0.398**	−1.482**
	(0.165)	(0.575)
Trend	−0.030***	0.032
	(0.006)	(0.019)
R-squared	0.997	0.947
SER	0.018	0.044
Serial correlation	2.268	0.373
	[0.113]	[0.544]
Functional form	4.066	0.426
	[0.048]	[0.518]
Normality	2.775	12.541
	[0.249]	[0.001]
Heteroscedasticity	6.553	0.681
	[0.000]	[0.640]
Bounds Test	2.960	11.211***
F-Statistics	10% 3.54 4.23	10% 3.62 4.33
Actual sample size	5% 4.18 4.93	5% 4.33 5.07
	1% 5.62 6.50	1% 5.87 6.87

Table B.44 Results of ARDL bounds test: South Africa (with unemployment)

	Profit1 *1980–2014* *ARDL (2, 1, 1, 0)*	*Profit2* *1980–2008* *ARDL (1, 0, 1, 0)*
Short-Run Coefficients		
Profit (−1)	0.710***	0.476***
	(0.159)	(0.131)
Profit (−2)	0.194	
	(0.169)	
Milex	−0.013	−0.019
	(0.106)	(0.045)
Milex (−1)	0.008	
	(0.094)	
GDP	0.942**	0.956***
	(0.354)	(0.335)
GDP (−1)	−1.311***	−1.324***
	(0.288)	(0.285)
Unemployment	0.078	0.010
	(0.100)	(0.094)
Trend	0.006	0.017*
	(0.009)	(0.008)
Intercept	4.449	5.650**
	(2.630)	(2.104)
Long-Run Coefficients		
Milex	−0.052	−0.038
	(0.513)	(0.083)
GDP	−3.899	−0.702*
	(5.076)	(0.358)
Unemployment	0.832	0.019
	(0.878)	(0.180)
Trend	0.064	0.034**
	(0.145)	(0.016)
R-squared	0.938	0.971
SER	0.041	0.028
Serial correlation	0.416	2.716
	[0.664]	[0.114]
Functional form	5.177	0.439
	[0.031]	[0.514]
Normality	7.279	0.050
	[0.026]	[0.974]
Heteroscedasticity	3.906	4.417
	[0.003]	[0.004]
Bounds Test	5.326**	7.057***
F-Statistics	10% 3.29 4.17	10% 3.37 4.27
Actual sample size	5% 3.93 4.91	5% 4.04 5.09
	1% 5.65 6.92	1% 5.66 6.98

Table B.45 Results of ARDL bounds test: South Africa (without unemployment)

	Profit1 *1951–2014* *ARDL (1, 0, 1)*	*Profit2* *1964–2008* *ARDL (1, 0, 1)*
Short-Run Coefficients		
Profit (−1)	0.941***	0.680***
	(0.041)	(0.066)
Milex	0.051***	−0.022
	(0.013)	(0.029)
Milex (−1)	0.746***	
	(0.135)	
GDP	0.942**	0.716***
	(0.354)	(0.169)
GDP (−1)	−1.027***	−1.134***
	(0.140)	(0.179)
Trend	0.009***	0.014***
	(0.002)	(0.002)
Intercept	3.269***	5.785***
	(0.669)	(0.939)
Long-Run Coefficients		
Milex	0.879	−0.071
	(0.738)	(0.079)
GDP	−4.802	−1.309***
	(3.782)	(0.305)
Trend	0.158	0.045***
	(0.128)	(0.010)
R-squared	0.945	0.970
SER	0.034	0.031
Serial correlation	0.468	0.912
	[0.496]	[0.345]
Functional form	0.726	2.302
	[0.397]	[0.137]
Normality	94.382	2.598
	[0.000]	[0.273]
Heteroscedasticity	1.001	3.710
	[0.425]	[0.007]
Bounds Test	7.396***	17.563***
F-Statistics	10% 3.53 4.20	10% 3.62 4.33
Actual sample size	5% 4.12 4.90	5% 4.33 5.07
	1% 5.54 6.45	1% 5.87 6.87

Table B.46 Results of ARDL bounds test: South Korea (with unemployment)

	Profit1 *1973–2014* *ARDL (1, 1, 1, 0)*	*Profit2* *1976–2008* *ARDL (3, 0, 1, 3)*	*Profit3* *1973–2010* *ARDL (2, 0, 2, 0)*
Short-Run Coefficients			
Profit (−1)	0.810***	1.033***	1.045***
	(0.090)	(0.186)	(0.184)
Profit (−2)		−0.739***	−0.467**
		(0.254)	(0.189)
Profit (−3)		0.205	
		(0.152)	
Milex	0.033	−0.528***	0.120
	(0.141)	(0.161)	(0.115)
Milex (−1)	0.106		
	(0.125)		
GDP	0.760***	0.452*	1.639***
	(0.258)	(0.242)	(0.397)
GDP (−1)	−0.637***	−0.421*	−1.778***
	(0.213)	(0.217)	(0.483)
GDP (−2)			0.600
			(0.460)
Unemployment	0.067*	0.018	−0.020
	(0.038)	(0.058)	(0.077)
Unemployment (−1)		0.104	
		(0.080)	
Unemployment (−2)		−0.109	
		(0.072)	
Unemployment (−3)		0.146	
		(0.052)	
Trend	−0.005	−0.039***	−0.055*
	(0.005)	(0.011)	(0.029)
Intercept	−1.208	3.281	−2.617
	(0.988)	(2.426)	(2.249)
Long-Run Coefficients			
Milex	0.739*	−1.054***	0.284
	(0.408)	(0.304)	(0.287)
GDP	0.648	0.062	1.094***
	(0.384)	(0.382)	(0.365)
Unemployment	0.354	0.319**	−0.047
	(0.270)	(0.133)	(0.185)
Trend	−0.028	−0.078***	−0.132***
	(0.022)	(0.020)	(0.026)
R-squared	0.918	0.994	0.990
SER	0.050	0.036	0.081
Serial correlation	0.162	0.895	0.026
	[0.689]	[0.462]	[0.973]
Functional form	7.730	0.612	2.939
	[0.993]	[0.443]	[0.097]

	Profit1 *1973–2014* *ARDL (1, 1, 1, 0)*	*Profit2* *1976–2008* *ARDL (3, 0, 1, 3)*	*Profit3* *1973–2010* *ARDL (2, 0, 2, 0)*
Long-Run Coefficients			
Normality	1.064	1.053	1.478
	[0.587]	[0.590]	[0.477]
Heteroscedasticity	2.949	1.473	1.477
	[0.015]	[0.213]	[0.208]
Bounds Test	2.471	6.540**	2.509
F-Statistics	10% 3.26 4.09	10% 3.29 4.17	10% 3.26 4.09
Actual sample size	5% 3.85 4.78	5% 3.93 4.91	5% 3.85 4.78
	1% 5.25 6.52	1% 5.65 6.92	1% 5.25 6.52

Note: Profit3 is taken from E. Maito.

Table B.47 Results of ARDL bounds test: South Korea (without unemployment)

	Profit1 *1954–2014* *ARDL (1, 0, 1)*	*Profit2* *1964–2008* *ARDL (1, 0, 1)*	*Profit3* *1957–2010* *ARDL (1, 0, 1)*
Short-Run Coefficients			
Profit (−1)	0.839***	0.622***	0.852***
	(0.057)	(0.095)	(0.054)
Milex	0.073**	−0.181***	0.064
	(0.033)	(0.060)	(0.077)
GDP	0.572***	0.529***	1.603***
	(0.128)	(0.195)	(0.290)
GDP (−1)	−0.542***	−0.483**	−1.661***
	(0.125)	(0.209)	(0.285)
Trend	−0.001	−0.023***	7.91E−05
	(0.003)	(0.008)	(0.011)
Intercept	−1.208	1.754**	0.961
	(0.988)	(0.750)	(0.902)
Long-Run Coefficients			
Milex	0.456*	−0.481***	0.439
	(0.239)	(0.151)	(0.557)
GDP	0.189	0.122	−0.392
	(0.214)	(0.184)	(0.888)
Trend	−0.007	−0.062***	0.0005
	(0.019)	(0.018)	(0.081)
R-squared	0.923	0.988	0.981
SER	0.046	0.064	0.099
Serial correlation	1.682	1.874	1.267
	[0.200]	[0.179]	[0.266]

(*Continued*)

Table B.47 (Continued)

	Profit1 1954–2014 ARDL (1, 0, 1)	*Profit2* 1964–2008 ARDL (1, 0, 1)	*Profit3* 1957–2010 ARDL (1, 0, 1)
Long-Run Coefficients			
Functional form	0.035	7.666	0.065
	[0.850]	[0.008]	[0.799]
Normality	1.479	10.356	0.769
	[0.477]	[0.005]	[0.680]
Heteroscedasticity	0.581	2.456	1.862
	[0.713]	[0.049]	[0.118]
Bounds Test	3.628	4.487**	4.851**
F-Statistics	10% 3.54 4.23	10% 3.62 4.33	10% 3.55 4.23
Actual sample size	5% 4.18 4.93	5% 4.33 5.07	5% 4.18 4.95
	1% 5.62 6.50	1% 5.87 6.87	1% 5.67 6.57
	Inconclusive		

Note: Profit3 is taken from E. Maito.

Table B.48 Results of ARDL bounds test: Spain (with unemployment)

	Profit1 1967–2014 ARDL (2, 0, 0, 0)	*Profit2* 1967–2008 ARDL (1, 0, 1, 0)	*Profit3* 1967–2011 ARDL (1, 0, 1, 0)
Short-Run Coefficients			
Profit (−1)	1.533***	0.680***	0.655***
	(0.126)	(0.072)	(0.089)
Profit (−2)	−0.671***		
	(0.139)		
Milex	0.051	0.120**	0.174*
	(0.056)	(0.055)	(0.089)
GDP	−0.039	0.138	0.525**
	(0.068)	(0.142)	(0.249)
GDP (−1)		−0.485***	−0.834***
		(0.163)	(0.245)
Unemployment	−0.019	−0.022**	−0.053***
	(0.011)	(0.009)	(0.018)
Trend	0.001	0.014***	0.015***
	(0.002)	(0.003)	(0.003)
Intercept	0.795	5.134***	4.686***
	(0.853)	(1.433)	(1.512)
Long-Run Coefficients			
Milex	0.376	0.377	0.507
	(0.466)	(0.228)	(0.308)
GDP	−0.283	−1.087***	−0.899***
	(0.524)	(0.165)	(0.302)

	Profit1 *1967–2014* *ARDL (2, 0, 0, 0)*	*Profit2* *1967–2008* *ARDL (1, 0, 1, 0)*	*Profit3* *1967–2011* *ARDL (1, 0, 1, 0)*
Long-Run Coefficients			
Unemployment	−0.143	−0.070**	−0.156***
	(0.086)	(0.032)	(0.056)
Trend	0.009	0.045***	0.043***
	(0.021)	(0.006)	(0.012)
R-squared	0.985	0.957	0.890
SER	0.029	0.023	0.044
Serial correlation	2.254	0.107	0.730
	[0.118]	[0.744]	[0.398]
Functional form	0.586	0.431	0.002
	[0.448]	[0.515]	[0.956]
Normality	7.740	14.070	2.248
	[0.020]	[0.000]	[0.324]
Heteroscedasticity	1.707	1.471	0.689
	[0.143]	[0.216]	[0.659]
Bounds Test	2.289	14.278***	6.636***
F-Statistics	10% 3.17 4.00	10% 3.26 4.09	10% 3.22 4.05
Actual sample size	5% 3.73 4.66	5% 3.85 4.78	5% 3.82 4.71
	1% 5.05 6.18	1% 5.25 6.52	1% 5.15 6.28

Note: Profit3 is taken from E. Maito.

Table B.49 Results of ARDL bounds test: Spain (without unemployment)

	Profit1 *1954–2014* *ARDL (2, 0, 1)*	*Profit2* *1964–2008* *ARDL (1, 0, 1)*	*Profit3* *1956–2011* *ARDL (2, 0, 1)*
Short-Run Coefficients			
Profit (−1)	1.428***	0.688***	0.896***
	(0.105)	(0.075)	(0.124)
Profit (−2)	−0.584***		−0.200
	(0.122)		(0.138)
Milex	−0.001	0.016	−0.015
	(0.026)	(0.040)	(0.056)
GDP	0.316**	0.158	0.540***
	(0.134)	(0.138)	(0.195)
GDP (−1)	−0.343	−0.529***	−0.775***
	(0.119)	(0.168)	(0.211)
Trend	−0.001	0.012***	0.007***
	(0.002)	(0.002)	(0.002)
Intercept	0.744*	5.511***	3.872***
	(0.404)	(1.402)	(1.035)

(*Continued*)

Table B.49 (Continued)

	Profit1 1954–2014 ARDL (2, 0, 1)	*Profit2* 1964–2008 ARDL (1, 0, 1)	*Profit3* 1956–2011 ARDL (2, 0, 1)
Long-Run Coefficients			
Milex	−0.007	0.053	−0.050
	(0.167)	(0.140)	(0.173)
GDP	−0.176	−1.188***	−0.773***
	(0.305)	(0.142)	(0.203)
Trend	−0.006	0.040***	0.023**
	(0.013)	(0.005)	(0.009)
R-squared	0.989	0.966	0.952
SER	0.028	0.024	0.044
Serial correlation	0.347	0.299	1.264
	[0.708]	[0.587]	[0.273]
Functional form	1.016	0.057	0.047
	[0.318]	[0.812]	[0.828]
Normality	9.730	34.024	0.224
	[0.007]	[0.000]	[0.893]
Heteroscedasticity	1.061	0.244	2.641
	[0.397]	[0.940]	[0.026]
Bounds Test	4.915*	16.187***	6.801***
F-Statistics	10% 3.54 4.23	10% 3.62 4.33	10% 3.55 4.23
Actual sample size	5% 4.18 4.93	5% 4.33 5.07	5% 4.18 4.95
	1% 5.62 6.50	1% 5.87 6.87	1% 5.67 6.57

Note: Profit3 is taken from E. Maito.

Table B.50 Results of ARDL bounds test: Sweden (with unemployment)

	Profit1 1967–2014 ARDL (2, 2, 2, 0)	*Profit2* 1968–2008 ARDL (1, 1, 2, 1)	*Profit3* 1967–2011 ARDL (2, 0, 2, 0)	*Profit4* 1967–2011 ARDL (2, 0, 2, 0)
Short-Run Coefficients				
Profit (−1)	1.386***	0.805***	0.877***	0.897***
	(0.136)	(0.106)	(0.170)	(0.169)
Profit (−2)	−0.593***		−0.230*	−0.271*
	(0.158)		(0.135)	(0.145)
Milex	−0.311**	−0.388**	0.013	0.064
	(0.152)	(0.181)	(0.228)	(0.374)
Milex (−1)	−0.053	0.449**		
	(0.162)	(0.202)		

	Profit1 1967–2014 ARDL (2, 2, 2, 0)	*Profit2* 1968–2008 ARDL (1, 1, 2, 1)	*Profit3* 1967–2011 ARDL (2, 0, 2, 0)	*Profit4* 1967–2011 ARDL (2, 0, 2, 0)
Short-Run Coefficients				
Milex (−2)	0.374**			
	(0.148)			
GDP	1.034***	0.406	3.810***	5.426***
	(0.183)	(0.288)	(0.817)	(1.368)
GDP (−1)	−1.512***	−1.080***	−5.111***	−6.510***
	(0.244)	(0.337)	(1.079)	(1.772)
GDP (−2)	0.904***	0.378	2.207**	2.405
	(0.227)	(0.267)	(0.945)	(1.520)
Unemployment	0.014	−0.014	0.146**	0.222*
	(0.012)	(0.028)	(0.072)	(0.114)
Unemployment (−1)		0.051*		
		(0.029)		
Trend	−0.012*	0.009	−0.025	−0.035
	(0.006)	(0.005)	(0.026)	(0.042)
Intercept	−4.288*	3.829	−9.556	−14.590
	(2.232)	(2.363)	(10.110)	(17.049)
Long-Run Coefficients				
Milex	0.042	0.313	0.039	0.171
	(0.310)	(0.490)	(0.651)	(1.013)
GDP	2.064***	−1.524	2.567	3.526
	(0.691)	(1.686)	(2.117)	(3.446)
Unemployment	0.068	0.188*	0.414***	0.594**
	(0.064)	(0.103)	(0.149)	(0.241)
Trend	−0.061**	0.047	−0.073	−0.093
	(0.020)	(0.047)	(0.059)	(0.095)
R-squared	0.964	0.961	0.886	0.877
SER	0.026	0.032	0.118	0.201
Serial correlation	0.640	1.128	0.510	0.554
	[0.532]	[0.337]	[0.604]	[0.579]
Functional form	1.720	4.759	4.750	5.163
	[0.198]	[0.037]	[0.036]	[0.029]
Normality	0.631	0.196	0.851	1.483
	[0.729]	[0.905]	[0.653]	[0.476]
Heteroscedasticity	2.848	1.828	2.360	6.744
	[0.009]	[0.102]	[0.037]	[0.000]
Bounds Test	2.979	5.700**	2.392	2.609
F-Statistics	10% 3.17 4.00	10% 3.26 4.09	10% 3.22 4.05	10% 3.22 4.05
Actual sample size	5% 3.73 4.66	5% 3.85 4.78	5% 3.82 4.71	5% 3.82 4.71
	1% 5.05 6.18	1% 5.25 6.52	1% 5.15 6.28	1% 5.15 6.28

Note: Profit3 and Profit4 are taken from E. Maito. While the calculation of the former includes mixed income, that of the latter excludes mixed income.

Table B.51 Results of ARDL bounds test: Sweden (without unemployment)

	Profit1 1960–2014 ARDL (2, 0, 2)	*Profit2* 1965–2008 ARDL (2, 1, 2)	*Profit3* 1960–2011 ARDL (1, 0, 2)	*Profit4* 1960–2011 ARDL (2, 0, 2)
Short-Run Coefficients				
Profit (−1)	1.462***	1.122***	0.833***	1.024***
	(0.135)	(0.156)	(0.079)	(0.149)
Profit (−2)	−0.518***	−0.257*		−0.241*
	(0.154)	(0.141)		(0.124)
Milex	0.020	−0.357**	0.129	0.108
	(0.062)	(0.171)	(0.206)	(0.323)
Milex (−1)		0.420**		
		(0.189)		
GDP	0.777***	0.443*	3.054***	4.326***
	(0.157)	(0.243)	(0.676)	(1.112)
GDP (−1)	−1.398***	−1.198***	−5.324***	−7.404***
	(0.227)	(0.321)	(0.948)	(1.584)
GDP (−2)	0.574***	0.425	1.515*	2.298*
	(0.200)	(0.276)	(0.774)	(1.346)
Trend	0.001	0.011**	0.026**	0.028
	(0.004)	(0.004)	(0.012)	(0.021)
Intercept	0.622	3.990*	8.477*	8.701
	(1.187)	(2.156)	(4.603)	(7.684)
Long-Run Coefficients				
Milex	0.364	0.463	0.778	0.501
	(1.418)	(0.712)	(1.467)	(1.587)
GDP	−0.842	−2.426	−4.533	−3.599
	(2.706)	(1.939)	(3.123)	(3.480)
Trend	0.027	0.083	0.157	0.131
	(0.101)	(0.058)	(0.109)	(0.114)
R-squared	0.966	0.956	0.866	0.860
SER	0.027	0.032	0.119	0.195
Serial correlation	1.778	0.464	0.850	0.554
	[0.180]	[0.632]	[0.434]	[0.579]
Functional form	0.234	0.982	2.497	0.310
	[0.630]	[0.328]	[0.121]	[0.734]
Normality	6.543	0.620	0.557	0.912
	[0.037]	[0.733]	[0.756]	[0.633]
Heteroscedasticity	3.457	0.828	3.591	9.048
	[0.004]	[0.559]	[0.005]	[0.000]
Bounds Test	1.078	3.324	2.996	2.602
F-Statistics	10% 3.55 4.23	10% 3.62 4.33	10% 3.57 4.28	10% 3.57 4.28
Actual sample size	5% 4.18 4.95	5% 4.33 5.07	5% 4.22 5.03	5% 4.22 5.03
	1% 5.67 6.57	1% 5.87 6.87	1% 5.80 6.79	1% 5.80 6.79

Note: Profit3 and Profit4 are taken from E. Maito. While the calculation of the former includes mixed income, that of the latter excludes mixed income.

Table B.52 Results of ARDL bounds test: Switzerland (with unemployment)

	Profit1 *1973–2014* *ARDL (1, 0, 2, 0)*	*Profit2* *1973–2007* *ARDL (1, 0, 1, 0)*
Short-Run Coefficients		
Profit (−1)	0.850***	0.709***
	(0.088)	(0.085)
Milex	−0.014	−0.062
	(0.079)	(0.051)
GDP	0.488***	0.904***
	(0.154)	(0.144)
GDP (−1)	−0.902***	−1.192***
	(0.227)	(0.143)
GDP (−2)	0.319**	
	(0.150)	
Unemployment	0.007	−0.001
	(0.009)	(0.008)
Trend	0.001	0.003
	(0.002)	(0.002)
Intercept	1.416*	4.288***
	(0.764)	(1.503)
Long-Run Coefficients		
Milex	−0.099	−0.213
	(0.489)	(0.202)
GDP	−0.638	−0.991
	(0.587)	(0.696)
Unemployment	0.050	−0.005
	(0.063)	(0.027)
Trend	0.011	0.010
	(0.025)	(0.010)
R-squared	0.869	0.928
SER	0.025	0.018
Serial correlation	1.215	1.170
	[0.309]	[0.288]
Functional form	0.007	0.327
	[0.932]	[0.571]
Normality	0.631	1.020
	[0.729]	[0.600]
Heteroscedasticity	4.373	1.903
	[0.001]	[0.115]
Bounds Test	3.251	9.758***
F-Statistics	10% 3.26 4.09	10% 3.29 4.17
Actual sample size	5% 3.85 4.78	5% 3.93 4.91
	1% 5.25 6.52	1% 5.65 6.92
	inconclusive	

Table B.53 Results of ARDL bounds test: Switzerland (without unemployment)

	Profit1 *1957–2014* *ARDL (1, 0, 1)*	*Profit2* *1964–2007* *ARDL (1, 0, 1)*
Short-Run Coefficients		
Profit (−1)	0.945***	0.677***
	(0.056)	(0.049)
Milex	0.046	−0.062*
	(0.060)	(0.036)
GDP	0.523***	0.999***
	(0.117)	(0.117)
GDP (−1)	−0.628***	−1.206***
	(0.113)	(0.108)
Trend	0.003*	0.0008
	(0.001)	(0.001)
Intercept	1.234**	3.461***
	(0.503)	(0.828)
Long-Run Coefficients		
Milex	0.848	−0.192*
	(1.865)	(0.108)
GDP	−1.932	−0.639**
	(2.158)	(0.259)
Trend	0.069	0.002
	(0.102)	(0.005)
R-squared	0.970	0.981
SER	0.024	0.016
Serial correlation	0.415	1.367
	[0.522]	[0.249]
Functional form	0.287	0.287
	[0.594]	[0.595]
Normality	6.015	1.713
	[0.049]	[0.424]
Heteroscedasticity	6.661	2.319
	[0.0001]	[0.062]
Bounds Test	5.147**	20.707***
F-Statistics	10% 3.54 4.23	10% 3.62 4.33
Actual sample size	5% 4.18 4.93	5% 4.33 5.07
	1% 5.62 6.50	1% 5.87 6.87

Table B.54 Results of ARDL bounds test: Turkey (with unemployment)

	Profit1 1963–2014 ARDL(2, 2, 1, 0)	*Profit3* 1963–2008 ARDL(1, 0, 0, 0)	*Profit4* 1969–2000 ARDL (1, 0, 0, 1)
Short-Run Coefficients			
Profit (−1)	0.995***	0.872***	0.968***
	(0.091)	(0.070)	(0.291)
Profit (−2)	−0.533***		
	(0.189)		
Milex	−0.105	0.163	−0.335
	(0.142)	(0.148)	(0.271)
Milex (−1)	0.254		
	(0.225)		
Milex (−2)	−0.207		
	(0.157)		
GDP	0.560**	0.419	0.426
	(0.225)	(0.291)	(0.780)
GDP (−1)	−0.759***		
	(0.253)		
Unemployment	−0.002	−0.210**	−0.474
	(0.041)	(0.100)	(0.483)
Unemployment (−1)			0.848
			(0.501)
Trend	0.006	−0.013	−0.021
	(0.004)	(0.011)	(0.028)
Intercept	4.016***	−4.365	−5.093
	(1.431)	(3.318)	(9.166)
Long-Run Coefficients			
Milex	−0.109	1.281	−10.542
	(0.120)	(0.910)	(93.642)
GDP	−0.370**	3.284	13.397
	(0.172)	(2.759)	(105.174)
Unemployment	−0.003	−1.650*	11.726
	(0.078)	(0.872)	(104.321)
Trend	0.011	−0.104	−0.682
	(0.007)	(0.109)	(6.202)
R-squared	0.745	0.932	0.894
SER	0.070	0.141	0.231
Serial correlation	0.588	1.268	0.255
	[0.560]	[0.267]	[0.617]
Functional form	0.140	0.164	3.778
	[0.710]	[0.687]	[0.063]
Normality	152.609	0.509	8.230
	[0.0000]	[0.775]	[0.016]

(*Continued*)

Table B.54 (Continued)

	Profit1 *1963–2014* *ARDL(2, 2, 1, 0)*	*Profit3* *1963–2008* *ARDL(1, 0, 0, 0)*	*Profit4* *1969–2000* *ARDL (1, 0, 0, 1)*
Long-Run Coefficients			
Heteroscedasticity	1.919	0.172	1.255
	[0.075]	[0.971]	[0.312]
Bounds Test	5.922**	1.230	1.978
F-Statistics	10% 3.13–3.95	10% 3.22–4.05	10% 3.378
Actual Sample Size	5% 3.69–4.58	5% 3.82–4.714	4.274
	1% 4.99–6.02	1% 5.15–6.28	5% 4.048 5.09
			1% 5.666 6.988

Note: Profit3 is taken from Ongan (2011). Following the method adopted by Eres (2005) and Memis (2007), Ongan (2011) computes profit rates for the manufacturing sector in Turkey based on national accounts by generating the capital stock data by using Organization for Economic Co-operation and Development's perpetual inventory model (OECD, 2001). Profit4 is taken from Eres (2005). It is the profit rate for the manufacturing sector. The total manufacturing capital stock figures are calculated according to the perpetual inventory method (OECD, 2001).

Table B.55 Results of ARDL bounds test: Turkey (without unemployment)

	Profit1 *1960–2014* *ARDL(2, 0, 1)*	*Profit3* *1960–2008* *ARDL(1, 0, 0)*	*Profit4* *1969–2000* *ARDL (1, 0, 0)*
Short-Run Coefficients			
Profit (−1)	0.975***	0.961***	1.075***
	(0.119)	(0.058)	(0.149)
Profit (−2)	−0.518***		
	(0.127)		
Milex	−0.026	0.046	−0.145
	(0.058)	(0.136)	(0.355)
GDP	0.726***	0.335	0.177
	(0.208)	(0.234)	(0.831)
GDP (−1)	−0.880***		
	(0.209)		
Trend	0.004	−0.013	−0.021
	(0.004)	(0.010)	(0.029)
Intercept	3.456***	−3.834	−1.518
	(1.261)	(2.666)	(9.499)
Long-Run Coefficients			
Milex	−0.049	1.194	1.924
	(0.104)	(3.404)	(6.417)
GDP	−0.284	8.642	−2.345
	(0.207)	(16.021)	(13.495)

	Profit1 *1960–2014* *ARDL(2, 0, 1)*	*Profit3* *1960–2008* *ARDL(1, 0, 0)*	*Profit4* *1969–2000* *ARDL (1, 0, 0)*
Long-Run Coefficients			
Trend	0.008	−0.337	0.284
	(0.008)	(0.671)	(0.719)
R-squared	0.713	0.927	0.018
SER	0.070	0.140	0.245
Serial correlation	0.133	1.520	0.502
	[0.875]	[0.224]	[0.484]
Functional form	1.502	0.202	1.022
	[0.226]	[0.655]	[0.321]
Normality	418.713	0.072	6.566
	[0.0000]	[0.964]	[0.037]
Heteroscedasticity	1.795	0.411	1.805
	[0.120]	[0.799]	[0.156]
Bounds Test	8.110***	1.034	1.330
F-Statistics	10% 3.55 4.23	10% 3.57 4.28	10% 3.77 4.53
Actual Sample Size	5% 4.18 4.95	5% 4.22 5.03	5% 4.53 5.41
	1% 5.67 6.57	1% 5.80 6.79	1% 6.42 7.50

Note: See notes for Table B.54.

Table B.56 Results of ARDL bounds test: U.K. (with unemployment)

	Profit1 *1952–2014* *ARDL* *(2, 0, 2, 1)*	*Profit2* *1964–2008* *ARDL* *(1, 0, 1, 2)*	*Profit3* *1952–2010* *ARDL* *(2, 0, 1, 2)*	*Profit4* *1962–2014* *ARDL* *(2, 0, 2, 2)*
Short-Run Coefficients				
Profit (−1)	1.093***	0.870***	1.003***	1.138***
	(0.130)	(0.058)	(0.135)	(0.133)
Profit (−2)	−0.252*		−0.326**	−0.225
	(0.132)		(0.145)	(0.142)
Milex	−0.067	0.064	−0.042	−0.029
	(0.041)	(0.052)	(0.193)	(0.111)
Milex (−1)				
Milex (−2)				
GDP	0.633***	0.689***	0.972	0.967**
	(0.198)	(0.227)	(0.940)	(0.452)
GDP (−1)	−0.831***	−0.694**	−2.863***	−1.729***
	(0.245)	(0.224)	(0.994)	(0.613)
GDP (−2)	0.420**			0.727
	(0.171)			(0.449)

(*Continued*)

Table B.56 (Continued)

	Profit1 *1952–2014* *ARDL* *(2, 0, 2, 1)*	*Profit2* *1964–2008* *ARDL* *(1, 0, 1, 2)*	*Profit3* *1952–2010* *ARDL* *(2, 0, 1, 2)*	*Profit4* *1962–2014* *ARDL* *(2, 0, 2, 2)*
Short-Run Coefficients				
Unemployment	−0.006	−0.001	−0.298*	−0.048
	(0.031)	(0.047)	(0.167)	(0.091)
Unemployment (−1)	0.058*	0.152**	0.150	0.258*
	(0.033)	(0.066)	(0.218)	(0.132)
Unemployment (−2)		−0.120***	−0.249**	−0.210**
		(0.038)	(0.119)	(0.083)
Trend	−0.010**	0.001	0.057***	0.001
	(0.004)	(0.004)	(0.016)	(0.005)
Intercept	−2.385	0.311	25.713***	0.647
	(1.909)	(1.956)	(7.998)	(3.032)
Long-Run Coefficients				
Milex	−0.427	0.500	−0.131	−0.342
	(0.305)	(0.433)	(0.590)	(1.274)
GDP	1.401**	−0.038	−5.839***	−0.390
	(0.633)	(1.124)	(2.175)	(2.511)
Unemployment	0.327***	0.232	−1.202***	−0.009
	(0.083)	(0.174)	(0.176)	(0.420)
Trend	−0.063***	0.014	0.177***	0.016
	(0.014)	(0.032)	(0.062)	(0.063)
R-squared	0.977	0.929	0.944	0.928
SER	0.025	0.025	0.117	0.055
Serial correlation	1.441	0.096	0.379	0.172
	[0.245]	[0.907]	[0.686]	[0.842]
Functional form	0.102	1.223	1.909	7.442
	[0.750]	[0.276]	[0.173]	[0.009]
Normality	25.846	0.910	1.639	0.317
	[0.000]	[0.634]	[0.440]	[0.853]
Heteroscedasticity	3.128	1.330	1.967	1.612
	[0.004]	[0.260]	[0.063]	[0.136]
Bounds Test	3.382	5.078**	3.554	0.775
F-Statistics	10% 3.12 3.94	10% 3.22 4.05	10% 3.13 3.96	10% 3.13 3.95
Actual sample size	5% 3.62 4.53	5% 3.82 4.71	5% 3.68 4.58	5% 3.69 4.58
	1% 4.84 5.84	1% 5.15 6.28	1% 4.92 5.95	1% 4.99 6.01
	Inconclusive		inconclusive	

Note: Profit3 is taken from E. Maito. Profit4 is from Roberts (2015), calculated based on AMECO.

Table B.57 Results of ARDL bounds test: U.K. (without unemployment)

	Profit1 *1952–2014* *ARDL (2, 0, 2)*	*Profit2* *1964–2008* *ARDL (1, 0, 1)*	*Profit3* *1953–2010* *ARDL (3, 0, 3)*	*Profit4* *1962–2014* *ARDL (2, 0, 2)*
Short-Run Coefficients				
Profit (−1)	1.250***	0.790***	1.136***	1.181***
	(0.129)	(0.050)	(0.132)	(0.134)
Profit (−2)	−0.256*		−0.390*	−0.293**
	(0.139)		(0.200)	(0.136)
Profit (−3)			0.259*	
			(0.141)	
Milex	−0.032	0.144***	−0.093	−0.030
	(0.042)	(0.049)	(0.193)	(0.111)
Milex (−1)				
Milex (−2)				
GDP	0.632***	0.817***	1.465*	1.175***
	(0.183)	(0.220)	(0.760)	(0.421)
GDP (−1)	−1.105***	−1.001**	−3.103***	−2.542***
	(0.242)	(0.190)	(1.088)	(0.531)
GDP (−2)	0.375**		−0.998	1.353***
	(0.183)		(1.285)	(0.372)
GDP (−3)			1.784**	
			(0.857)	
Trend	0.001	0.009***	0.022	0.0007
	(0.003)	(0.003)	(0.017)	(0.004)
Intercept	1.367	2.810	11.271	0.468
	(1.635)	(1.826)	(8.106)	(3.044)
Long-Run Coefficients				
Milex	−4.892	0.687**	17.938	−0.273
	(34.593)	(0.282)	(199.797)	(0.932)
GDP	−14.971	−0.879	162.841	−0.127
	(111.153)	(0.644)	(1592.080)	(1.978)
Trend	0.218	0.043**	−4.373	0.006
	(1.770)	(0.016)	(42.160)	(0.045)
R-squared	0.973	0.904	0.948	0.917
SER	0.027	0.028	0.112	0.057
Serial correlation	1.214	1.653	1.119	0.183
	[0.305]	[0.206]	[0.351]	[0.833]
Functional form	0.813	1.619	1.945	4.331
	[0.371]	[0.210]	[0.169]	[0.043]
Normality	16.321	0.511	5.081	2.057
	[0.000]	[0.774]	[0.078]	[0.357]
Heteroscedasticity	4.851	3.893	1.805	1.927
	[0.0003]	[0.005]	[0.091]	[0.087]
Bounds Test	1.252	9.369***	1.243	1.030
F-Statistics	10% 3.53 4.20	10% 3.62 4.33	10% 3.54 4.23	10% 3.55 4.23
Actual sample size	5% 4.12 4.90	5% 4.33 5.07	5% 4.18 4.93	5% 4.18 4.95
	1% 5.54 6.45	1% 5.87 6.87	1% 5.62 6.50	1% 5.67 6.57

Note: Profit3 is taken from E. Maito. Profit4 is from Roberts (2015), calculated based on AMECO.

References

AMECO. Available at: http://ec.europa.eu/economy_finance/ameco/user/serie/SelectSerie.cfm

Eres, B. (2005). The profit rate in the Turkish economy: 1968–2000. PhD dissertation, University of Utah, Salt Lake City, UT.

Memis, E. (2007). A disaggregate analysis of profit rates in Turkish manufacturing. *Review of Radical Political Economics*, 39(3), pp. 398–406.

OECD. (2001). *Measuring capital – OECD manual measurement of capital stocks, consumption of fixed capital and capital services*. Paris: OECD.

Ongan, T. H. (2011). Profit rate of Turkish manufacturing sector in a Marxian perspective. *Sosyal Bilimler Dergisi*, 1, pp. 1–10.

Roberts, M. (2015). Revisiting a world rate of profit. *Paper for the 2015 conference of the association of heterodox economists*, Southampton Solent University, July 2015.

Appendix C: Toda-Yamamoto procedure results

Table C.1 Cointegration test results of Greece (profit1)

Unrestricted Cointegration Rank Test (Trace)				
Hypothesised No. of CE(s)	Eigenvalue	Trace Statistic	0.05 Critical Value	Prob.**
None*	0.554708	70.70654	63.87610	0.0119
At most 1	0.405909	39.15459	42.91525	0.1131
At most 2	0.301067	18.84641	25.87211	0.2900
At most 3	0.117539	4.876570	12.51798	0.6142
Unrestricted Cointegration Rank Test (Maximum Eigenvalue)				
Hypothesised No. of CE(s)	Eigenvalue	Max-Eigen Statistic	0.05 Critical Value	Prob.**
None	0.554708	31.55196	32.11832	0.0585
At most 1	0.405909	20.30817	25.82321	0.2259
At most 2	0.301067	13.96984	19.38704	0.2562
At most 3	0.117539	4.876570	12.51798	0.6142

Max-eigenvalue test indicates no cointegration at the 0.05 level
*denotes rejection of the hypothesis at the 0.05 level
**MacKinnon-Haug-Michelis (1999) p-values

Table C.2 VAR Granger causality tests of Greece

Dependent variable: PROFIT1			
Excluded	Chi-sq	df	Prob.
MILEX	3.900083	3	0.2725
GDP	6.406789	3	0.0934
UNEMPLOYMENT	8.929944	3	0.0302
All	12.74088	9	0.1747

(*Continued*)

Table C.2 (Continued)

Dependent variable: MILEX			
Excluded	Chi-sq	df	Prob.
PROFIT1	3.705590	3	0.2951
GDP	1.272605	3	0.7356
UNEMPLOYMENT	2.375591	3	0.4982
All	6.134201	9	0.7264

Table C.3 Cointegration test results of Greece (profit1, without unemployment)

Unrestricted Cointegration Rank Test (Trace)

Hypothesised No. of CE(s)	Eigenvalue	Trace Statistic	0.05 Critical Value	Prob.**
None*	0.326098	45.29350	42.91525	0.0283
At most 1	0.197983	21.21856	25.87211	0.1704
At most 2	0.119460	7.760428	12.51798	0.2719

Unrestricted Cointegration Rank Test (Maximum Eigenvalue)

Hypothesised No. of CE(s)	Eigenvalue	Max-Eigen Statistic	0.05 Critical Value	Prob.**
None	0.326098	24.07493	25.82321	0.0836
At most 1	0.197983	13.45814	19.38704	0.2925
At most 2	0.119460	7.760428	12.51798	0.2719

Max-eigenvalue test indicates no cointegration at the 0.05 level
*denotes rejection of the hypothesis at the 0.05 level
**MacKinnon-Haug-Michelis (1999) p-values

Table C.4 VAR Granger causality tests of Greece

Dependent variable: PROFIT1			
Excluded	Chi-sq	df	Prob.
MILEX	3.695529	2	0.1576
GDP	0.426165	2	0.8081
All	4.945711	4	0.2929

Dependent variable: MILEX			
Excluded	Chi-sq	df	Prob.
PROFIT1	5.268390	2	0.0718
GDP	5.858490	2	0.0534
All	7.825204	4	0.0982

Table C.5 Cointegration test results of Greece (for profit2)

Unrestricted Cointegration Rank Test (Trace)

Hypothesised No. of CE(s)	Eigenvalue	Trace Statistic	0.05 Critical Value	Prob.**
None*	0.732085	88.61703	63.87610	0.0001
At most 1	0.479124	42.51908	42.91525	0.0547
At most 2	0.364774	19.69060	25.87211	0.2420
At most 3	0.103103	3.808512	12.51798	0.7696

Unrestricted Cointegration Rank Test (Maximum Eigenvalue)

Hypothesised No. of CE(s)	Eigenvalue	Max-Eigen Statistic	0.05 Critical Value	Prob.**
None*	0.732085	46.09795	32.11832	0.0005
At most 1	0.479124	22.82849	25.82321	0.1184
At most 2	0.364774	15.88209	19.38704	0.1503
At most 3	0.103103	3.808512	12.51798	0.7696

Max-eigenvalue test indicates 1 cointegrating eqn(s) at the 0.05 level
*denotes rejection of the hypothesis at the 0.05 level
**MacKinnon-Haug-Michelis (1999) p-values

Table C.6 VAR Granger causality tests of Greece

Dependent variable: PROFIT2

Excluded	Chi-sq	df	Prob.
MILEX	0.055858	1	0.8132
GDP	0.022910	1	0.8797
UNEMPLOYMENT	0.146930	1	0.7015
All	0.552980	3	0.9071

Dependent variable: MILEX

Excluded	Chi-sq	df	Prob.
PROFIT2	0.364632	1	0.5459
GDP	1.468095	1	0.2256
UNEMPLOYMENT	0.004416	1	0.9470
All	2.183265	3	0.5353

Table C.7 Cointegration test results of Greece (for profit2, without unemployment)

Unrestricted Cointegration Rank Test (Trace)

Hypothesised No. of CE(s)	Eigenvalue	Trace Statistic	0.05 Critical Value	Prob.**
None*	0.532464	53.05718	42.91525	0.0036
At most 1	0.354468	23.40630	25.87211	0.0983
At most 2	0.149968	6.336779	12.51798	0.4188

Unrestricted Cointegration Rank Test (Maximum Eigenvalue)

Hypothesised No. of CE(s)	Eigenvalue	Max-Eigen Statistic	0.05 Critical Value	Prob.**
None*	0.532464	29.65089	25.82321	0.0149
At most 1	0.354468	17.06952	19.38704	0.1052
At most 2	0.149968	6.336779	12.51798	0.4188

Max-eigenvalue test indicates 1 cointegrating eqn(s) at the 0.05 level
* denotes rejection of the hypothesis at the 0.05 level
**MacKinnon-Haug-Michelis (1999) p-values

Table C.8 VAR Granger causality tests of Greece

Dependent variable: PROFIT2

Excluded	Chi-sq	df	Prob.
MILEX	10.94265	5	0.0525
GDP	20.01839	5	0.0012
All	31.82177	10	0.0004

Dependent variable: MILEX

Excluded	Chi-sq	df	Prob.
PROFIT2	8.445344	5	0.1333
GDP	7.635265	5	0.1775
All	12.00730	10	0.2846

Table C.9 Cointegration test results of India (for profit1)

Unrestricted Cointegration Rank Test (Trace)

Hypothesised No. of CE(s)	Eigenvalue	Trace Statistic	0.05 Critical Value	Prob.**
None	0.154471	11.54249	25.87211	0.8425
At most 1	0.034112	1.978309	12.51798	0.9700

Unrestricted Cointegration Rank Test (Maximum Eigenvalue)

Hypothesised		Max-Eigen	0.05	
No. of CE(s)	Eigenvalue	Statistic	Critical Value	Prob.**
None	0.154471	9.564183	19.38704	0.6654
At most 1	0.034112	1.978309	12.51798	0.9700

Max-eigenvalue test indicates no cointegration at the 0.05 level
*denotes rejection of the hypothesis at the 0.05 level
**MacKinnon-Haug-Michelis (1999) p-values

Table C.10 VAR Granger causality tests of India

Dependent variable: PROFIT1

Excluded	Chi-sq	df	Prob.
MILEX	1.872945	1	0.1711
All	1.872945	1	0.1711

Dependent variable: MILEX

Excluded	Chi-sq	df	Prob.
PROFIT1	2.826700	1	0.0927
All	2.826700	1	0.0927

Table C.11 Cointegration test results of Italy

Unrestricted Cointegration Rank Test (Trace)

Hypothesised No. of CE(s)	Eigenvalue	Trace Statistic	0.05 Critical Value	Prob.**
None	0.219378	34.31996	42.91525	0.2741
At most 1	0.174135	19.70774	25.87211	0.2411
At most 2	0.132991	8.419636	12.51798	0.2193

Unrestricted Cointegration Rank Test (Maximum Eigenvalue)

Hypothesised No. of CE(s)	Eigenvalue	Max-Eigen Statistic	0.05 Critical Value	Prob.**
None	0.219378	14.61221	25.82321	0.6691
At most 1	0.174135	11.28810	19.38704	0.4841
At most 2	0.132991	8.419636	12.51798	0.2193

Max-eigenvalue test indicates no cointegration at the 0.05 level
*denotes rejection of the hypothesis at the 0.05 level
**MacKinnon-Haug-Michelis (1999) p-values

Table C.12 VAR Granger causality tests of Italy

Dependent variable: PROFIT1

Excluded	Chi-sq	df	Prob.
MILEX	13.15506	4	0.0105
GDP	7.841797	4	0.0975
All	20.50895	8	0.0086

Dependent variable: MILEX

Excluded	Chi-sq	df	Prob.
PROFIT1	4.205272	4	0.3789
GDP	0.829356	4	0.9345
All	4.310619	8	0.8281

Table C.13 Cointegration test results of Italy (with unemployment)

Unrestricted Cointegration Rank Test (Trace)

Hypothesised No. of CE(s)	Eigenvalue	Trace Statistic	0.05 Critical Value	Prob.**
None	0.438971	52.12532	63.87610	0.3244
At most 1	0.279797	26.69407	42.91525	0.6987
At most 2	0.174845	12.25228	25.87211	0.7943
At most 3	0.082660	3.796211	12.51798	0.7714

Unrestricted Cointegration Rank Test (Maximum Eigenvalue)

Hypothesised No. of CE(s)	Eigenvalue	Max-Eigen Statistic	0.05 Critical Value	Prob.**
None	0.438971	25.43125	32.11832	0.2620
At most 1	0.279797	14.44178	25.82321	0.6841
At most 2	0.174845	8.456071	19.38704	0.7789
At most 3	0.082660	3.796211	12.51798	0.7714

Max-eigenvalue test indicates no cointegration at the 0.05 level
*denotes rejection of the hypothesis at the 0.05 level
**MacKinnon-Haug-Michelis (1999) p-values

Table C.14 VAR Granger causality tests of Italy (with unemployment)

Dependent variable: PROFIT1

Excluded	Chi-sq	df	Prob.
MILEX	0.067154	2	0.9670
GDP	2.147587	2	0.3417
UNEMPLOYMENT	3.033509	2	0.2194
All	5.737307	6	0.4533

Dependent variable: MILEX

Excluded	Chi-sq	df	Prob.
PROFIT1	4.386005	2	0.1116
GDP	0.213994	2	0.8985
UNEMPLOYMENT	1.811885	2	0.4042
All	5.793273	6	0.4467

Index

For Product Safety Concerns and Information please contact our EU representative GPSR@taylorandfrancis.com Taylor & Francis Verlag GmbH, Kaufingerstraße 24, 80331 München, Germany